Water Needs
for the Future

Other Titles in This Series

The Changing Economics of World Energy, edited by Bernhard J. Abrahamsson

Indonesia's Oil, Sevinc Carlson

Desertification: Environmental Degradation in and around Arid Lands, edited by Michael H. Glantz

The Nuclear Impact: A Case Study of the Plowshare Program to Produce Natural Gas by Underground Nuclear Stimulation in the Rocky Mountains, Frank Kreith and Catherine B. Wrenn

Natural Resources for a Democratic Society: Public Participation in Decision-Making, edited by Albert Utton, W. R. Derrick Sewell, and Timothy O'Riordan

Social Assessment Manual: A Guide to the Preparation of the Social Well-Being Account for Planning Water Resource Projects, Stephen J. Fitzsimmons, Lorrie I. Stuart, and Peter C. Wolff

Environmental Effects of Complex River Development: International Experience, edited by Gilbert F. White

Food from the Sea, Frederick W. Bell

The Geopolitics of Energy, Melvin A. Conant and Fern Racine Gold

EARTHCARE: Global Protection of Natural Areas, edited by Edmund A. Schofield

Westview Special Studies in Natural Resources and Energy Management

Water Needs for the Future:
Political, Economic, Legal, and Technological Issues
in a National and International Framework
edited by Ved P. Nanda

Water is crucial to our very lives, but water resources are limited. The drought in parts of the United States and Europe in 1977 has driven home the lesson that we need to develop water policies based on knowledge, understanding, and mature judgment. Choices must be made as to how to allocate, distribute, conserve, and augment our water resources, and those choices will directly affect all of us.

This volume is designed to stimulate interest in this area and to broaden the focus of discussion to a full range of legal, political, economic, social, and ethical considerations. It will increase the body of knowledge upon which future decisions will be based and will serve as a starting point for ongoing discussion among all sectors of the public.

Ved P. Nanda is professor of law and director of the International Legal Studies Program at the University of Denver.

Water Needs for the Future

Political, Economic, Legal, and Technological Issues in a National and International Framework

edited by Ved P. Nanda

Westview Press
Boulder, Colorado

Westview Special Studies in Natural Resources and Energy Management

Published in 1977 in the United States of America by
  Westview Press, Inc.
  1898 Flatiron Court
  Boulder, Colorado 80301
  Frederick A. Praeger, Publisher and Editorial Director

Library of Congress Cataloging in Publication Data
Main entry under title:
Water needs for the future.
  (Westview special studies in natural resources and energy management)
  Most of the papers originally presented at a conference sponsored by the University of Denver College of Law, Oct. 1976.
  1. Water-supply—Addresses, essays, lectures. I. Nanda, Ved P. II. Denver. University. College of Law.
TD355.W37   333.9'1   77-12273
ISBN 0-89158-236-3

Printed and bound in the United States of America

Contents

Water Needs for the Future

Ved P. Nanda[*]

Water is crucial to every type of human endeavor, indeed to human life itself. Water resources, while renewable, are limited. The drought situations in the Sahel in the early 1970s, in Western Europe in 1976, and in the United States in 1977 have merely accentuated the long-term problems of imbalance caused by short supply and increasing demand for water. These problems are likely to become critical unless urgent and immediate action is taken both to increase and to conserve existing supplies of water resources.

A desirable first step is the recognition that problems of water resources are not merely of regional or national concern but are of worldwide concern. For example, the recent United Nations conferences on global issues, especially those on the environment, food, and human settlements have emphasized the crucial role of water in the quality of life of all the world's inhabitants. The 1977 U.N. Water Conference has further focused world attention on the need for safe drinking water, for irrigation water, and for coordinated regional and global policies, planning, and action to meet the water demands of a growing world population.

As the population grows and the demand for clean water accelerates, choices must be made as to how to allocate, distribute, conserve, and augment existing water resources. Since the choices that are made will directly affect the lives and livelihoods of all citizens of the world community, these choices should be made by a public which is informed and knowledgeable about the nature of competing claims, interests, and values, and is aware of the complex issues which need to be intelli-

* Professor of Law, University of Denver College of Law; Chairman, Water Needs for the Future Conference, University of Denver, Oct. 8-9, 1976.

gently considered and weighed before policies are formulated
and action is undertaken.

Water Needs for the Future is designed to stimulate interest in these issues, to broaden the focus of discussion to a full
range of legal, political, economic, social, technological, and
ethical considerations, to increase the body of knowledge upon
which future choices will be made, and to serve as a starting
point for ongoing discussion among all sectors of the public.

Most of the essays in this volume were originally presented
at the conference, "Water Needs for the Future: Colorado, the
United States and the World," sponsored by the University of
Denver College of Law in October 1976. Nearly 500 attorneys,
engineers, planners, public officials, academicians, and concerned citizens assembled in Denver to discuss the local,
regional, national, and international aspects of water problems. The conference brought together participants with diverse backgrounds, skills, and disciplines, and the outcome of
the various panels, workshops, and informal sessions was a
heightened understanding and awareness of the full range of
social, political, economic, legal, and ethical considerations
which affect decisionmaking in water resource management.

A number of highly qualified experts contributed papers
and commentaries which provide the necessary framework for
the discussion of these issues. Thomas Oliver, the Executive
Secretary of the U.N. Water Conference, sets the stage for such
discussion. He makes a strong plea for identification and clear
understanding of the underlying issues of the global water crisis
and for rational conduct and behavior on the part of nation
states in the management of water resources.

Papers, case studies, and commentaries which follow Mr.
Oliver's presentation are conveniently divided into three parts:
(1) legal; (2) political and economic; and (3) technological.

In setting the legal framework, the first paper surveys the
emerging trends in the international legal and institutional
contexts in which water resource questions are being addressed. An appraisal of the trends in decision leads the author
to conclude that "[t]he common interest in the optimal utilization of international waters demands a definite worldwide
move toward integrated basin management, administration,
and development." Professors Frank Trelease and George

Radosevich have made valuable contributions in their studies of the various national legal systems throughout the world. Jerome Muys addresses the question of interstate allocation of water, concluding that the federal-interstate compact concept provides the greatest efficiency and equity in allocation amongst states. Raphael Moses examines the important issue of transmountain diversion, concluding that such interbasin transfers, while often of great value in distributing sorely needed water resources, face serious obstacles. The commentaries by Michael White and Robert Emmet Clark reflect the consensus position of the conference that legal and institutional mechanisms must be developed to allow for greater public input in the decisionmaking process and increased public management of scarce water resources.

The next section offers a detailed study of the political and economic contexts in which decisions regarding allocation of water are made. Senator Gary Hart presents an overview of the political and economic aspects of water problems, calling for greater public participation in the decisionmaking process. Federal-state relations are examined by Professor Henry Caulfield, a former federal official, who concludes that much of the federal apparatus should be dismantled, leaving the bulk of water development to the states. Professor Timothy Tregarthen then analyzes the economics of water allocation, recommending changes to increase the efficiency of the allocation system. A nonmarket model for evaluating the social impacts of resource decisions, which often go unevaluated for lack of a means to do so, is suggested by Professor David Freeman.

A series of case studies further elaborates the political and economic issues of resource management. David Lavender examines the historical development of water law and systems in the western United States, while Ival Goslin details the impact on Colorado of equitable apportionment with sister states. Governor Richard Lamm of Colorado further analyzes the need for comprehensive planning of water use and development and the interrelationship of water planning to land use and other resource planning. The relationship of surface to groundwater, one of the key questions facing water planners, is examined by C.J. Kuiper, the Colorado State Engineer. Comments by representatives of municipal, industrial, energy, and agricultural interests round out the discussion on conflicting political and economic demands for allocation of water.

The technological context often determines what may or may not be accomplished in the legal and political spheres. Dr. Gordon Milliken, and Professor Lewis Grant and Kelvin Danielson evaluate the various technological approaches to increasing the supply of water. While Dr. Milliken examines ten specific alternatives for increasing water supplies, Messrs. Grant and Danielson concentrate on the techniques of water augmentation and watershed management. The controversial subject of weather modification and the ramifications of present laws to this new source of augmentation are studied by Messrs. Danielson, Sherk, and Grant, who conclude that new laws will be necessary to adequately provide for such projects.

Case studies include the Sahel and Denver, Colorado. Dr. Michael Glantz's paper plays the valuable role of pinpointing the limitations on "technological fixes" by analyzing the problem of "inappropriate technologies" in the context of the Sahel, while Kenneth Miller outlines the attempts of Denver, Colorado—one of the leaders in the United States—in municipal recycling efforts.

One theme that clearly emerges even after a cursory glance at these papers and commentaries is the interrelatedness of water problems cutting across various disciplines and various geographical and ideological boundaries of the world and the resulting need for coordinated action. It is imperative that a recent warning by the U.N. Secretary-General, Kurt Waldheim, be heeded:

> [W]ater [is] a vulnerable resource that must be protected and developed through international cooperation to avoid disastrous shortages when the world's population reaches six billion to seven billion people by the end of this century.[1]

The conference "Water Needs for the Future" owes its success to a large number of individuals. As the chairman of the conference and the special editor of this volume, I gratefully acknowledge the assistance of the Board of Editors and staff of the DENVER JOURNAL OF INTERNATIONAL LAW AND POLICY, the officers and members of the Denver International Law So-

---

1. N.Y. Times, Mar. 15, 1977, at 3, cols. 1-2.

ciety, my colleagues at the College of Law, and my secretary, Jackie Mijares. The Colorado Humanities Program was of immense help in providing a matching grant which considerably eased the financial demands of such an undertaking.

I am especially indebted to Dr. Maurice Mitchell, Chancellor of the University of Denver, Dean Robert B. Yegge and Professor John A. Carver, Jr. of the College of Law, and my students and friends: Ian Bruce Bird, former managing editor; Mark S. Caldwell, former business editor; Gilbert D. Porter, managing editor; and Douglas G. Scrivner, editor-in-chief of the JOURNAL and conference coordinator, whose invaluable advice, help, and understanding not only made my task easier and more enjoyable but also contributed significantly to the success of the conference.

Spaceship Earth and Water for the Future

Thomas Oliver[*]

A discussion of water problems reminds me of my favorite water man—the late Sextus Frontinius—who was appointed Rome's water commissioner in the first century, A.D. He found himself in the position classic to water managers; he was told, "We need more water, go and get it—and by the way, you cannot have any more money." So, being a man of ingenuity, he looked around and decided to find out where the water went. He found that it mostly went to waste. He thought of various ways to overcome the waste and is today known as being the first to enunciate the great principle: halving the demand is the equivalent of doubling the supply. He did very well; he did not have to build any more aqueducts, and one would have thought he was destined for glory. Unfortunately there is a sad end to the story—he eventually committed suicide in order to avoid being put to death by Nero. One only hopes that those who are tackling similar problems in the United States, and elsewhere, will not find themselves as hard pressed.

I must confess that the title of the talk has caused me a certain degree of anguish. The analogy of Spaceship Earth is somewhat disturbing. It is perhaps seductive, but certainly misleading, for two reasons. In the first place the spaceship concept suggests the totally false premise that we are careening through space in this purpose-built object with a mission—knowing what we are going to do. But the problems faced by this conference, and the United Nations Water Conference at Mar del Plata are decidedly different. Certainly we are careening through space, but do not quite know why. We do not even know what we are trying to do as we careen through space, and the whole process is a disorderly, fascinating, potentially productive and exciting one.

A second point also troubles me about the analogy. As the Apollo astronauts sat in their capsule atop the rocket at Cape Kennedy, they could be certain of one thing: they knew that they numbered three at lift-off, and that there would be no

---

[*] Executive Secretary, U.N. Water Conference at Mar del Plata, Argentina, March 14-25, 1977.

more than three when the thing splashed down again. We in Spaceship Earth, if it is a spaceship, can not be sure of that. As we whirl through space, we simply do not know how many of us there will be tomorrow, the next day, or the next week. We do know that every time the planet spins around there are more people, there are more people demanding more water and demanding better water; each new person needs more water in order to stay alive and enjoy the blessings of the civilization that he has grown accustomed to—and to which he is entitled. This is the kind of problem that one does not have in a spaceship.

Our concerns demonstrate the failure of the spaceship analogy. The conference at Mar del Plata is but one of the series of conferences that have been organized under the auspices of the United Nations to deal with what Lady Jackson (Barbara Ward) has come to call global housekeeping. We are concerned with one central issue: How do we, inhabitants of this planet and the governments that represent us, so arrange our affairs as to ensure that there will be no water crisis—or rather, no serious, recurring, or more rapidly recurring water crisis—before the end of this century. It is a big job, but one the conference can successfully handle.

In this perspective, the conference falls into the long series of conferences organized by the United Nations. The first was the conference on the conservation and utilization of resources which was convened in the mid-1940s. That conference was convened as a result of a very imaginative initiative by the then-U.S. Secretary of the Interior. It brought together with great success a very large number of scientists, technologists, and administrators to consider how the world could best use and conserve its resources. It preceded the environmentalists, but was a successful attempt to deal with one of the vital housekeeping problems that arises in the course of managing this one earth that we all occupy.

A number of conferences have followed. There has been, for example, a conference on the application of science and technology to development. There have been conferences on the peaceful uses of atomic energy, on the peaceful uses of outer space, on the environment (Stockholm), on population (Bucharest), and on women (Mexico City), each of which attempted to deal with one of the problems faced by the majority of the occupants of Spaceship Earth. In addition, there was the recent human settlements conference in Vancouver, the food conference in Rome, and the water conference at Mar del Plata. Down the road is a conference, to be held in Nairobi, on the problems of desertification—how you create deserts by applying water to them, and how you eliminate deserts by applying water more intelligently.

At the Mar del Plata water conference, we have attempted to bring to the attention of governments the specific water and water-related problems that stem from the earlier conferences. For example, it is quite obvious that if the world is to achieve the ambitious food goals set in Rome there will have to be an almost frightening array of activities affecting water. I do not mean that the rich countries will merely have to dig into their pockets, but that there will have to be improvements in irrigation, in the use of water in agriculture, and in other vital water uses. Similarly, at the human settlements conference, the participants agreed that there should be action taken between now and 1990 to provide safe drinking water and reasonably adequate waste disposal facilities to the vast majority of the world's population, who now have neither. What is needed is a practical program—a set of commitments by developed countries to give those problems priority, to provide some of the finances and some of the technical cooperation that will be necessary to achieve the habitat goal.

The Mar del Plata conference was preceded by a very successful period of regional preparatory meetings; the first of these was held in Bangkok in July 1976, the second at Lima during August 1976, the third at Addis Ababa at the end of September 1976, and the fourth in Geneva at the beginning of October 1976. At each of these preparatory conferences the member governments produced reports on water problems in their countries and the likely demands, problems, and solutions considered by the governments. These reports have been collated in a set of regional reports which are to be published.

During the regional meetings the governments considered recommendations to be proposed at the Mar del Plata conference. These recommendations vary in style from region to region. For example, the African region placed a great deal of emphasis on measures to improve net worth—the assessment of water resources. They did so for two reasons: partly because Africa needs significant development in that area, and partly because its regional meeting was preceded by a meeting of hydrologists.

Nonetheless, the general contents of these recommendations are generally uniform. An example might be the Latin American recommendations. They cover a fairly obvious set of topics: planning; water management; institutions for water management, laws, and regulations; assessment of supply and demand; efficiency in water use; community water supplies; use of water for agriculture, energy, recreation, and navigation; technology, conservation, and the environment; floods and droughts, cooperation in hydrological studies, and international rivers.

On each of these subjects, the recommendations note what would be nice to do, but contain no stirring call for action. In the case of international rivers, a very large element of compromise is evident. The proposal adopted in Latin America is virtually the same as the one adopted in Bangkok, and it is obvious that a recommendation adopted, by consensus, by a group that includes a downriver country like Bangladesh and an upriver country like India, is likely to be a meek proposal.

However, international agreement on difficult political and economic questions, such as those of international rivers and the use of shared water resources, cannot be resolved in a one or two week meeting. The resolution will take place through the normal processes of treaty-making, and of law-making at the international level. Hopefully, the International Law Commission will draft appropriate legal texts.[1] The scholarly and professional communities, through organizations like the International Law Association, will also, hopefully, continue their efforts to propose the sort of formulae that governments might eventually accept.[2]

When agreement does come it will come because the force of circumstances propels people in that direction. I know of one

---

1. A brief sketch of the current activities of the International Law Commission on the legal aspects of international water-courses is contained in Nanda, *infra*.

2. For a summary report on the legal norms recommended by these organizations see Nanda, *id.*

developing country which has a somewhat successful treaty for the common use of an international river with one of its neighbors. It is trying unsuccessfully, however, to establish a similar arrangement with another neighbor. The reason the arrangement can not be brought to fruition, I am told, is not political, but is because the other neighbor has not yet reached a point of development where it needs to make use of that water; until that time it is not going to enter into commitments whose outcome it can not foresee. Nevertheless, we can be sure that the discussions and decisions taken at Mar del Plata and regional conferences will propel the international community further along the road to agreement.

A major issue affecting the management of water is conservation, and the resulting set of environmental considerations, with which environmental programs are concerned. The U.N. Environment Program has therefore been most generous in helping us to organize the regional meetings, and in the case of the Mar del Plata meeting it assisted the neediest among the developing countries to send representatives.

An additional important contribution made by the conference is certainly the series of reports and papers submitted by governments and discussed at the conference. Earlier we had asked governments to present papers at the conference relating to their national experiences in broad problems of water management. The compilation of these papers and the preparation and analysis involved in each were invaluable in creating a new-found awareness of water management concerns on both the national and international levels.

There is no guarantee that the Mar del Plata conference or a similar intergovernmental conference would bring about what Barbara Ward considers necessary to make Spaceship Earth a flyable object: "Rational behavior is the condition of survival. Rational rules of behavior are what we largely lack," or what Buckminster Fuller wants everybody to do, "to think clearly." However, as the preamble to the Latin American proposal has aptly stated, the conference at Mar del Plata has provided a magnificent opportunity, "to raise problems, to exchange experience, and to identify techniques and solutions' that may help governments to take decisions in this matter, focusing their attention on the major issues in the water sector which demand the attention of the world community." If even half of the delegations to Mar del Plata sensed that we should focus our efforts in these directions, the conference will have achieved something worthwhile.

Part 1
Legal

1
Emerging Trends in the Use of International Law and Institutions for the Management of International Water Resources[*]

Ved P. Nanda[**]

I. The Problem

A recent United Nations study[1] notes that presently at least 20 percent of the world's urban population and 75 percent of the rural population (in many countries the number is as high as 50 percent of the urban population and 90 percent of the rural population) suffer from a lack of reasonably safe supplies of drinking water.[2] The quality of water supplies, and in turn the quality of life and environmental health, suffers for many reasons, including: (1) the increasing and unplanned concentration of population and industry in large urban areas; (2) the increase of toxic compounds and other pollutants caused by the proliferation of industrial processes, greater use of energy, and increased agricultural activity; (3) water-logging, salinization and erosion, exhaustion of groundwater supplies, and deterioration of both ground and surface water sources in many regions; (4) needlessly inefficient and wasteful water use; and (5) intensified conflicts about rights and priorities as the demand for available water accelerates.[3]

Since there is a fixed total stock of water[4]—even though it may be potentially inexhaustible—the future worldwide accelerating demand is likely to strain water resources not only in several countries but also in several regions of the world. Thus

---

* This paper is an adaptation of the author's remarks made at the Water Resources Conference at the University of Denver on Oct. 9, 1976.

** Professor of Law and Director of the International Legal Studies Program, University of Denver College of Law; Chairman, Water Needs for the Future Conference, University of Denver, Oct. 8-9, 1976.

1. U.N. Water Conference, *Resources and Needs: Assessment of the World Water Situation*, U.N. Doc. E/CONF. 70/CBP/1 (1976) [hereinafter cited as *U.N. Assessment of the World Water Situation*].

2. *Id.* at 5.

3. *Id.*

4. *Id.* at 4.

the study concludes that there exists a potential world water crisis even though "globally there may be potentially enough water to meet forthcoming needs. But, frustratingly, it tends to be available in the wrong place, at the wrong time, or with the wrong quality."[5] Consequently, all societies, rich and poor, are likely to be affected.

A recent study by the United Nations Economic Commission for Europe has concluded that water resources are inadequate to meet current needs in five European countries—Cyprus, the German Democratic Republic, Hungary, Malta, and the Ukrainian S.S.R.—and that seven more countries—Belgium, Bulgaria, Luxembourg, Poland, Portugal, Romania, and Turkey—will face similar problems by the year 2000.[6]

In September 1976, United Nations Secretary-General Kurt Waldheim described the main concern of the 1977 U.N. Water Conference: "[to ensure] that the world manages its water supply [so that] this vital resource is available in sufficient quantities and of sufficiently good quality to meet the mounting needs of a world population which is not only growing, but is seeking improved economic and social conditions for all."[7] Subsequently, in November 1976, the consensus adopted by the General Assembly on the dispute between India and Bangladesh pertaining to the use of waters of the Ganges River[8] highlighted the world community's interest in avoiding conflicts and in seeking cooperative action in the management of international water resources.

Invoking Article 14 of the U.N. Charter, Bangladesh brought the dispute before the Assembly, stating that "[f]ailure to resolve this issue expeditiously and satisfactorily carries with it the potential threat of conflict affecting peace and security in the area and the region as a whole."[9]

---

5. *Id.* at 5.

6. U.N. Economic Commission for Europe, *Problems of Europe's Water Suppliers*, Press Release ECE/GEN/F/4, ECE/ENV/9 (1976), cited in Report of the International Law Commission on the Work of its 28th Session, 31 U.N. GAOR, Supp. 10, at 384, U.N. Doc. A/31/10 (1976) [hereinafter cited as *Report of the 28th Session of Int'l L. Comm'n*].

7. In a letter to the author, *supra* at 225.

8. 13 *U.N. Monthly Chronicle*, Dec. 1976, at 35.

9. *Id.* at 35-36. *See also* U.N. Doc. A/31/195 & Add. 1, 2 (1976).

Bangladesh contended that India's construction of a barrier on the Ganges River at Farakka, a few miles from the Bangladesh-India border, for the purpose of diverting the river into the Hooghly River in India, and India's continued unilateral withdrawal of a large volume of water from the Ganges had a devastating impact on Bangladesh, causing "cumulative and permanent" damage.[10] India expressed "serious misgivings about the desirability of involving the Assembly in an issue which was intrinsically bilateral."[11] It considered Bangladesh's insistence on the continued natural flow of an international river to be inconsistent with the concept of "equitable utilization."[12] Asserting that India "had always subscribed to the view that each riparian State was entitled to a reasonable and equitable share of the waters of an international river," it showed willingness not only to consult with Bangladesh on finding a short-term solution "to avoid the common hardship that might be caused by a shortage of water during the lean months, but also to co-operate in the search for a long-term solution by augmenting the flow."[13] Accordingly, the parties "decided to meet urgently at Dacca at the ministerial level for negotiations with a view to arriving at a fair and expeditious settlement."[14]

If the Assembly involvement in the Ganges waters dispute were to be construed to be an emerging trend toward the internationalization of bilateral water management issues, or at least some of them, it would be a trend I would consider desirable, necessary, and long overdue; critical questions pertaining to water management and their proposed solutions have been traditionally considered primarily as local, regional, and national issues. These issues include the setting of priorities among multiple and often competing uses of water; the allocation, distribution, conservation, augmentation, and optimization of existing water resources; and the prevention of pollution and exhaustion. Obviously, experience of water resource management accrued at all these levels can be benefi-

---

10. 13 *U.N. Monthly Chronicle*, Dec. 1976, at 36.

11. *Id.*

12. *Id.*

13. *Id.*

14. *Id.* at 35. Negotiations, however, were stalled in January 1977. N.Y. Times, Mar. 14, 1977, at 12, col. 2.

cially shared by others. Similarly, experience in integrated development and management of international river basins[15] can be helpful both in the devising of new plans and in their implementation. A brief inquiry into the role of international law and institutions in facilitating the management of international river resources, primarily for non-navigational uses, will be attempted in the following sections.

II. POLICY CONSIDERATIONS

⌐ Unilateral attempts by states to solve water problems are likely to produce limited results⌐for at least two reasons: (1) many nations lack adequate scientific data about water supply and its rational use, and adequate technical know-how and resources to develop local water systems and to appraise their long range effects and implications, and (2) there is likely to be unnecessary and wasteful duplication of effort.[16] Efficient, rational development and use of water resources demands cooperative, concerted efforts by nation states.

The need for such concerted efforts is especially striking where internationally interconnected water resources—surface or underground—are involved. The emergence of the international drainage basin concept and its wide acceptance, contrasted with the "international river" and "international river system," can be attributed to a better understanding of hydrologic facts.[17] This development has created expectations that

---

15. The concept of "international drainage basin" is used in article 2 of the Helsinki Rules, INT'L LAW ASS'N, HELSINKI RULES ON THE USES OF THE WATERS OF INTERNATIONAL RIVERS art. II (1967). For a discussion of various aspects of this concept *see* L. TECLAFF, THE RIVER BASIN IN HISTORY AND LAW (1967); U.N., *Integrated River Basin Development*, U.N. Doc. E/3066/Rev. 1 (1970); THE LAW OF INTERNATIONAL DRAINAGE BASINS (A. Garretson, R. Hayton & C. Olmstead eds. 1967); *Developments in the Field of Natural Resources—Water, Energy and Minerals—Technical and Economic Aspects of International River Basin Development*, U.N. Doc. E/C.7/35 (1972) [hereinafter cited as *The 1972 U.N. Report*]; U.N. Secretary-General's Supplementary Report, *Legal Problems Relating to the Non-Navigational Uses of International Watercourses*, U.N. Doc. A/CN.4/274 (1974) [hereinafter cited as 1-2 *The 1974 Supplementary Report of the Secretary-General*]; Report of the Panel of Experts on the Legal and Institutional Aspects of International Water Resources Development, *Management of International Water Resources: Institutional and Legal Aspects*, U.N. Doc. ST/ESA/5 (1975) [hereinafter cited as *The 1975 U.N. Panel of Experts Report*]; Bourne, *The Development of International Water Resources: The "Drainage Basin Approach"*, 47 CAN. B. REV. 62 (1969); Menon, *Water Resources Development of International Rivers With Special Reference to the Developing World*, 9 INT'L LAW 441 (1975) [hereinafter cited as Menon].

16. *U.N. Assessment of the World Water Situation* at 6.

17. *The 1975 U.N. Panel of Experts Report* at 9.

when two or more states, sharing uses of international water resources, establish a regime to regulate or govern such uses, the scope of such a regime would, barring special agreements, extend to the entire basin.[18]

The next step beyond the international drainage basin concept is the international water resources system concept. The latter concept allows the optimal utilization of all water resources, for the concept encompasses "a complete transnational, non-maritime hydrosystem"[19] by recognizing: (1) the value and functioning of all portions of the hydrologic cycle—surface water, groundwater, and atmospheric water; (2) international frozen water resources including glaciers and polar ice; and (3) the many interrelationships which exist among various natural and human resources affected by such a system.[19.1]

Figure I.   Hydrologic cycle

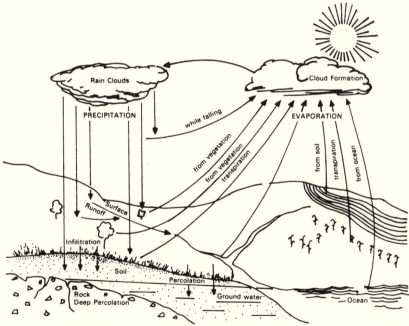

Source: THE WATER ENCYCLOPEDIA: COMPENDIUM OF USEFUL INFORMATION ON WATER RESOURCES 59 (D. Todd ed. 1970), cited in U.N. Doc. St/ESA/5, at 13 (1975).

---

18. *Id.* For an illustration of special agreements see *id.* at 48-54. *But see* Bourne, *supra* note 15, at 83-87.

19. *The 1975 U.N. Panel of Experts Report* at 12.

19.1. *Id.* at 12-15. Figure 1 illustrates the hydrologic cycle.

The major impetus for evolving legal norms and institutional structures on the uses of international watercourses can be traced to the growing awareness and realization among states sharing international watercourses of their common interest in rational utilization and optimal development of these water resources.[20] In turn, these norms and institutions influence and shape policies affecting (1) water balance efficiency, and (2) mechanisms for regulating a balanced demand/supply relationship when supply is scarce.[21]

However, despite a significant trend toward cooperative action by states on international watercourses, which has already "reached international solutions in about 20 [international river] basins" and in about 300 related bilateral and multilateral treaties,[22] states are still split on the appropriate scope of the definition of an international watercourse for the purpose of studying the legal aspects of the uses and pollution of such waters.[23] In reply to a recent International Law Commission questionnaire,[24] several states expressed opposition to the use of an international drainage basin concept as the appropriate basis for a study of the legal aspects both of non-navigational uses and the pollution of international watercourses.[25] Poland suggested that "from the legal point of view one cannot speak of the unity of the international drainage basin extending on the territory of more than one State until the States of this basin will not recognize the restriction of their territorial sovereignty on internal waters under their control."[26]

---

20. Such a growing awareness and realization is reflected in a large number of recent agreements on the subject among nation states. *See, e.g.*, 1 *The 1974 Supplementary Report of the Secretary General* at 79-183; U.N. Secretary-General's Report, *Legal Problems Relating to the Utilization and Use of International Rivers*, Pt. II, U.N. Doc. A/5409 (1963), which is conveniently contained in 2 Y.B. Int'l L. Comm'n Pt. II, at 33, U.N. Doc. A/CN.4/SER.A/1974/Add.1 (Part 2) (1974) [hereinafter cited as *The 1963 Report of the Secretary-General*, citation to pages being to the 1974 Int'l L. Comm'n Yearbook]; U.N., *Legislative Texts and Treaty Provisions Concerning the Utilization of International Rivers for Other Purposes than Navigation*, U.N. Doc. ST/LEG/SER.B/12 (1963).

21. *U.N. Assessment of the World Water Situation* at 52-53.

22. *Supra* note 20; *The 1972 U.N. Report* at 13.

23. *Report of the 28th Session of Int'l L. Comm'n* at 376-78.

24. *The Law of the Non-Navigational Uses of International Watercourses* at 8-9, U.N. Doc. A/CN.4/294 (1976).

25. *Id.* at 14 (Austria); 15-16, 35, 42 (Brazil); 17, 35 (Columbia); 18, 36, 42-43 (Ecuador); 27-28, 39-40, 45 (Poland); and 28-29 (Spain).

26. *Id.* at 39.

Acknowledging that the existence of a clear trend is "manifest in the legalizing of the river basin as the basis for cooperation" between the member basin states,[27] a commentator has recently noted that most existing international river institutions "have authority only to advise and supervise the execution of waterworks already approved,"[28] and are unable to initiate water resource projects.

What legal norms and what kind of institutions can encourage, facilitate, and accelerate integrated aproaches to international watercourse management and development is a useful inquiry. The first step which will be attempted here is to outline in the next section the trends in decision; this will be followed by an appraisal of these trends and a few concluding recommendations.

III. TRENDS IN DECISION

Although legal rules to regulate and govern the use of water have existed since ancient times and civilizations,[29] the development of international water law can be traced back only to the end of World War I when peace treaties declared many European rivers to be international.[30] These treaties in many instances contained provisions concerning the regimes not only for the regulation of navigational uses of such rivers but also for their non-navigational uses.[31] However, during the last 50 years, international law has played an increasingly influential role in dealing with questions pertaining to water resources. A brief sketch of this more recent development follows.

A. *General Conventions*

The first treaty on the subject was adopted by a General Conference on Freedom of Communications and Transit, convened in 1921 at Barcelona under the auspices of the League of Nations.[32] The Conference also adopted a Statute on the regime of navigable waterways of international concern.[33] Al-

---

27. Teclaff, *The Influence of Recent Trends in Water Legislation on the Structure and Functions of Water Administration*, 9 LAND & WATER L. REV. 1, 2 (1974).

28. *Id.* at 3.

29. Menon at 443 n. 4-9.

30. *The 1975 U.N. Panel of Experts Report* at 21-22.

31. *The 1963 Report of the Secretary-General* at 57-61.

32. *Id.* at 60.

33. *Id.*

though both the Convention and the Statute, which entered into force in 1922, are primarily concerned with navigation, they contain provisions regarding the utilization and use of rivers for non-navigational purposes as well.[34]

The following year, the League of Nations convened the Second General Conference on Freedom of Communications and Transit which adopted a convention on the development of hydraulic power affecting two or more states.[35] The convention formulated principles to accomplish the goal of "facilitating the exploitation and increasing the yield of hydraulic power."[36] Although the Conference did not require a state party to reach agreement with other states to ensure the hydroelectric development of an international river, it did provide "principles by means of which the interested States may negotiate and come to an agreement with a view to developing international rivers for the generation of hydro-electric power."[37]

B. *Multilateral, Regional, and Bilateral Conventions*

The latest United Nations reports[38] list more than 300 agreements between and among states. However, more than half the treaties listed are in Europe and, while 23 of a total of 45 European basins are covered by treaties, only 38 of the 155 basins located in Africa, the Americas, and Asia have become the subject of international compacts.[39]

One can surmise that this lopsided development in Europe is to a large measure attributable to industrialization and the resulting common interest and need perceived by European nations to enter into cooperative agreements, initially on navigational aspects of international rivers and subsequently on non-navigational uses of international water resources. With industrialization, a similar pressure for more extensive use and development of international water resources is likely to be felt in other regions as well. As a result, the need will be increasingly felt to enter into cooperative agreements both on regional

---

34. *Id.* at 60-61.
35. *Id.* at 57.
36. *Id.* at 58.
37. *Id.*
38. *Supra* notes 20-21.
39. *The 1972 U.N. Report*, Annex VI, at 21. For a discussion of selected bilateral and regional agreements see Nanda, *The Establishment of International Standards for Transnational Environmental Injury*, 60 Iowa L. Rev. 1089, 1101-08 (1975).

and bilateral levels. Three recent developments portend this direction: (1) in the post-World War II period, especially during the last two decades, a large number of multilateral treaties have been signed in Africa, the Americas, and in Europe;[40] (2) many recent multilateral conventions extend the scope of their coverage to the entire basins of international water resources in question;[41] and (3) at least a few such conventions, such as the Senegal River Basin Authority, have set up institutions capable not only of settling disputes but also of providing the needed initiative and leadership in the management of international water resources.[42]

C. *Intergovernmental Organizations*

A large number of intergovernmental organizations have been actively associated with various aspects of the uses of international watercourses. These organizations include the United Nations under whose auspices several international conferences, such as the 1972 Conference on the Human Environment,[43] the 1976 Conference on the Habitat,[44] and the 1977 Water Conference,[45] have studied various aspects of the problem. The United Nations Economic and Social Council and its subsidiary bodies have prepared several useful studies and reports regarding the development and utilization of water resources.[46]

The U.N. Secretariat itself took the lead in 1968 in assembling an interdisciplinary panel of experts to study the legal and institutional aspects of international water resources development.[47] The Panel, which was composed of economists, engineers, lawyers, public administration specialists, and exec-

---

40. *Supra* note 20.

41. Treaties on the Senegal River basin, the Niger basin, the Chad basin, and the River Plate basin provide recent examples. *See* 1 *The 1974 Supplementary Report of the Secretary-General* at 79-83, 87-88.

42. *See generally* Parnall & Utton, *The Senegal Valley Authority: A Unique Experiment in International River Basin Planning*, 51 IND. L.J. 235 (1976).

43. *See Report of the United Nations Conference on the Human Environment*, U.N. Doc. A/CONF.48/14/Rev.1 (1973).

44. The Conference met in Vancouver, Canada, from May 31 to June 11, 1976. For a report of the Conference see U.N. Doc. A/CONF./70/15 (1976).

45. The Conference took place from March 14-25, 1977. The Work Programme of the Conference is contained in U.N. Doc. E/C.7/SR.96 (1976).

46. 2 *The 1974 Supplementary Report of the Secretary-General* at 190-212.

47. *The 1975 U.N. Panel of Experts Report* at iii.

utives from different parts of the world, held sessions in 1968 and 1969.[48] These sessions were also attended by participants from interested U.N. agencies.[49] The resulting Panel Report is an impressive document containing specific proposals.[50] Countries seeking help on the issue of international water resources planning will find the report of considerable assistance.

Among the specialized agencies of the United Nations, the Food and Agriculture Organization (FAO)[51] and the World Meteorological Organization (WMO)[52] have shown special concern for the problem. In 1972 the FAO legal office prepared a draft agreement on water utilization and conservation in the Lake Chad Basin.[53] WMO is presently conducting two studies: (1) on the effects of salinity caused by the erection of dams and other watercourse structures; and (2) on the thermal pollution of·waters caused by effluents from energy-producing installations.[54] Additionally, the World Health Organization has conducted a comparative survey of health legislation on the control of water pollution,[55] and, in conjunction with the International Atomic Energy Agency, it convened in 1969 a panel of experts which prepared a report on the pollution of fresh waters by radioactive material.[56] The report makes specific recommendations to "control the quantities of radioactive materials passing from one country to another."[57]

As early as 1933, the American states adopted the Declaration of Montivideo on the industrial and agricultural use of international rivers at the Seventh Inter-American Conference.[58] The Declaration, applicable to both contiguous and successive rivers, conditions the exercise of a state's "right to exploit, for industrial or agricultural purposes, the margin which is under their jurisdiction of the waters of international rivers . . . upon the necessity of not injuring the equal right due to

---

48. *Id.* at 3.
49. *Id.*, Annex I, at 187.
50. Specific proposals are contained in *id.* at 181-84.
51. *See 2 The 1974 Supplementary Report of the Secretary-General* at 216-22.
52. *See id.* at 223.
53. *Id.* at 217.
54. *Id.* at 223.
55. *Id.* at 222-23.
56. *Id.* at 223-25.
57. *Id.* at 225.
58. *The 1963 Report of the Secretary-General,* Annex I(A) at 212.

the neighboring State on the margin under its jurisdiction."[59]
Thus no state "may, without the consent of the other riparian
State, introduce into watercourses of an international character, for the industrial or agricultural exploitation of their waters, any alteration which may prove injurious to the margin
of the other interested State."[60] It provides for joint action pertaining to studies regarding the utilization of such waters,[61]
prior consultation between and among riparian states on the
projects contemplated on these waters,[62] reparation and compensation,[63] and dispute settlement mechanisms.[64] Subsequent
reports, declarations, and resolutions adopted in the Western
Hemisphere on the use of international watercourses include:
(1) a 1941 resolution concerning the establishment of joint
technical commissions to study the hydrographic system of the
River Plate;[65] (2) a 1965 draft convention on the industrial and
agricultural use of international rivers and lakes, prepared by
the Inter-American Judicial Committee;[66] (3) a 1966 resolution
on control and economic utilization of hydrographic basins and
streams in Latin America, adopted by the Inter-American Economic and Social Council;[67] and (4) various declarations and
resolutions adopted by Argentina, Bolivia, Brazil, Paraguay,
and Uruguay pertaining to their joint efforts for the development of the Plate Basin, including the 1971 Act of Asuncion.[68]

The Inter-American practices may be highlighted by noting a few provisions from the 1965 draft convention and the
1971 Act of Asuncion. Articles 5 and 6 of the draft convention
read:

> 5.   The utilization of the waters of an international river or lake
> for industrial or agricultural purposes must not prejudice the free
> navigation thereof in accordance with the applicable legal rules,
> or cause substantial injury, according to international law, to the
> riparian States or alterations to their boundaries.

---

59. *Id.* art. 2.
60. *Id.*
61. *Id.* art. 6.
62. *Id.* arts. 7-8.
63. *Id.* art. 3.
64. *Id.* arts. 9-10.
65. *See The 1963 of the Secretary-General,* Annex I(B) at 212.
66. *See 2 The 1974 Supplementary Report of the Secretary-General* at 264.
67. *See id.* at 267.
68. *See 1 id.* at 173-79.

6. In cases in which the utilization of an international river or lake results or may result in damage or injury to another interested State, the consent of that interested State shall be required, as well as the payment or indemnification for any damage or harm done, when such is claimed.[69]

Articles 1 and 2 of the Act of Asuncion provide:

1. In contiguous international rivers, which are under dual sovereignty, there must be a prior bilateral agreement between the riparian States before any use is made of the waters.
2. In successive international rivers, where there is no dual sovereignty, each State may use the waters in accordance with its needs provided that it causes no appreciable damage to any other State of the Basin.[70]

Intergovernmental efforts in Africa and Asia have resulted in (1) a 1961 report, adopted at the first Inter-African Conference on Hydrology in Nairobi,[71] which called for the establishment of effective consultation mechanisms, especially regarding the River Niger and Lake Chad,[72] and (2) the 1973 draft propositions on the law of international rivers formulated under the auspices of the Asian-African Legal Consultative Committee,[73] which accepted the concept of an international drainage basin "except as may be provided otherwise by convention, agreement or binding custom among the basin states."[74] The draft propositions define the international drainage basin area as "a geographical area extending over two or more states determined by the watershed limits of the system of waters, including surface and underground waters, flowing into a common terminus."[75] They accept the principle of equitable utilization,[76] require a state to "act in good faith in the exercise of its rights on the waters of an international drainage basin in accordance with the principles governing good neighbourly relations,"[77] prefer consumptive uses over other competing uses,[78] provide for prior consultation, and for inter-

---

69. *Supra* note 66, at 265-66.
70. *Supra* note 68, at 179.
71. *See The 1963 Report of the Secretary-General* at 217.
72. *Id.* at 218.
73. *See supra* note 66, at 226.
74. Proposition I, *id.* at 227.
75. Proposition II(1), *id.* at 228.
76. Proposition III, *id.*
77. Proposition IV(1), *id.* at 228-29.
78. Proposition V, *id.* at 229.

national arbitration and adjudication as dispute settlement mechanisms,[79] and impose state responsibility on violating states with injunctive and compensatory remedies.[80]

European efforts, which have centered around water pollution problems, include: (1) the report of the 1961 Geneva Conference on Water Pollution Problems in Europe;[81] (2) a 1965 report on fresh water pollution control in Europe submitted to the Consultative Assembly, Council of Europe,[82] and a resulting recommendation adopted by the Assembly, calling upon member states to undertake joint action;[83] (3) the 1967 European Water Charter,[84] which calls for international cooperation "to conserve the quality and quantity of water," since water "knows no frontiers,"[85] and calls for the management of water resources to be based on their natural drainage basins rather than on political and administrative boundaries;[86] and (4) a 1969 draft European Convention on the Protection of Fresh Water against Pollution,[87] which has been further refined in a 1974 draft.[88] It should be noted that the 1974 draft defines an international watercourse as "any watercourse, canal or lake which separates or passes through the territories of two or more States,"[89] and prohibits or restricts the "discharge into the waters of international hydrographic basins of any of the [enumerated] dangerous or harmful substances."[90] It contains elaborate provisions on joint action including negotiations,[91] joint agreements,[92] the setting of standards,[93] the establishment of appropriate commissions,[94] and dispute settlement mechanisms.[95] Finally, the 1971 recommendation of the Con-

---

79. Proposition X, *id.* at 230.
80. Proposition IX, *id.*
81. *Supra* note 71, at 218.
82. *Supra* note 66, at 230-34.
83. *Id.* at 235-39.
84. *Id.* at 239-42.
85. *Id.* at 242.
86. *Id.*
87. *Id.* at 243-50.
88. *Id.* at 251-61.
89. Art. 1(a), *id.* at 252.
90. Art. 5(1), *id.* at 253.
91. Art. 12, *id.* at 255.
92. Arts. 12, 14, *id.* at 255-56.
93. Art. 4(1)(b), Appendix I, *id.* at 253, 259.
94. Arts. 15, 16, *id.* at 256-57.
95. Arts. 20, 22, Appendix A, *id.* at 258, 260-61.

sultative Assembly, calling for urgent action by all the countries bordering on the River Rhine, concerning the pollution of the Rhine Valley watertable should be noted.[96]

D. *Nongovernmental Organizations*

Among scholarly and professional associations which have studied the uses of international watercourses, perhaps the one most widely known for its work in this field is the International Law Association.[97] The Rules on the Uses of the Waters of International Rivers adopted at the Fifty-Second Conference of the Association at Helsinki in 1966,[98] known as the Helsinki Rules, contain the "key principle" that "[e]ach basin State is entitled, within its territory, to a reasonable and equitable share in the beneficial uses of the waters of an international drainage basin."[99] What is a "reasonable and equitable share . . . is to be determined in the light of all the relevant factors in each particular case."[100] Some relevant factors are enumerated for illustrative purposes.[101] According to the Rules, a "use or category of uses is not entitled to any inherent preference over any other use or category of uses."[102] In addition to providing rules for the equitable utilization of the waters of an international drainage basin,[103] the Helsinki Rules cover many other areas such as pollution,[104] navigation,[105] and timber floating.[106] They also provide for dispute settlement mechanisms.[107] Since the Helsinki Conference, the Association has been actively pursuing the study of

> certain selected aspects of water resources law [such as] underground waters; the relationship of water to other natural resources; domestic uses of water; hydraulic uses of water, including the generation of power and irrigation; flood control and silta-

---

96. *See id.* at 262-63.

97. For a summary of the work of the International Law Associaton in this field *see supra* note 71, at 202-208; *supra* note 66, at 287-304.

98. Int'l Law Ass'n, Helsinki Rules on the Uses of the Waters of International Rivers (1967). The Helsinki Rules are contained in *supra* note 66, at 288-94.

99. Art. IV, *supra* note 66, at 288.

100. Art. V(1), *id.*

101. Art. V(2), *id.* at 288-89.

102. Art. VI, *id.* at 289.

103. Ch. 2, arts. IV-VIII, *id.* at 288-90.

104. Ch. 3, arts. IX-XI, *id.* at 290.

105. Ch. 4, arts. XII-XX, *id.* at 290-91.

106. Ch. 5, arts. XXI-XXV, *id.* at 291.

107. Ch. 6, arts. XXVI-XXXVII, *id.* at 292-94.

tion; regulation of water flow; detailed rules on the navigation of rivers; and further consideration of the subject of pollution of coastal areas and enclosed seas.[108]

The work is being done by the Association's Committee on International Water Resources Law.[109] One of the Committee's six working groups, the Working Group on Management of International Waters, was set up to study legal aspects concerning: (1) obligation (if any) to establish international administration; (2) functions, powers, and composition of international management; (3) economic and financial problems of international management; (4) questions concerning the constitutional requirements of certain states to accept the binding force of the decisions of international management; and (5) national water legislation of the co-basin states regarding the use of water under international management.[110] Earlier, in 1958, the Committee on the Uses of Waters of International Rivers of the American Branch of the Association asserted a principle of law that a riparian "is under a duty to refrain from increasing the level of pollution of a system of international waters to the substantial detriment of a co-riparian."[111]

Among other similar groups, the Institute of International Law and the Inter-American Bar Association have also studied the questions pertaining to the uses of international waterways and have made specific recommendations.[112] For instance, the Institute of International Law decided as early as 1910 to study the question of "determining the rules of international law relating to international rivers from the point of view of the utilization of their energy."[113] The following year, the Institute adopted a resolution on "international regulations regarding the use of international watercourses."[114] Fifty years later, in

---

108. *Id.* at 295.

109. For a report on the work of the Committee *see id.* at 294-304.

110. *Id.* at 300-02.

111. COMMITTEE ON THE USES OF THE WATERS OF INT'L RIVERS OF THE AMERICAN BRANCH OF THE INT'L LAW ASS'N, PRINCIPLES OF LAW AND RECOMMENDATIONS ON THE USES OF INTERNATIONAL RIVERS xii (1958).

112. For a summary of the work of these organizations *see* 3 M. WHITEMAN, DIGEST OF INTERNATIONAL LAW 921-24, 929-30 (1964); *supra* note 71, at 199-202, 208-09; *supra* note 66, at 283-86.

113. *Supra* note 71, at 199.

114. *Id.* at 200.

1961, at its Salzburg session the Institute adopted a resolution on utilization of non-maritime international waters (except for navigation).[114.1] The principle of equitable utilization is recognized[115] and provisions are contained (1) for prior notice before undertaking "works or utilizations of the waters of a watercourse or hydrographic basin which seriously affect the possibility of utilization of the same waters by other States,"[116] (2) for adequate compensation for any loss or damage,[117] and (3) for settlement of disputes.[118] Similar principles are outlined in a 1957 resolution of the Inter-American Bar Association,[119] which also created a Permanent Committee on the Law Governing the Uses of International Rivers.[120] At the 16th Conference of the Association, held at Caracas in November 1969, the Association adopted a resolution recommending that "the laws of the American countries on the industrial and agricultural utilization of rivers and lakes be unified or harmonized in order to avoid international controversies."[121]

E. *The International Law Commission Study*

Pursuant to a General Assembly resolution of December 8, 1970,[122] that the International Law Commission should study the law of the non-navigational uses of international watercourses with a view to its progressive development and codification, and the Assembly resolution of December 3, 1971,[123] recommending that the Commission give priority to the topic, the Commission appointed a Subcommittee and subsequently a special rapporteur to deal with the question.[124]

In its report to the Commission,[125] the Subcommittee noted that the recent studies on the subject, as well as the more recent treaties and state practices, showed the use of varying

---

114.1. *Id.* at 202.

115. Arts. 2-4, *id.*

116. Arts. 4-5, *id.*

117. Art. 4, *id.*

118. Arts. 6-9, *id.*

119. *See id.* at 208.

120. *See id.* at 208-09.

121. *Supra* note 66 at 286.

122. G.A. Res. 2669, 25 U.N. GAOR Supp. 28, at 127, U.N. Doc. A/8028 (1970).

123. G.A. Res. 2780, 26 U.N. GAOR Supp. 29, at 136, U.N. Doc. A/8429 (1971).

124. For a report on the Commission's response to the General Assembly's recommendations *see Report of the 28th Session of Int'l L. Comm'n* at 367-69.

125. *See* [1974] 2 Y.B. Int'l L. Comm'n Pt. 1, at 301, U.N. Doc. A/CN.4/SER. A/1974/Add.1 (Part 1) (1974).

terms to determine the scope of "international watercourses." These terms include "river basin," "drainage basin," "international drainage basin," "hydrographic basin," and "successive and contiguous international rivers" as a basis for the solution of legal problems.[126] In view of these variations in practice and theory, showing that the term "international watercourses" lacks "a sufficiently well-defined meaning to delimit, with any degree of precision, the scope of the work which the Commission should undertake on the uses of fresh water,"[127] the Subcommittee proposed that the Commission request states to comment on the questions pertaining to: (1) "the appropriate scope of the definition of an international watercourse, in a study of the legal aspects" of fresh water uses and of fresh water pollution; and (2) the geographical concept of an international drainage basin as being the appropriate basis for a study of the legal aspects of non-navigational uses, as well as the pollution of international watercourses.[128]

State responses confirmed the Subcommittee's initial conclusion that there is a lack of consensus on the subject.[129] Several states preferred the traditional definition of an international river, as contained in the Final Act of the Congress of Vienna of June 9, 1815—that international watercourses are those which separate or cut across the territory of two or more states.[130] However, several states supported the Commission's adoption of the concept of the drainage basin to determine the scope of its work,[131] while others expressed some reservations.[132]

A similar variation in the view of states was evident during the course of the subsequent discussion of the subject in July 1976 at the Commission's 28th Session.[133] While many members supported the traditional definition of an international

---

126. *Id.* at 301-02.

127. *Id.* at 302.

128. *Id.*

129. *The Law of the Non-Navigational Uses of International Watercourses* 13-47, U.N. Doc. A/CN.4/294 (1976).

130. *See, e.g., id.* at 15 (Brazil); 17 (Columbia); 20 (Federal Republic of Germany); and 27 (Poland).

131. *Id.* at 13-14 (Argentina); 15 (Barbados); 19 (Finland); 26 (Pakistan); 26 (Philippines); 30 (Sweden); and 30-31 (United States of America).

132. *Id.* at 21-25 (Hungary); and 31-32 (Venezuela).

133. *See Report of the 28th Session of Int'l L. Comm'n* at 385-87.

river embodied in the Final Act of the Congress of Vienna,[134] one member suggested that the subject was not yet "ripe for codification because experience was rapidly accumulating and scientific progress was opening many doors, with the result that it was impossible to predict new developments in irrigation and the proper economic uses of water."[135] He warned against making generalizations at this stage. Another member suggested that since river basins varied considerably—encompassing very limited or very large portions of the territory of a state or parts of the territory of different states, some of them covering areas as huge as the Amazon Basin and the River Plate Basin, which cover areas of 4,787,000 square kilometers and 2.4 million kilometers respectively—there could not be a serious contention "that the Commission had the authority to formulate rules that would be valid for the whole of such huge areas, imposing a kind of dual or multiple sovereignty."[136]

In its deliberations the Commission was influenced by the following comments contained in the Subcommittee report:

> Almost all of the States responding recognized, either expressly or implicitly, that the purpose of a definition of international watercourses should be to provide a context for examination of the legal problems that arise when two or more States are present in the same fresh water system and that a definition should not ineluctably bring with it corollary requirements as to the manner in which those legal problems should be solved. Thus some States objected to use of the drainage basin concept because they considered that its use implied the existence of certain principles, especially in the field of river management. Other States considered that traditional concepts such as contiguous and successive waterways would be too restricted a basis on which to carry out the study in view of the need to take account of the hydrologic unity of a water system.
>
> Consequently, it would seem wise for the Commission to follow the advice proffered by a number of the commenting States that the work on international watercourses should not be held up by disputes over definitions. This approach is, of course, in line with the customary practice of the Commission in deferring the adoption of definitions, or at the most adopting them on

134. *Id.* at 385.
135. *Id.*
136. *Id.*

a provisional basis, pending the development of substantive provisions regarding the legal subject under review.[137]

The Commission reached a general agreement that it need not determine the range of the term "international watercourses" at the outset of the work, and that, instead, it should begin formulating general principles applicable to legal aspects of the uses of these watercourses.[138] On the nature of these principles it was agreed that

> every effort should be made to devise rules which would maintain a delicate balance between those which were too detailed to be generally applicable and those which were so general that they would not be effective. Further, the rules should be designed to promote the adoption of regimes for individual international rivers and for that reason should have a residual character. Effort should be devoted to making the rules as widely acceptable as possible and the sensitivity of States regarding their interests in water must be taken into account.[139]

On the Subcommittee's recommendation, the Commission had also sought state responses to the question of what uses should be included in the study.[140] The suggested Subcommittee outline, containing the following three items, was generally endorsed: (1) agricultural uses—irrigation, drainage, waste disposal, and aquatic food production; (2) economic and commercial uses—energy production, manufacturing, construction, transportation other than navigation, timber floating, waste disposal, and extractive; and (3) domestic and social uses—consumptive, waste disposal, and recreational.[141] However, the list was supplemented by proposals to include commercial fishing, gravel extraction, aquatic food control, stockraising, pollution from inland shipping, sediment discharge, forestry, and heat dissipation.[142] There was general agreement that (1) flood control, erosion problems, and sedimentation be included in the Commission study[143] and (2) the interaction between the uses of international watercourses for navigational and other purposes had to be taken into account.[144] Thirteen

---

137. Cited in *id.* at 382.
138. *See id.* at 387.
139. *Id.*
140. *See id.* at 373-74.
141. *Id.* at 378, 388.
142. *Id.* at 378.
143. *Id.* at 388.
144. *Id.*

out of twenty states responding to the question whether the Commission should give priority to the problem of pollution answered that the question of uses should be taken up first;[145] six suggested that pollution problems should be taken up first;[146] while suggestions were made to study these problems simultaneously.[147] The Commission decided to study the pollution problems to the extent possible in connection with the particular uses that give rise to the pollution.[148]

IV. Appraisal and Recommendations

It seems that although the interplay over a period of the last several decades between customary practices and specific multilateral, regional, and bilateral treaties has resulted in some broad, general guidelines on the use of international watercourses, no cohesive body of rules has yet been widely accepted by states. At the basis of these guidelines lies the Roman maxim, *sic utere tuo ut alienum non laedas* (one must so use his own not to do injury to others). Implicit in the acceptance of this maxim is the rejection of the absolute territorial sovereignty theory,[149] a classical example of which is United States Attorney-General Harmon's assertion in 1895 of U.S. claims against Mexico in a conflict concerning the utilization of the Rio Grande.[150] According to this theory, a state's rights as an upper riparian over water within its jurisdiction are unlimited since it has absolute territorial sovereignty under international law. Thus it would be held to be unaccountable to the co-riparian for the use of those waters in a manner that adversely affected the latter. Additionally, the generally accepted guideline—reasonable and equitable utilization of waters—implicitly rejects the territorial integrity theory,[151] according to which a lower riparian is entitled to demand the continuation of the natural flow of waters from upstream.

---

145. *Id.* at 379.

146. *Id.*

147. *Id.*

148. *Id.* at 388.

149. For a discussion of the various theories *see* Lipper, *Equitable Utilization,* in The Law of International Drainage Basins, *supra* note 15, at 18; Menon at 445-46. *See also* Witaschek, *International Control of River Water Pollution,* 2 Denver J. Int'l L. & Pol. 35 (1972).

150. The statement is contained in 21 Op. Att'y Gen. 274, 283 (1895).

151. *Supra* note 149.

Under this theory, no interruption, augmentation, or diminution of the flow would be permitted.

However, while there seems to be consensus that territorial sovereignty and integrity have to be limited, no generally agreed formulation exists of the criteria to be used in weighing and balancing the co-riparian's interests. The often-used prescription—prohibition from causing substantial damage or injury to a co-riparian[152]—is negative, again lacking precision.

A recommendation that the community interest be a guiding principle in determining the use of international waterways was made by a member of the International Law Commission at the most recent discussion of the subject by the Commission. The member reportedly

> stressed that sovereignty was not a basis for dealing with the uses of international watercourses. The Commission must realize that there was another principle of international law to which it should attach greater importance, namely, the principle of the development of international law in the direction of a social law dealing with the delimitation of competence and sovereignty and with the interests of the international community as a whole in using all natural resources for the benefit of all mankind.[153]

The Commission felt the need to further explore legal concepts, such as abuse of rights, good faith, good neighborliness, and humanitarian treatment, in the elaboration of legal rules for water use.[154]

If the community approach to international watercourses were to be generally accepted, adequate institutional arrangements would be needed to give effect to this approach. Clearly, the nature of the institutional structures which would bring about integrated management of international water resources will vary with their purposes, states' capabilities, and various economic, political, and social factors. However, there are many similarities and general patterns in several experiments to date which could offer lessons for future development. Examples both among developed and developing states where

---

152. The prescription prohibiting "substantial injury" in the territory of a co-basin state is contained in art. X(1)(a) of the Helsinki Rules, *supra* note 66, at 290. The term "substantial damage" is used in Proposition VIII of the draft propositions prepared by the Asian-African Legal Consultative Committee, *id.*, at 229.

153. *Supra* note 133, at 387.

154. *Id.*

agreements have been reached on the utilization of water resources include the following international watercourses: the Danube, Rhine, Indus, Moselle, Niger, Senegal, Columbia, Nile, Mekong, Rio Grande, Chad, Plate, the Great Lakes, and St. Lawrence waters.[155]

In commenting recently on the inadequacy of the many existing institutional arrangements to provide for a rational and coordinated development of water resources, Professors Parnall and Utton have noted that "the inability of river basin organizations to make decisions and to draw up resource management plans that have at least some binding effect on the member basin states is probably the single most important weakness of the majority of international river organizations."[156] They relate the example of an international watercourse institution which is modeled on the concept of integrated river basin development, l'Organisation Pour la Mise en Valeur du Fleuve Senegal (OMVS).[157] An appraisal of the structure of the OMVS has led them to suggest that "[p]erhaps uniquely, the OMVS is endowed with [the] highly desirable planning and management authority,"[158] which is a prerequisite for the optimal management of the international watercourse resources within the jurisdiction of such an authority. Of course such development presumes joint action by states treating the basin as a geoeconomic unit. And the establishment of an institution with the kind of jurisdiction, functions, and authority enjoyed by the OMVS presumes that basin states have balanced their interests between following the traditional notion of national sovereignty and opting for rational utilization and optimal development of the international basin resources, and have chosen the latter.

To accomplish the objective of optimal development and

---

155. Institutional arrangements of multipartite and bipartite commissions established for some of these watercourses are contained in *supra* note 66, at 270-81. *See also* Israel & Zupkus, *Model Statute: International Drainage Basin Pollution Control*, 2 DENVER J. INT'L L. & POL. 89 (1972).

156. Parnall & Utton, *supra* note 42, at 236. *See also* Menon, *The Lower Mekong River Basin—Some Proposals for the Establishment of a Development Authority*, 6 INT'L LAW. 796 (1972); Utton, *International Water Quality Law*, 13 NAT. RES. J. 382 (1973); Israel & Zupkus, *supra* note 155.

157. *Supra* note 42.

158. *Id.* at 253-54.

utilization, it is essential to investigate the basin resources, to collect scientific data, and to know the potential benefits before any planning is undertaken for joint, coordinated action. These joint actions will usually take the form of basin-wide programs and multi-purpose projects.[159] Of course, at the basis of such efforts lies the concept of community interest, which implies the equality of all basin states in the use of the whole of the course of the river, without any discrimination or preference of any one state in relation to others. To finance specific projects the assistance of U.N. organizations, such as the U.N. Development Program and various U.N. specialized agencies, regional and bilateral economic commissions, and financing institutions, should be actively explored.

The building of new institutional arrangements or the upgrading of existing ones requires taking into account necessary technical information and the political and legal framework. Beginning with the establishment of consultation mechanisms, nations may create permanent joint agencies, undertake joint construction programs, and reach agreements on many important issues such as customs, immigration, labor, taxation, and dispute settlement mechanisms.[160] Such joint agencies could be linked with the United Nations and its various specialized agencies and commissions. The common interest in the optimal utilization of international waters demands a definite worldwide move toward integrated basin management, administration, and development. The development of appropriate legal norms by the International Law Commission and the establishment of more institutional structures on the model of the OMVS will facilitate and accelerate this desirable trend.

---

159. *See generally The 1975 U.N. Panel of Experts Report*, at 92-143, 174-84.
160. *Id.*

2
Global Water Law Systems and Water Control

George Radosevich[*]

I. WATER LAW

Water is a fundamental natural resource with complex characteristics. The ability to apply water for beneficial uses is as much subject to natural laws of the physical universe as the laws of human institutions. The greatest benefit from water is derived when it is used in combination with other natural resources (soil, mineral, or vegetative) and economic resources (labor and capital). The more efficiently it can be used in combination with other resources, whether by technological or institutional innovation, the greater the benefit to the water user and to society.

A quick review of water activities around the globe clearly indicates that this resourse has rapidly become one of the critical elements in determining local, national, and regional growth. In the past three decades, particularly the last five years, the trend has been away from treating water as a free good, subject to nearly unrestricted control, to a recognition of the resource as a capital commodity whose spatial and temporal availability dictate policy formulation and new directions in both macro and micro planning and development. Nations in all stages of development have accorded control and management of water resources a high priority.

Water laws are an expression of policy. Substantive provisions dealing w   of water resources are the basis fc   ulations to implement the law.   of each particular system of water law has a direct connection to the surrounding physical factors of its origin. Where water is plentiful, regulation is aimed at ameliorating the harmful effects of water (floods, salination, etc.). Where water is scarce, however, regulation is aimed at ensuring an adequate supply by providing, for example, that water is not owned by any one individual,

* Associate Professor of Water Law & Economics, Colorado State University; Director, International Conference on Global Water Law Systems, Valencia, Spain, Sept. 1975.

but, rather, is owned collectively so that all might use what is available.

Over time distinct regional or national systems emerged which reflect particular physical conditions and social goals. Elaborate water laws and administrative systems evolved where the greatest needs and most serious natural constraints existed. Through adoption or imposition many of these sytems have also influenced or directed water use and control in other countries or regions. While retaining many of the basic characteristics of the original system, these variations have incorporated modifications to meet indigenous conditions. (See figure 1.)

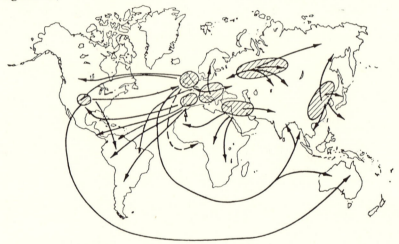

Figure 1   A Descriptive Map of Proposed Examination of Major Legal Systems (⬭) and Their Variations or Paths of Influence (———▶). (This is not an Exhaustive Description but Only Indicative Categorizations.)

Water laws must be dynamic and should be the product of evolutionary processes. However, the water laws and organizational structures that at one point in time were designed to be solutions to particular problems often become the problem at a later time. Through inflexibility—lack of explicit policy provisions and gaps in subjects included—constraints to the introduction of new technologies and improved water management practices frequently emerge. Three key issues, in light of needed changes in the law, impede water resources optimization: (1) allocation and reallocation of water supplies; (2) integration of water quantity and quality control; and (3) management and conjunctive use of ground and surface waters.

Past practices have, in many countries, created vested rights in the continued use of a source of water. In most cases, efficiency in transmission by the purveyor of water (which may be the sovereign) or the user of the supply is low, due to costs of reducing seepage, evapotranspiration, percolation, and other system losses. The tasks facing most water decision makers are now more related to water reallocation than allocation, and how this can be done with a minimum of social disruption.

The problems and pressures are not only at the micro levels, but exist at the macro (policy and program) levels as well. Policies toward development and water resource use of one nation have a consequence upon its neighbors where such neighbors are hydrologically connected. A well-known example is the impact on Northwestern Mexico from the western reclamation policies of the United States. Further, technology has not only provided more efficient and effective means for using water in or out of the natural basin regime, but has also placed an additional task upon decision makers to prepare programs and promulgate laws and regulations with scientific awareness.

Projections in water demands, as many proclaim, should not remain bleak if rational remedial action is taken. It is not a matter of reaching a plateau of subsistence with our water supply. There is little reason why the development, use, and management of available resources cannot take place harmoniously with an enhanced quality of life if decisions executed and legal controls enacted are systematically made.

Water law and administration consist of a wide variety of alternative approaches which have evolved over time and under different demand situations. Identifying a set of these major systems provides the decision maker with a spectrum of alternative doctrinal and organizational approaches. These can be of value in preparing proposed legal machinery or evaluating present effectiveness in light of potential changes.

In September 1975, a conference was convened in Valencia, Spain to systematically describe and analyze the major systems of water law in the world. Among the water law systems reviewed were the Spanish, French, British, Italian, Soviet, Hindu-Bali, Moslem, Latin American, Israeli, and the variations found in both the United States and selected Asiatic countries. The relationship of water law to the human and physical environment was discussed from the social, economic, and technical perspectives. Presentations concerning national water planning, drafting water codes, and bilateral and multilateral assistance available to developing countries in preparing or revising water codes and administrative arrangements concluded the conference.

The following summary of selected systems of water law and administration is based upon the reports prepared for the conference.[1] These systems have been arranged into three categories: customary, traditional, and modern water law systems.

II. Systems of Customary-Religious Base

These systems are represented by the Moslem system of water law and the Subak system for water administration in Bali, Indonesia. Both systems have in common their religious origin. In both, water is treated as part of man's cosmogony. Water is not subject to private appropriation in either system. Water is the object of a right to use, not own, the corpus, with the exception of the cases in which the Islamic law recognizes private rights in waters. This recognition is limited to small volumes of water contained in well-defined boundaries, such as the water contained in a cistern.

The Islamic water law is not a national system of water law in the western style.[2] Rather, it is a system of religious and traditional doctrines and uses. It goes beyond country boundaries pervading local customs. In turn, the religious element which gives commonality to the system is influenced by the particular uses of each place and locality. In this respect, it should be stressed that Islam did respect local practices, as long as they were not in opposition to the basic set of religious rules. The basic egalitarian concept of Islam prevails throughout all aspects of Moslem water law and is easily identified in the common water ownership and equitable apportionment principles of the law. Water is spread, for example, to enable all farmers to irrigate the maximum possible area of land. An-

---

1. For the complete text prepared by specialists in the various water law systems, see 1-4 Proceedings of the International Conference on Global Water Law Systems (G. Radosevich, V. Giner, D. Daines, G. Skogerboe & E. Vlachos eds. 1976) (Colorado State University, Fort Collins) [hereinafter cited as Proceedings].

2. Maktari, *Islamic Water Law*, in 1 Proceedings at 295-308.

other reason is that taxes are based on irrigated land. Water rights are also attached to the land. With the spread of Islam, concepts of common ownership, and equitable apportionment, the appurtenancy principle and local administration spread to Spain and to regions of North and South America.

Great rivers are absolutely common property. Small natural rivers are predominantly for the use of the riparian, and artificial rivers are for the common use of those who dig them. Surplus waters are to be always offered for the use of other persons.

Water for irrigation is to be allocated on the basis of: (1) the crops; (2) the season; and (3) the local customs and the quality of the water. It is allocated by time and volume and the order of preference is: (1) thirst; (2) domestic uses; (3) irrigation and commerce; and (4) industry.

Rules against abuse and waste pervade the use of the waters. Any member of the community can claim judicial redress to establish or protect a water right. The most rational use of wells is restricted because every person does have the right to drill a well on his land, even when it affects the rights of other water users.

Islamic principles on national or provincial water administration are not very relevant in that the law says very little about high levels of administration. The Islamic law, as a prevailing system of belief and tradition, does not offer solutions for centralization of water management; but it has had a fundamental influence at local levels, where it results in a local authority controlling water rights. The administration and organization that does exist results from ancient customs. Local water masters carry out water administration.

Another system of customary-religious based law that is significant to local water use is the Subak.[3] The Subak is the traditional water management technique of Bali in the Indonesian Archipelago. It is based on the Hindu cosmogony. It survived the brief domination of Buddhist dynasties and was modified only slightly by Islam, which reduced the unit for water administration to the level of the village. The Subak

---

3. Wohlwend, *Hindu Water Law and Administration*, in 2 PROCEEDINGS at 536-85.

included not only one, but several villages for the purpose of water administration.

The Subak is basically a community of farmers that irrigates. The common bond is irrigation, and, for this reason, it encompasses several villages. The limits are not set by the village boundaries but by the irrigated lands. It is governed by rules of customary law.

Administration is through a Subak meeting (assembly) which has sovereign water jurisdiction and whose decisions are implemented by a chief water master. The latter is assisted by deputies, by assistants, and by criers, who control, respectively, each subunit of the water network, the end of the water network, and the distribution of water to individual users.

Water can never become an element of appropriation. It is subject only to the rights of use and is distributed in proportion to crop needs.

III. The Latin American Systems

In Latin America there are two systems of water law.[4] The first is the traditional system, influenced by the riparian system of France and by the system of the Spanish Water Law of 1879.

Second are the modern water laws, inspired by the principles of comprehensive water management under the control of the state. These laws have attempted to translate principles of water management into principles of water law. They are the laws of Mexico, Panama, Colombia, Peru, Ecuador, and Chile.

The laws of each country in this vast region are easily the topic of a regional conference, so it is preferable to quote part of the abstract from the report by Dr. Joaquin Lopez to illustrate the range of differences that exist. It must be said that Dr. Lopez did not feel comfortable with his description of the Latin American systems even in a three hundred page report because there are still topics of importance that were not included.

> The countries of South and Central America which were colonized by Spain and Portugal have a system of water law with

---

4. Lopez, *Water Law and Water Administration in Latin America*, in 3 PROCEEDINGS at 699-848.

particular features. The judicial regulations of these countries have similarity of principles, norms, institutions, origins and customary uses respect[ing] waters. The system was influenced by the colonial legislation, the metropolitan legislation, the Civil Code of France and the Constitution of the United States. The laws for Indians, the laws of the "Siete Partidas" and the Spanish water law of 1866 were also influential. In Brazil the metropolitan legislation was constituted of several ordinances: the Alfonsianas of 1447; the Manoelinas of 1521; and the Philipinas of 1603.

The different legal criteria between the Spanish and Brazilian legislations determined the existence of marked differences between the system of the water law of Brazil and the system of the water law of the other Iberoamerican countries.

In the former colonies of Spain prevailed the principle by virtue of which the waters were common to all the people, modified in some degree by the principles of the French Civil Code; in Brazil, instead, the riparian system, of French and Anglosaxon ascendancy was followed.

Regarding their constitutional organization, some countries adopted a federal regime, while others adopted unitarian systems of government. Among the former, despite their federal systems, there are some countries in which the domain of the waters and the jurisdiction to regulate their use appertains to the Federal Government; and there are other countries in which these attributions correspond to the provinces.

The administration in the unitarian countries is carried out by decentralized national organisms, by autarchical entities, or by the central government. In the federal countries there are some which maintain centralized systems of legislation and administration of the waters; while in others the provinces are attributed broad faculties regarding water.[5]

The greatest problem in Latin America is the system for the administration of water resources which, in most countries, is highly fragmented. There are problems of interference and duplication of functions. The problem is twofold: on the one hand, lack of united decisionmaking processes; and, on the other, lack of adequate input from the water users. There is a significant lack of effective channels of communication from the users to the highest levels of administration. In most of the countries there is a lack of general coherent policies which, translated to the water resources field, would give criteria for

---

5. *Abstracts*, in 1 PROCEEDINGS at 45.

the guidance of the particular activities of each national water agency.

Significant attempts to overcome these constraints are represented in Mexico by united decisionmaking which is combined with the maximum possible user participation, in Cuba, where there is an autonomous institute for water administration, and in Ecuador, which has implemented a comprehensive scheme for water administration.

Water administration can be carried out by federal and state agencies, as in Argentina, or at a centralized center of autonomous decisions, as in Mexico. Attempts of regional structures for water administration are carried out in Brazil, where the input of the central government is very significant. In Venezuela, an attempt for comprehensive planning and management is at present being carried out. Peru has most of the responsibility for water management delegated to the General Directorate of Waters and Irrigation.

Examples of countries in which water administration is divided among several institutions are Uruguay, the Dominican Republic, Paraguay, Nicaragua, Guatemala, and El Salvador. In Chile, there is a proposal for the creation of an Institute of Water Resources which would be charged with the coordination of all water resources activities.

There is a growing awareness in South America of the importance of water resources for the developmental process. There are serious attempts at implementation of new legal systems for the most correct management of the resource. There are, however, difficulties created by the particular socioeconomic structures of the Latin American countries. The subject deserves special attention, for new legal codes cannot be severed from the conditions of each country. If abstraction is made of the facts, the seeds for failure will accompany any intent of legal change. The law is not only an instrument for the change of a particular socio-economic milieu, it is also a consequence of it.

IV. SELECT SYSTEMS OF WATER LAW IN EUROPE[6] AND THE MID-EAST

A brief summary follows of the system of water law in the

---

6. For an analysis of the legal aspects of water quality management in Europe, see R. JOHNSON & G. BROWN, CLEANING UP EUROPE'S WATERS (1976).

United Kingdom, France, Spain, Italy, the Soviet Union, and Israel. These systems were selected due to their global influence or unique and potentially transferable features. They range from traditional to modern systems of water law.

In the United Kingdom statutory regulations have been enacted in the public interest.[7] England has placed a high premium on water as resource needs have transformed the plentiful commodity into an item of scarcity.

For this reason, common law has been substituted by statutory law. The provisions which have evolved from traditional common to modern laws have been designed: (1) to secure an adequate supply of water both in quantity and quality; (2) to satisfy all needs and prevent waste; (3) to secure water quality and pollution control; (4) to promote flood control and land drainage; (5) to clean the rivers of the country; (6) to assure recreational, wildlife, and fisheries opportunities; and (7) to protect the interests of affected water users.

Under common law the rivers are considered in the public domain and cannot be owned. Ownership is significant only in relation to waterbeds. The beds of tidal rivers are owned by the Crown. The use of water in riparian land is an incident of the right of ownership. The quality and quantity of the water cannot be diminished, unless authorized by grant, statute, or prescription. Rights regarding artificial watercourses are always acquired by grant or arrangement. Underground water can be freely used, according to the English absolute-ownership rule. Many changes were made in the common law after the enactment of the Water Resources Act of 1963 and its coming into operation on July 1, 1965. It is now necessary to obtain a license for the use of inland underground waters. Exceptions are given for small abstractions, riparian domestic or agricultural uses, and abstraction of underground water for household use. The Act has substituted for the common law rights of the riparians a system of compulsory licensing. Rights to the use of waters are legally protected and administered. Water authorities are given broad powers for the control of the use and abuse of water rights. Under the common law, water was not to be impaired

---

7. Richardson, *Systems of Water Law and Organization in the United Kingdom*, in 2 PROCEEDINGS at 309-408.

in quality. Water pollution control laws have been enacted which strengthen and further define the common law concept in the context of new and projected uses.

The evolution of water administration in the United Kingdom is important in that it illustrates the dynamic growth and maturation process of a national system of water law. From the 1945 and 1963 Water Resources Acts to the present 1973 and 1974 Acts, the concept of the river basin authorities has been developed and tested under centralized to decentralized control. All functions associated with the water cycle are under the control of a single authority in any one region which attempts to closely correlate to a natural hydrological unit. This leads to an integrated system of water management combining water quantity and quality control and conjunctive use of ground and surface waters. The guidelines of these control and management activities are set by water policies elaborated by the Secretary of State and by the Minister of Agriculture, Fisheries, and Food. The intent is to jointly promote a water policy for water management in England and Wales. The regional authorities execute the policy.

There is a National Water Resources Council which consists of a chairman appointed by the Secretary of State, the chairman of the water authorities and other members appointed by the Secretary of State, and the Minister of Agriculture, Fisheries, and Food. The Council assists and gives advice in water-related matters to the Ministers requiring it, assists and controls in the effective performance of duties of the water authorities, and must elaborate a scheme for training and education in water-related functions.

There are nine regional water authorities in England and one in Wales. The area of a water authority may be different for the performance of different functions, but the intent is to organize around natural watersheds where possible, with, however, alterations in the boundaries where social and economic reasons prevail. Water authorities are presided over by a chairman appointed by the Secretary of State, and consist of two or four members appointed by the Ministry of Agriculture, and a variable number of representatives of the local population. The water authorities provide an integrated control system for water within the confines of national policy laid down by the ministries, and can take every necessary action to insure the best use and administration of the water.

In France the waters are considered a source of life, and the legislature has recognized, with reluctance, private appropriation.[8] Common rights have been readily recognized in favor of the riparian owners of watercourses. The need to legislate pollution control has produced a deep change in the system of water law, as well as in the system for water administration. France has abandoned the old system of water classification which was based on the navigability or floatability of the waters. Waters were public that were navigable or floatable. At present, water resources can be declared public because of their utility or importance for uses considered vital by the state for the socioeconomic well-being of the population. Waters can be declared public because of their relevance to agriculture, industry, domestic uses, and navigation as well as for their damaging potential, as when the waters can produce dangerous floodings, according to the Law of December 16, 1964. This new classification includes the waters that were considered public in the old system; and, at the same time, broadens the category to include waters that, even when not navigable or floatable, do have public importance, either for their utility or for their dangerous potential.

There are also "mixed" watercourses in which the waters are public and the beds are private. Public and mixed watercourses are part of the general category of public waters. Private waters are a residual category. They are what is left after the former two categories have been determined.

Private property rights are recognized over springs and underground waters, but with important limitations. These limitations derive from several facts. For example, a landowner cannot make free use of spring water that, even when arising on his land, is used by towns or other domestic needs. The use of underground water is subject to health regulation. The right to underground water is only acquired in the abstracted water. The consequences are quite similar to the application of the English rule. Flowing, nonpublic waters are common waters

---

8. Depox, *The French Water Law*, in 2 PROCEEDINGS at 409-15.

subject to common use. For the use of public waters authorization is required. Navigation always has preference.

France has also developed an extensive system for the protection of water against pollution. Water administration at the national level is spread among several ministries due to the public or nonpublic nature of the waters according to the uses to which they are dedicated. For concrete management, it is unified at basin level. The interministerial coordination is carried out by the Ministry of the Quality of the Human Life under the Decrees of March 2, 1971 and June 1975. The important decisions are taken by the interministerial Committee for the Action for Environment. Final decisions or arbitrations are taken up by the Prime Minister. At the basin level, water administration is carried out by basin agencies in which local interests have representation.

Spanish water law proclaims all water flowing in natural beds as being public property.[9] The category of flowing waters is interpreted broadly to include large as well as small rivers and arroyos. Spring waters flowing in natural beds are also considered public. Also classified as public waters, flowing or not, are waters located on lands of the public domain, or lands affected by public water works. The waters, which do not flow in natural waterbeds and which are located in private lands, are private property. The Spanish water law thus combines two criteria: (1) waters flowing in natural waterbeds are public; and (2) if the waters do not flow in natural waterbeds, their condition depends upon the legal conditions of the lands in which they are located.

The allocation of public waters for individual or private uses is by concession from the Ministry of Public Works. These concessions are not required for limited domestic or natural uses such as water for thirst and washing, but are a necessary prerequisite to uses of "special developments." A priority in allocation is set out in Article 160 of the Water Act of 1879, placing uses in the following order—towns, railways, irrigated agriculture, navigation channels, mills and other factories, and aquatic life and habitats. Public waters are totally administered by the Ministry of Public Works through the Directorate

---

9. Arrieta, *Spain's Legal Water Ordinance System*, in 1 PROCEEDINGS at 234-94.

of Water Works. The country is divided into ten basin administration entities which provide logical management consistent
with the natural flow regime.

The agencies for water administration at basin level are:
the Water Commissioner and the Hydrographic Confederation,
integrated by the individual users; Communities of Irrigators;
and Central Syndicator of the Basin. It can be said that,
through this sytem of organization, Spain has greatly harmonized the need for unified decisionmaking at central level with
the requirement of participation of the local water users. Central decisions are conveyed in each river basin through the
Water Commissioner. User and local institutional inputs are
furnished through the Hydrographic Confederation. The disputes on water can be solved by Special Administrative Courts,
by the Civil Courts, or by the Criminal Courts, depending on
the kind of issue.[10]

In spite of a very workable system for water allocation and
management, it is important to take note of changes in the
Spanish law. Conditions and demands have so significantly
developed in the country that, with the advances of technology,
the law is required to evolve to a new plateau. Presently, a draft
of a modern Spanish water code is being discussed which places
emphasis upon the two major deficiencies under the old
law—conjunctive use of both ground and surface water and
integration of water quantity and quality control. Thus, Spain
is rapidly moving toward a more modern system of water law.

Italy defines as public all the waters which have or can
have qualities useful for satisfaction of needs of the public and
general interest.[11] This classification is influenced by the magnitude, volume, flow, or width of the waters, as well as by their
relationship to the hydrological system of which they form a
part. The administrative authority determines the particular
condition of each corpus of water, trying to assure adequate
protection to pre-existing water rights.

The public waters are listed in registers of public waters.
Nonpublic (private) waters are a residual category whose use

---

10. Fairen-Guillen, *The Process of the Tribunal of Water of Valencia*, in 1 PRO-
CEEDINGS at 136-58.
11. Caponera & Burchi, *Italian Water Law System*, in 1 PROCEEDINGS at 193-233.

is also regulated by the laws. These waters are springs or waters wholly within lands under private ownership. Public waters are allocated to use through a permit system which includes an elaborate review of the application to determine the appropriateness of the use and quantity requested.

Water administration is delegated throughout several different levels: national, regional, provincial, and municipal. The centralized administration of prewar Italy gave way to a more fragmented system. Nevertheless, a resources approach has been retained in the juridical arena. Italy's water courts are composed of a Supreme Tribunal for Public Waters and eight regional courts.

It was pointed out by Dr. Caponera that even though the Italian water law functions well, the lack of continuity between basins as physical units for water control and the political entities of water administration act as a constraint on the best use of the water. This constraint remains even though the existence of a Ministry of Public Works offers a unitary center of decision.

The basic principles of Soviet water law are contained in the Fundamentals of Water Legislation of the U.S.S.R., in force since September 1, 1971.[12] They contain the basic concepts and conditions for water use and control. In their elaboration, water codes have been adopted by each of the 15 Republics of the Union. There are, in addition, many subsidiary normative acts.

The law regulates state agencies, state and public enterprises, organizations, and individual citizens in connection with water ownership, management, use, conservation, control, and protection against the harmful effects of the waters. Thus, regulation refers only to water resources available as separate natural water bodies. When waters are no longer part of the environment, they are regulated by other bodies of law.

The policies are to ensure the most rational and economical use of the waters; to preserve, maintain, and improve water bodies; and to prevent the harmful effects of the waters. The basic principles of the law are: (1) exclusive state ownership;

---

12. Kolbasov, *Soviet System of Water Law*, in 2 PROCEEDINGS at 416-52.

(2) national and comprehensive use; (3) priority of domestic uses; (4) strict requirement of water pollution control; (5) development of technology for water conservation; (6) registration and control of water uses; (7) adoption of the basin as the hydrologic unit for water administration; and (8) active participation of the population in water uses. It is considered fundamental that water resources, within basins, form a definitive and economical unit. Water administration is carried out through several levels of government and through agencies of general state administration, agencies of special state administration, and agencies of branch administration.

An examination of the water laws and administrative organisms of Israel provides an excellent opportunity to observe the dynamic role and process of change served by a legal resources control system placed under extreme needs to optimize scarce water supplies.[13] Many other examples exist in national or subgovernmental jurisdiction in the case of federated systems, but the laboratory process of developing water laws found in Israel illustrates the ultimate role in extensive and intensive water control through formalized laws and regulations. All waters, regardless of their form or location, are under the strict control and jurisdiction of the state. The state holds the water in trust for the citizens of Israel and is dutybound to allocate and administer this limited resource in the most beneficial and efficient manner possible. This power and duty is placed with the Ministry of Agriculture and under the specific jurisdiction of the Water Commissioner.

The general proposition that water is public property entitles every citizen of the country to the right to use the resource. However, an important feature of this right is the set of conditions placed upon its exercise. Water is allocated for use by term and reviewable permit. The process of application and final actions for water use insure that the proposed use is beneficial to the individual and country. The results of the use must be within the range of maximum output, and other users should not be unreasonably affected if the proposed use is approved. All water rights are registered, which enables effective

13. Tamir, *Legal and Administrative Aspects of the Water Laws of Israel*, in 3 PROCEEDINGS at 849-911.

administration and the ability to prepare appropriate water plans and projections. The important feature of this modern code is the policy declaration that provides the basis for subsequent administrative operation. The policy reflects the national goals, just as water serves as an input to achieving them.

Administratively, the law empowers the Water Commissioner or his agents with the right of exclusive control over withdrawals as provided in the permits. The Commissioner can cancel or amend any permit and permanently or temporarily alter or suspend uses under it. All water use is metered and water fees charged according to volumetric uses, with rates varying throughout the country to reflect different uses and use conditions. The Water Commissioner also has full power to prevent degradation to the nation's water quality. Water pollution control is imperative and infractions are dealt with quickly.

In addition to the Water Commissioner, there are numerous boards and authorities to provide advice and assistance in water matters. Water users play an important role as members of many of the entities. Disputes are under the jurisdiction of a Special Tribunal for Water Affairs. Any person who feels aggrieved by the actions of a government official or of another water user can bring his case before this Tribunal.

V. Water Law in the United States

Although many other papers in this work describe the legal aspects of water control in the United States, their focus is upon particular issues or problem areas. Thus, a brief overview is provided here to enable some comparison between the other major systems discussed.

Water law in the United States is a federated system of complex proportions.[14] Federal (national) and state water laws exist in both the water quantity and quality aspects of this resource. At the federal level, jurisdiction over water originates with the Constitution. The property, commerce, general welfare, treaty, and compact clauses provide the basis for federal involvement in navigation, pollution abatement, and allocation and management of water resources. Particular laws

---

14. Radosevich & Daines, *Water Law and Administration in the United States*, in 2 Proceedings at 453-502.

have been enacted to provide the substantive control and organizational structures to carry out federal policies and programs.

State water laws are less cognizant of the hydrologic aspects of water resources. Each state, being an autonomous political entity, has rights to develop policies, laws, and organizations according to local and state needs. Thus, there are virtually 50 separate water law systems for quantity and quality control, often with lack of uniformity between states causing interstate conflicts. The states are primarily concerned with methods of allocation, distribution, and administration of ground and surface waters given the wide variety of geographical conditions in the country.

Ownership of water is either public, as in the case of the federal government jurisdiction over certain classes of water, or public or state in the case of rights over water vested in state control. The use of water depends upon the state systems of water law and ranges from common law right in the riparian system to a permit, license, or decree under the appropriation system. A form of contract water rights is becoming increasingly popular.

The past 10 years have witnessed the emergence of federal involvement from water development to management in the national and regional interests. Population shifts in a mobile society, industrialization, energy development, increased needs for food and fiber, conflicts and complementarities of water use with the interface of economic sectors, and new technologies have brought about this involvement. States, faced with the same issues at a more concentrated and grassroots level, have likewise been experiencing a significant evolution in their quantity and quality control laws with an emphasis upon developing planning and management capabilities to make conscious decisions based upon an evaluation of alternatives, impacts, and opportunity costs.

Water-administration at the federal level is under the jurisdiction of the Water Resources Council and a multitude of ministerial land departments and departmental agencies, bureaus, and authorities. State administration is hierarchical from central control at the political jurisdictional level down to the level of hydrologic units within the state. Normally, water quantity and quality control is vested in different agencies. The water law systems in the United States are in a dynamic and evolutionary process brought about by changing conditions and can constantly benefit by an awarness of experiences of other nations.

VI. ASIATIC SYSTEMS

Professor Clark, a well-known expert in water law systems of Oceania and Asiatic regions, has repeatedly proclaimed the difficulty of summarily discussing this topic due to the great diversity that exists between countries in the region.[15] This single topic was the subject of a meeting of experts in the field held in Bangkok, Thailand in 1967, convened by the Economic Commission for Asia and the Far East.

To summarize the complexity of these systems, Mr. Clark states in the abstract to his report:

> Water legislation in Asia has been profoundly influenced by Common Law, Civilian and Roman-Dutch models. There is thus great diversity in the theoretical bases for water administration, but a common pattern of relying on administrative bodies to allocate and adjust private rights to use water. In this sense, systems of judicial apportionment of rights, through litigation, are most uncommon.
>
> There is remarkable similarity in the techniques used for granting and controlling rights to water, although the primary emphasis of the legislative schemes naturally differs with the hydrological problems encountered. There is increasing reliance on techniques of multi-objective planning, but care must be taken in adapting systems of environmental planning to the different economic and social goals of developing countries.[16]

The range of features in the law extend ownership from state to public to private; acquisition of rights according to custom without administrative intervention to systems granting permits or concessions; allocations according to a nonpreference or to limited preference of user classes; and administration under centralized to decentralized systems. A major concern of many systems is with water removal, as in flood and drainage programs, rather than water allocation.

VII. SUMMARY

In summary, the water law systems illustrate a wide range of approaches in control of allocation, distribution, and regula-

---

15. Clark, *The Asian Region*, in 2 PROCEEDINGS at 503-35.
16. *Abstracts*, in 1 PROCEEDINGS at 39.

tion of the resource under diverse conditions. Ownership of the resource extends from state ownership in the U.S.S.R., to public ownership in the vast majority of countries, to some private ownership, as found in Spain and other countries. Often the lack of a water policy inhibits the control and management of the government agency administering the laws. It is recommended that the "policy" should be given serious attention in any attempt to stimulate water-use efficiency and promote formation of collaborative efforts among water users.

Allocation of water likewise varies considerably, extending from: no evidence of a right; to customary rights; to government concessions, permits or titles; to court decrees. The success of public irrigation programs will partly depend upon the assurance of continued water availability to the water users in order to elicit their willingness to invest time and money beyond the present practice. While the assurance of right or privilege should be definable and dependable, it must also be flexible to react to changing demands and technologies.

From an examination of the systems, the following statements can be made:

1. There is a clear tendency towards the public ownership of all water. This tendency is dramatically exemplified by the legislative amendments of France and the United Kingdom. The public character of the waters has always been a strong component of the Spanish, North American, and Israeli systems. As water resources become relatively scarce, public pressures for regulation demand more state activity in the field. The opposite of public ownership of water in the realm of state activity is state ownership, as found in the Soviet Union. The conclusion is, however, the same—a direct correlation between the degree of state control and "scarcity" of resources regardless of ownership.

2. The basin as a unit of water management is recognized as an imperative for improved and rational management.

3. Where water users have a voice in the decisionmaking process by means of direct input at various levels of that process, greater continuity and realism exists in resource use.

4. The value of a unitary or coordinated system of water decisionmaking is discernable from the documents analyzed. It is observed that unitary decisionmaking does not imply the

subjugation of local interests at provincial, state, or regional levels. Adequate mechanisms for harmonic integration can be devised.

5.   Some countries, like Italy, Spain, and Israel, do have special courts for water problems. As water conflicts become more technical and complex and water issues involve more people and interests, the need for special water courts becomes increasingly apparent.

6.   The increase in the role of the state in water resources management, the increasingly public nature of water law, and the growing relative scarcity of water demand a redefinition of the concept of "acquired" water rights.

7.   The problems of improving water-use effectiveness, especially for developing countries, demand the development of new forms of compensation for the condemnation of land and water-related resources. Vested rights should not be a permanent constraint to optimum water use.

8.   In light of the growing complexity and interrelatedness of water problems, it is imperative for water law specialists to have an interdisciplinary foundation and communication network.

3
Alternatives to Appropriation Law

*Frank J. Trelease**

In recent years many water laws throughout the world have been subjected to review and reconsideration. The continued suitability of current law is questioned and a search is made for a new and modern form of water law. Older systems of self-generating rights—"private waters" and riparian rights —are to be discarded; "concessions" bring ugly memories of exploitation; and "prior appropriation" to many means some sort of Wild West rip-off of the public domain. In the search for a new system something called "administrative allocation of water" is frequently advocated, although what is meant is not always clear. In the course of a long career of teaching and writing about water law, and of acting as a consultant to several states and developing countries, I have been exposed to many variations on this theme. Most of them are prefaced by a rejection of prior appropriation; it is made clear that this is not what is wanted.

As a resident of the American West I have lived with prior appropriation a long time. I used to think that prior appropriation was an American invention, and I have done my share of repeating the familiar tale of how the '49ers protected their gold claims and water ditches with Colt and Winchester, how courts adopted these "customs" as American common law, and how the farmers that came after them adapted the miners' law to agriculture. But today I read in a compilation of the world's water laws that the protection of vested rights and a preference for the eldest rights is the most common of all systems of distribution of water, and many of these go back to antiquity and can in no sense be said to be derived from American law.[1] Thus it is natural to wonder why this prejudice against prior appropriation exists, why it is so often rejected by those who seek the best. Since it is so widely used there must be some good to it. As I look about and see the development that has taken place in the western states and review their history of transition from

* B.A., L.L.B., University of Colorado; J.S.D., University of Wisconsin. The author is Professor of Law at the University of Wyoming.
1. L. TECLAFF, ABSTRACTION AND USE OF WATER: A COMPARISON OF LEGAL REGIMES 81, U.N. Doc. No. ST/ECA/154 (1972).

gold rush to irrigated agriculture to great modern centers of commerce, I cannot help but think that we must have done something right.

What, then, are the objections to the spread of this common and proven system? Generally, they fall into two classes. The first type is founded on observed facts. Sometimes an example of waste is cited: excessive water use in Idaho or duplicating ditches in California. Sometimes dry streambeds in Arizona are pointed to as proving that instream uses, ecological balances, and environmental values cannot be protected under prior appropriation. The mistake in these cases is the assumption that because these examples of defects can be found the defects are inherent in the system. Most of these distortions and dislocations seem historical remnants of a pioneer system that need not be repeated today or minor aberrations that could be corrected by small adjustment of the system or tighter administration of the law.

The second class of objections is based on theory. Three recurrent reactions are voiced:

1. A dislike of the "property system"; appropriators seize valuable interests in the public domain and enrich themselves at the expense of the public.

2. A mistrust of the "market system"; a fear that under prior appropriation, water rights will become "frozen in the pioneer patterns," unsuitable for modern times and problems, and not subject to reallocation to new uses and needs.

3. A dislike of the "priority system"; in a shortage an "all-or-nothing" rule gives one of two essentially similarly situated water users all of his water while his neighbor gets none.

To a large extent these objections are based on lack of understanding—a failure to appreciate the flexibility and variety of operational methods available under controlled appropriation laws.

I. CONTROL OF INITIATION OF USES

Those who object to prior appropriation as a crude pioneer system are simply not up with the times. In the early days of western prior appropriation the pioneers did help themselves to water as they would "take berries from a bush or a rabbit from the plain."[2] The water was given away, but then so was the land. Even so the pioneer was hard put to survive, and as he broke the land to the plow and dug his ditches his "sweat equity" generally dispelled the charge of unearned increment. Today the water might be sold, but tradition is against it, and most governments are still willing to let water increase the wealth of their citizens rather than have it increase the balance in the state coffers.

The states did place some demands on the water users. The earliest limit on the appropriation of water was the legal concept of "beneficial use." Most of the pioneer uses met this test: water was used to mine the gold and silver from the hills, to dispell the myth of the "Great American Desert" by irrigated agriculture, to provide water for cities, railroads, and all forms of industry. By 1890 the need for more controls was seen by the people of Wyoming, who adopted the first permit system. A person who desires water must apply to a state official, who may deny the permit if there is no unappropriated water in the source or if the proposed appropriation will be contrary to the public interest. This statute became the model for most of the West, and today fifteen states have similar laws.[3] In 1910 the New Mexico court first gave the public interest concept some real content. The court was faced with two conflicting applications for the same water, and the first applicant to file demanded that he receive the permit. The court, however, said that the purpose of the statute was to secure the greatest possible benefit from the public waters for the public, and told the state water authorities to choose the better of the two projects, not merely the first proposal.[4] This is the legal expression of what the economist calls the efficiency principle, the notion that we should get the maximum net benefits from the use of our resources.

The power to control the initiation of water uses was seldom exercised, and few conflicts over unappropriated water occurred. Most beneficial uses were also found to be in the

---

2. Lasky, *From Prior Appropriation to Economic Distribution of Water by the State Via Irrigation Administration,* 1 ROCKY MTN. L. REV. 161 (1929).

3. Alaska, Arizona, California, Kansas, Nebraska, Nevada, New Mexico, North Dakota, Oklahoma, Oregon, South Dakota, Texas, Utah, Washington, and Wyoming.

4. Young & Norton v. Hinderlider, 15 N.M. 666, 110 P. 1045 (1910).

public interest, and although private initiative could be theoretically controlled by permits, in practice few were denied. However, there were some examples. An Oregon appropriation was denied when it was found that it could interfere with the state's plan for development of its lands and waters.[5] A limitation was placed on the height of a Wyoming dam to preserve the canyon for a future railroad link between two areas of the state.[6] In Utah the Bureau of Reclamation and the state government were cooperating on a plan for a large multipurpose project that would bring irrigation, municipal, and electric power benefits to three counties. An entrepreneur filed an application for a smaller project that would have seriously interfered with this development. Although he had filed first, the state authorities, backed by the courts, subordinated the small project to the large multipurpose project.[7]

These cases laid the groundwork for modern water planning. Today in many states an inventory has been taken of water resources and the alternative possibilities for their use. The goals of the state are carefully spelled out, policies are adopted to bring them to fruition, and the permit process is the mechanism for effectuating the plan. Strong efforts are being made in this direction in Wyoming, Alaska, the West Coast States, and others. A proposed private use that does not accord with the state plan will be denied, or brought into line by conditions attached to its permit. This technique is spreading eastward; the permit feature of western prior appropriation law is the one which has been most accepted in the Eastern States. Several of them, including Florida, Kentucky, Delaware, Mississippi, and New Jersey, now have very similar planning and permit processes.

II. THE DURATION OF THE WATER RIGHT

The major objective of any water law must be to achieve, or at least promote, the efficient allocation of water resources. Economic efficiency is the reference: that combination of labor, capital, and resources which will produce the greatest net benefits. Social and environmental factors will be worked into the adjustment of costs and benefits. State plans, programs, and

---

5. Cookinham v. Lewis, 58 Ore. 484, 114 P. 88 (1911).
6. Big Horn Power Co. v. State, 23 Wyo. 271, 148 P. 1110 (1915).
7. Tanner v. Bacon, 103 Utah 494, 136 P.2d 957 (1943).

policies may determine the optima to be sought, and state projects and agencies may play a large part in reaching them. Yet it is clear that in most countries a very large contribution toward optimum use of water for irrigation and industry will come from private sources. The water law system must foster and encourage water use and provide a climate conducive to investment in water-using enterprises. A person will put his capital and labor into such an enterprise if he has sufficient assurance that he will receive a fair return on his investment for a period long enough to make the venture worthwhile. This is the minimum the state must offer if it is to enlist the efforts of the private sector. The use of water by people and firms can be guided and controlled, but it cannot be forced. The state may screen the uses and weed out the undesirable ones to insure that state policies and plans are furthered, and it may impose conditions and limits to prevent undesirable practices and side effects, but it must give security to investments and opportunities for profit. With these assurances long term ventures and stable endeavors will be undertaken. Without them much will be lost, for if risks are great only those requiring little capital and promising quick returns will be taken, and cheap construction and short cuts can be expected.

In a dynamic society efficiency also requires change, if maximum benefits are to be continually obtained. New and better uses will arise that promise more than is being produced by existing, perhaps outmoded, uses. Demands will increase as population and industrialization expand, and if they can not be economically satisfied from unused supplies, changes in use must take place. The resulting shifts from present uses to new uses must meet the same test applied to an original use. Each must be another step towards maximization of the benefits from the resource. The economist, using the "Pareto criterion," tells us that a change will reach or approach a new optimum if it will make at least one person better off and if it makes no person worse off. A change that merely shifts wealth from one person to another does not increase economic welfare, and even if a new use will create greater wealth, the criterion requires the gainer to pay the loser. The person who is better off should receive the net gain from the change, not someone else's wealth as well.

The problem for the lawyer, then, is to draft a law, a system of water rights, that will promote this goal of efficiency by providing both security and flexibility of water rights. Some people see these two *desiderata* as opposites, and if too much of one is given, the other is thought to suffer. Yet they can be reconciled, and water rights can be made both secure and flexible.

A prime element of security is the tenure of the right. Prior appropriation rights are held "in perpetuity," although in view of the possibilities of loss through forfeiture or condemnation they might better be described as "of indefinite duration." The ideal water right should last as long as it is contemplated that the water use will last. Rights for cities, irrigation, and other purposes of a continuing nature should last indefinitely; there is no substantial reason to think that a need will arise in 10 or 50 years to take water from the inhabitants of a city and give it over to another use. If irrigation water furnishes a major component of the value of land, the titles to the land and the water should run concurrently. On the other hand, there is little utility in leaving a mining company with a water right after the mine has been exhausted.

Rights that last as long as the enterprise will give security of tenure to the water user. But how are flexibility and change to be accommodated if rights are perpetual or for long terms? As an analogy, consider the laws applied to another valuable resource: land. The state has exactly the same interests in seeing that the highest and best use of land is made and that those uses can change when needs change. Almost universally rights to land are as secure a form of property as there is, and land titles run "to him and his heirs forever." Yet land use is flexible, and a shift from a low productive use to a higher productive use is accomplished by the simple process of a sale of the land. A farm on the outskirts of a city may have a higher productive use as an industrial site or as a residential area. In either case the industrialist or the developer can afford to pay the farmer more than the land is worth as a farm, and the one with the best use can afford the most. Both buyer and seller profit. In this respect water resources are not too different from land resources.

This is not to say that unrestricted powers of sale are recommended. Legal mechanisms can be found that will permit economic forces to operate within a framework of government control. The government will generally favor a change in use that moves water to higher productivity. The government may disapprove of a change, however, and should be able to block a transfer of the water right that would interfere with the rights of third persons, result in a disfavored water use, or harm the public interest. Procedures that permit affected private persons to raise objections and the government to approve or disapprove can take the form of government confirmation of a sale or of cancelling the old right and issuing a new permit for the new use. On the other hand, the government may wish to force transfers that advance the public interest when private action does not produce the desired change. Again, consider the case of land. If the government needs the land, it takes it by expropriation or condemnation; if a favored enterprise needs it, the government gives those powers to it. Fair compensation is paid if the total value is taken and should similarly be paid if the value given by water is taken.

The desirability of this mechanism for change is not seen by all water lawyers. In fact, it seems quite popular nowadays to recommend that water rights should last only for fixed, fairly short periods.[8] The advantage is thought to be the attainment of flexibility, since at the end of the term the state has the power to reassign the water to new and better uses. There are disadvantages, however, to such a system, some of which accrue to the state in departures from optimum use and some of which impose unnecessary harm upon the water user. Most investments take many years to amortize, and the term must be a long one if capital is to be attracted. Repairs and replacements may be foregone by the water user towards the end of a fixed period. Flexibility is surrendered during the life of the right, and if an application for a new use does not coincide with the expiration of an old permit, the new user may have to wait a fairly long time before water becomes available. If to meet this the right is subject to condemnation or expropriation during its life, the usual compensation offered is the unamortized

---

8. F. Maloney, R. Ausness & J. Morris, A Model Water Code (1972).

portion of the investment. But the holder of the right will in many cases lose an asset more valuable than his sunk costs, that is, the going concern value of his enterprise—the continuing opportunity to make a profit—which is presumably a contribution to the economy.

It may be wise to remember that we are speaking of laws that affect people and that laws should be tested by thinking through their application to practical facts. The theoretical proposition is that water use should be flexible and that water should move from less productive to higher and better uses. The fact is that almost everywhere in the world irrigation of agricultural crops produces less wealth per unit of water than does almost any other use—hydroelectric power, food processing, raw material processing, mining, manufacturing, and domestic and commercial consumption within municipalities. So in practical operation a change to greater beneficial use will mean that water now used by farmers will be shifted to large enterprises or cities. There is nothing bad about this *per se*, in fact it is almost inevitable. However, it may need to be controlled. For example, in a country where food production has a high government priority the natural economic processes may have to be interrupted and such changes forbidden. This would force cities and industries to seek higher cost water not presently in use, and they might have to construct reservoirs or bring water long distances from places where use has not yet equalled supply.

But if these considerations do not apply and the change is desired, a change made by fiat, without payment or compensation, will impoverish the farmer and unnecessarily enrich the industrialist or city dweller. Inevitably the farmer is poorer than he was before; he can produce less on his dry land. The water he formerly used is now being used by a manufacturing or mining company, for which the water cost would be a small part of total operating costs and could be recouped in the price for the product. If the water has moved to municipal uses, it is now benefitting householders and owners of commercial establishments within the city, and the principle of requiring those who receive the benefits to pay for them can be realized by a simple adjustment of water rates. A very small addition to the water bill of everyone in the city would create a fund from which the payment could be made.

III. Distribution in Times of Shortage

Legal security given by tenure is only one-half the picture. So far it has been assumed that water was available to fulfill the right. But what if there is not enough to satisfy all rights? What physical security does the law provide—what guarantees that the holder of a right will get water? When there is a shortage of water, which water users get it? These questions go to the heart of the law. Indeed, shortages are what the law of water rights is all about. There is little need for water rights if there is plenty of water for all.

The word "shortage" needs to be defined. It is meaningless unless demand is considered as well as supply. On a variable stream there may be an annual shortage if the normal or average low flows cannot support existing uses, although much high water flows to the sea. There may be shortages induced by drought if a usually sufficient supply fails in some years. There may be a shortage although the stream is running full, if the full flow is needed for fisheries, navigation, or environmental concerns. There may be no shortage even though every drop is used if the stream is so controlled that annual and perennial flows are equated by storage and the smoothed-out supply is fully, but not excessively, allocated. Such a firm right to a firm supply puts the water user in the best of all worlds.

But for the most part the real world is not so ideal. Some aquifers with steady recharge may present an opportunity to limit water rights and match demand to supply, but most streams are subject to very large annual fluctuations and to marked variation in yearly total flows. Some are sufficiently predictable to allow a dependable flow to be determined and split among a fixed group of water users, but this either wastes the excess high water if no rights are given to it or casts most of the burden of shortage on the users of high water.

In all cases, however, the physically available supply limits the water that can be withdrawn, and the state, if it is to avoid chaos, must limit the claims to it. Inevitably, this limit will have an element of temporal priority to it. When claims equal supply, no more can be granted. New demands for better uses must then be accommodated by some mechanism for flexibility, as discussed above. Such a limit can be easily fixed if the supply is fixed. When the source fluctuates and sometimes can fill all needs but sometimes can not, some method of allocating or distributing the immediately available water must be devised.

There are at least five ways of doing this. One is to enforce strict temporal priority, as exemplified by American prior appropriation. Another is to apply equal sharing enforced by proportionate reduction, as among some riparian irrigators. A third is to follow a statutory list of preferences, giving priority according to a fixed ranking of the values of different uses. A fourth is to distribute the water as determined by administrative discretion based on various economic and social factors. A fifth is to put up the water for sale or auction, as practiced in some Moslem communities.

Since the criterion for the law is efficiency in obtaining maximum net benefits from water use, each of these must be evaluated against that standard before an intelligent choice can be made. Prima facie, each seems to have advantages and disadvantages. Temporal priority gives security, but it may sometimes seem to discriminate rather arbitrarily among people who are essentially similarly situated, and the earliest uses may not be the best ones. Sharing may be equitable among many farmers, but not if some have orchards or vineyards and others grow annual field crops; and a variable supply may be completely unsatisfactory for a factory or mine. Statutory lists may reflect prevailing notions of relative values, but they may embody obvious diseconomies or prevent the comparison of the relative merits of individual uses. Even if they do prefer the most efficient uses, they operate so that the rich get richer and the poor get poorer. Bidding on the water market would seem to insure that the water goes to those who can produce the most from it, but it can lead to speculation and gouging, and to enrichment of those who hold a monopoly on water rather than those who work with it.

This leaves administrative control, and a number of water lawyers have thought this to be the ideal. Their theory is to place all the water in the hands of a wise administrator; let him put it where it will do the most good, let him prorate, let him reduce the supply or suspend the rights of some so that others may receive the water.[9] I have serious reservations about this.

---

9. *Id.*; Clark, Guidelines for the Drafting of Water Codes, U.N. Water Resources Ser. No. 43 (1973).

We seldom give to a government official so much power over the lives and livelihood of people. This procedure may deter investment and development, since entrepreneurs hesitate to engage in enterprises when success or failure depends upon factors beyond their control. A rather ugly thought occurs — the human factor could be subjected to enormous temptations and tremendous pressures to play political favorites, yield to political coercion, and offer and receive bribes and graft. Even the most scrupulously honest administrators have complained of the personal strain such decisions cause, and have disclaimed the wisdom to make them with any assurance. And even if wisdom can be found, it must not only exist in higher echelons where policy is decided, but it must also be spread through all the regional subordinates and field men who must make the actual on-the-spot decisions in individual cases.

Those who advocate administrative distribution in case of shortage may urge that with this method the public interest, or the environment, can be protected. But it must be remembered that all of this has been taken care of in the initial allocation of rights. To understand the workings of administrative distribution, it must be very clearly kept in mind that all we are talking about is water already allocated to private use, that the state and its administrators have issued permits for its use, that every use is beneficial, and that all the uses can be made in times of water plenty. It must be remembered that all minimum flow requirements are met, that all other environmental factors are protected, and that the state water plan is observed or even furthered. The public interest stands neutral, and the only question is: Which people get to use the water?

If each system has its good and bad features, must we then choose the least of evils? I think not. It is possible to combine the best features of all of these and to eliminate the bad effects of each.

In the preferred solution, temporal priority is the starting point, but only that. It does give security; it does mean that the state, having granted water to *A,* will not later grant that same water to *B.* Temporal priority is not the grant of a special privilege. It is simply a necessary element of the description of the water right that marks its boundaries and distinguishes it from other rights. On a fluctuating source, it is the only way that new rights can be limited to water that is available in nature and is not already committed to existing uses. These virtues can be combined with those of sharing, if that is desirable. This is frequently done all over the world, even in western America, where a project or distribution scheme serves a number of irrigators who share the distributor's appropriated water right. If that right cannot be supplied in full, the consumers take a proportionate reduction. Much the same thing can be done even though no works are needed and it is contemplated that individuals will provide their own means of diversion. If a reasonably dependable supply is available and total withdrawals are held to that limit, all of the permits, although requested at different times, could be given the same priority date or number. The plan would replace the project; the plan would receive the priority. This would avoid overcrowding by too many seeking shares and would settle the relationships between the irrigators as a group and other irrigators, industrial users, and municipalities.

Next is the problem of seeing that the water goes to the best uses. If the more productive and valuable users have junior water rights, economic efficiency can still be served by using the market, under the supervision of the administrator. We have spoken of transfers of water rights, but there is also need for sales of water as a commodity. The State of New Mexico gives a good example of how this can work. A statute permits the "leasing of the use of water" by an appropriator to any other person, with the approval of the state authorities.[10] In a water-short year, growers of beans who anticipate a high price may hold junior water rights that give them no supply, while potato growers who face a glutted market can draw water under their senior rights. The bean growers buy water from the potato farmers. Maximum efficiency is reached, since the high-value crop is produced, and both water users share the profits. An administrator could not do as well. If he were charged with distributing the water on the basis of economic efficiency, he would allocate the water to the bean grower, but that lucky farmer would get all his profit while the unfortunate potato grower would suffer a total loss. If the administrator attempted

---

10. N.M. Comp. Laws, §§ 75-40-1 to -7 (1953).

to avoid this by a criterion of equity and gave half the water to each, the highest and best use would not be served and maximum production would not be reached.

Another example of how temporary transfers of rights or sales of water could be of great utility is that of the city which gambled on a junior water right and is faced with an unusual drought. If farmers hold the priority, I would assume that an administrator would say that the city has the better use and would cut off the farmers' supply. The city would get the water, but the farmer would be bankrupted. This is a social cost which must be reckoned, and the best way to account for it is to have the city pay for the farmers' lost crop. A country enacting a new law could improve on the New Mexico system by allowing only owners of permits to make purchases and by limiting quantities to enough to make up the shortage in the permitted supply. This would avoid the use of water by unauthorized persons or in unauthorized quantities. The administrator could also be given the power to force such temporary transfers and empower preferred users who are unable to make private arrangements to take temporary control of water rights at a fair compensation.

Up to now we have been dealing with shortages as if they were inevitable and uncontrollable. Both annual low flows and cyclic drought produce periods of plenty and periods of shortage, but in many areas storage of water can be used to equate the flow, to save high water for use in the low water period. Where storage is physically and economically available, the rule for dividing shortage is in practical fact a rule for determining who pays for the dam and reservoir. If an open-ended system of riparian sharing of a variable stream for irrigation eventually were to lead to too many and too small shares, all holders of rights might band together in some joint or communal organization to raise the dam. I think, however, that the costs of dislocation and the difficulties of organization would be great. If economic productivity is the criterion for determining who gets low flows, the burden of providing storage would be cast on those least able to afford it. But if temporal priority is the rule, the juniors who enter the field after the low water is all spoken for must pay. Is this fair? I think so, for reasons to be developed later. It certainly is desirable from the standpoint of securing the main goal, the efficient use of water. The persons who will get the direct benefit of the storage must consider whether it is worth the price. A large estate—a communal group of farmers, an industry, a city, or a government multipurpose agency—which wants the water must calculate whether its benefits will exceed its costs.

From the standpoint of equity and justice it should be remembered that development takes place over time. The first users take cheap, easily available, always available water. There is no shortage. When more and more uses are made, shortages are created as demands increase to meet or exceed low flow supply. Additional risks are created and additional costs must be met. It seems not unfair for the government to place those risks and those costs on those who create them.

Justice is difficult to identify. One American writer has said that injustice is easier to spot, that human beings hold in common many notions of when they are being abused or treated unfairly.[11] One of those notions is that when a person has taken, used, become accustomed to, and made a livelihood from water, it becomes "his water," and that one who takes it from him has "stolen his water." I used to think that prior appropriation was an American invention, but now I am convinced it was simply the verbal identification of a very widespread human trait.

Teclaff, in his survey of 57 countries, tells us that seniority in use is the most common of all bases for distributing water among users.[12] In its most explicit form, prior appropriation exists not only in 19 American states, but also in four western provinces of Canada, Taiwan, China, Iran, Rhodesia, Zambia, and the Philippines. There are strong elements of it in several South American countries.[13] The 1963 British Water Resources Act creates a "protected right" indistinguishable from an appropriation, though enforced in an unusual roundabout manner.[14]

Protection based on temporal priority is to some degree implicit in many other laws. Before state controls came into

---

11. E. Cahn, The Sense of Injustice: An Anthroporentic View of Law (1949).
12. L. Teclaff, *supra* note 1.
13. L. Teclaff, *supra* note 1, at 82-83.
14. Water Resources Act of 1964, 42 U.S.C. § 1961 *et seq.* (1970).

being, customary water rights, held from time immemorial or for prescriptive periods, were everywhere protected. When state authority to use water was instituted, the notion that a state should not make successive grants of the same water to different people appeared in most such laws. Permits, licenses, or concessions—whatever they may be called—are not to be issued to the detriment of existing uses in most of the Spanish American countries, in several of the eastern United States, in Tanzania, and in Italy. Practically every new water code has given some sort of group preference to uses in existence when the code was adopted.

Some evidence indicates a subliminal recognition of priority even where the law is specifically to the contrary. The natural flow theory of 19th century English riparianism has been said to have been a protection of mill owners, a law designed to keep the wheels of the Industrial Revolution turning.[15] The reasonable use theory of American riparian law is applied to require several types of adjustments which enable several riparian uses to coexist, but a recent study of the cases shows that when two uses are truly incompatible the American courts almost invariably hold that a new use is unreasonable if it takes the water supply of an existing user.[16] Empirical studies show the existence of a sort of "practical priority" in some American states, where riparians with theoretical rights to share in a stream voluntarily refrain from taking water after their neighbors have first captured the available supply. Even under modern statutes that subject the allocation and distribution of water to administrative discretion, the administrators in Great Britain, Kenya, and Mexico have eased their burden by issuing permits that authorize the withdrawal of water only when there is a surplus over the needs of existing users.

IV. EXAMPLES

I realize that, when I state my personal precepts for a desirable form of water rights, I take issue with a number of colleagues. In many personal conversations and exchanges of correspondence we have debated the merits of long term versus

---

15. Beuscher, *Appropriation Water Law Elements in Riparian Doctrine States,* 10 BUFFALO L. REV. 448 (1961).

16. RESTATEMENT (SECOND) OF TORTS, § 850B(h)(i), Notes at 115-18 (Tent. Draft No. 17, 1971).

short term water rights, voluntary transfers versus governmental shifts of water use, and priority versus administrative distribution of shortages. I seldom lose these debates, of course, but I seldom seem to win them either. Too often our arguments do not meet head on because my propositions seem hard to state and the full implications of prior appropriation seem difficult to understand, and my opponents assume that I advocate some kind of "robber baron" speculation in the national patrimony. It is not difficult to show that administrative control offers advantages over such a system. It seems very difficult to explain how a system of controlled rights—secure but transferable and limited to quantities available in the source and not previously committed to other uses—can incorporate each advantage claimed for discretionary administration.

Perhaps the propositions here set forth can be clarified by illustration. Two very new examples may be compared: one represents the ultimate in discretionary control of water use by officials, the other is based on the principles I have recommended.

Last year the President of the Philippines created a new National Water Resources Council and empowered it to issue rules and regulations for the exploitation and optimum utilization of water resources.[17] The superseded Irrigation Law of 1912 was modeled on an early form of American prior appropriation, implemented by a permit system. A number of contributing factors had made administration of the law ineffective, and permit procedures were overwhelmed by a flood of applications resulting from a new government program. The Council quickly adopted interim rules designed to expedite the processing of applications for water rights, and those rules make a fundamental departure from the nature of existing rights. The permits under the rules will not definitely fix the quantity of water allowed, the priority of the right, or the duration of the right. Each will be subject to these conditions:

> The Council may, after due notice and hearing, reduce at any time the quantity of water or adopt a system of apportionment, distribution or rotation thereof when the facts and circumstances

---

17. *See* Trelease, Current Developments in Philippine Water Law—Suggested Interim Groundwater Regulation (1975) (prepared for MIA-UNDP/FAO Ground-water Development Project).

in any situation would warrant the same in the interests of legal appropriators.

The Council may, after due notice and hearing, revoke the permit in favor of projects for greater beneficial use or for a multipurpose use.[18]

As explained by the Council's staff, these conditions were written into the permit for five reasons:

1. *Wasteful uses:* Some water users are wasteful, some can get along with less water, and, as water demand increases and technology progresses, all water users may be required to initiate more economical methods or facilities.

2. *Reduction of use:* Irrigated lands are frequently subjected to changes in land use. If a water right exists to serve an area of land and part of the land is sold for residential use, or if the water is concentrated on one part while another is more or less permanently devoted to a purpose such as storage or a barnyard, the right should be reduced in quantity or terminated in part.

3. *Sharing during drought:* In time of drought, it is inequitable that the entire burden of shortage fall on some farmers, while others, essentially similarly situated, get a full supply. "We wish to abolish priority" was the statement made.

4. *Incorporation into projects:* It is expected that many small irrigated plots will later be served by large multipurpose projects.

5. *Flexibility of use:* To "keep up with progress" under developing conditions and to permit "greater beneficial use" it will be necessary to shift water from one enterprise to new and different ones that will contribute more to the Philippine economy and development, and to permit multipurpose uses of greater public benefit.

Each of these reasons has a sound basis in fact, and each problem or need described exists. Each condition described can be corrected and each aim accomplished by administrative action under the terms of the permit. These conditions will protect the paramount interests of the state, preserve every right

18. Philippine National Water Resources Council, Interim Rules Governing Application for Water Permit, Dec. 17, 1974.

of the state, and subordinate private uses of water to state control at every stage.

Contrast the new water law recommended for Swaziland.[19] The Swaziland permit is a "protected right," following British terminology, and each permit bears the date on which the application therefor was filed. The law provides:

> Every water right shall be protected from derogation by the exercise of any permit bearing a later date and shall entitle the holder to abstract the whole amount of water specified in the permit before any water is distributed to the holder of a permit bearing a later date.

The permit lasts as long as water is needed:

> Every permit shall state the period of its duration, as determined by the Board in accordance with the following provisions: (a) any permit for [domestic] use, for urban and public water supply, for the irrigation of land and for other purposes of a continuing nature shall be of indefinite duration, and valid until revoked, varied or cancelled in accordance with § 23 [with compensation except in cases of three year nonuse or violation of law]; (b) any permit for industrial purposes shall lapse with the termination of the use of the water for such purposes or with the abandonment of the mine, plant or other facility for which it was used.

These provisions give the Swaziland water user the security denied to his Philippine counterpart. Yet every objective of the Philippine Government can be accomplished under the Swazi law. In Swaziland, as in the Philippines, physical waste can be found. Irrigators use large quantities of water, inefficient means of diversion, and wasteful practices. Cheap water is used instead of expensive equipment or labor. But a Swazi permit will be issued subject to:

> Such terms, conditions, restrictions and limitations as [the Board] deems necessary for the protection of others and the public interest including (a) any limitation whereby the quantity of water permitted to be extracted is restricted to that amount which may be beneficially and economically used and efficiently applied.

If future conditions require the state to impose an increase in efficiency, the permit is also subject to:

> Any requirement for the abstraction and use of the quantity al-

---

19. Trelease, A Proposed National Water Resources Order for Swaziland, U.N. Doc. No. OTC/SWA/73/002 (1975).

lowed by the permit to be made pursuant to the regulations or orders of the Board governing efficient water management.

These same conditions in the permit could be used to take care of the second case that bothers the Philippine Council, in which the amount of irrigated land is decreased and less water is therefore needed. Since the beneficial use is decreased the amount of water needed for the remainder of the land would decrease. Further, the Swazi law states that:

> The Board may cancel or vary any permit if the holder thereof voluntarily fails or neglects, without sufficient cause, to apply all or any part of the water to the use for which the permit was issued for a period of three successive years.

Thus, if the decrease in use were temporary, the decrease in water delivery would be temporary, but, if the decrease were permanent, a part of the water right would cease to exist.

In the third situation, the Philippine Council reserves the right to apportion and rotate a short supply among irrigators. The practical problem arises from the fact that the government, seeking to improve rice yields by prolonging the growing season with irrigation, has distributed a large number of pumps to individual farmers in order to enable them to use whatever water is available. Each farmer will have to apply for a permit, and it is felt that minor differences in the time of filing should not be the deciding factor in determining who gets the water. In Swaziland as well, projects are being studied that call for irrigation of small plots of new land by the Swazi people. On some of them the water is quite accessible and may be taken by individual works that may be initiated at different times; on others the government will construct large works and deliver the water to the farmers. In either type of settlement, equality and sharing among the irrigators is thought desirable. The law therefore states:

> If a government irrigation project or scheme or an irrigation project or scheme initiated by an organization or group of water users is to be effectuated by permits issued to individual water users, the government, industry, department or agency, or the organization or group, may apply to the Board for an order setting aside or reserving a specified quantity of water for the irrigation of all irrigable lands to be served by the project or scheme, and the Board may issue such order and thereafter all permits issued for the irrigation of such land shall bear the date of the application for such order.

All permits bearing the same date shall entitle the holders thereof
to a prorata share of the source of water insufficient to supply all
such rights in full.

The fourth concern of the Philippine Council is that of the
small farm which is swallowed up by a large project. It is contemplated that the land will continue to be irrigated, and what
is actually involved is the substitution of the project's right for
the old individual right. This would be done without compensation. The farmer's facilities would be rendered useless, however, and he would bear a double burden if he must pay for his
own works and a full share of project costs as well. Contrast the
Swazi solution:

If as a result of variation or revocation the holder of the varied
or revoked permit can be supplied with water by a government
or private scheme or project, or a local authority, in favor of
which the permit was revoked or varied, damages shall be limited
to the unamortized portion of the investment in water works
rendered useless or unnecessary.

Lastly, the Philippine permit was made revocable at the
will of the Council so that it might keep up with progress and
shift water to new enterprises that will contribute more to the
country's development, or to government multipurpose projects. Such opportunities for water to move to higher and better
uses will occur in Swaziland as well. If a new government
scheme is planned, and it is found that an incompatible existing use must be ended or that the water must be acquired for
the project, then:

If the [government], a local authority, the Electricity Board, or
any ministry, department or agency of the government constructing or operating a government scheme, project or water work,
desires to acquire for its purposes any existing water right, servitude or land, it may . . . acquire such water rights, servitude or
land, or such portion thereof as may be necessary, by expropriation and the Acquisition of Property Act shall . . . apply to such
expropriation and the compensation . . . to be paid therefor.

Swaziland has large reserves of coal and is highly mineral-
ized, and if a mining enterprise should in the future need a firm
supply of water it could approach any one of a number of farmers who have high priority water rights and work out a transfer:

The Board may authorize the use of all or part of the water to be
abstracted pursuant to permit to be changed or transferred to a
different use or place of use by the same or another person if a

change or transfer is effected by a surrender of the permit and the issuance of a new permit or permits bearing the same date.

In proceedings for obtaining approval of the Board for any change or transfer, . . . the Board shall approve and allow changes and transfers . . . only if it is satisfied that no injury will occur to the water rights of other persons, that the new use or place of use will be in the public interest and in conformity to or compatible with a water resources plan relating to the source or area, provided, that in appropriate cases the Board may inquire into the adequacy of the consideration paid to the person making the transfer and as to whether permitting the transfer will be to the best interests of such person.

The transaction would be the same as if the mining company needed the farmer's land. Since the company will in fact produce greater wealth than does the farmer, it will be able to afford to buy out the farmer's interest to give him a substitute in money that will replace the foregone income from farming. The state will control the transaction, protect its interest, and must agree that its goals and plans are furthered by the shift. The last proviso illustrates state retention of control over a social factor. If the transferor is a Swazi farmer, the transaction can be scrutinized to see that he was not overreached in the bargaining process and that he has other opportunities he can grasp, and has not merely sold his birthright for a mess of pottage.

To summarize, in both countries and under either form of law waste can be prevented, forfeiture imposed for nonuse, shortages prorated among similarly situated irrigators, large projects substituted for individual works, and water moved to higher and better uses. Under the interim rules of the Philippines this is accomplished by telling the water user that the initial quantity of water allotted to him may be reduced at any time for someone else's benefit, and that his entire water right may be taken from him at any time the government or someone else needs it. This is overkill—more than is necessary for the purpose. Though these same objectives are reached in Swaziland, there the water user, whether African farmer or mining executive, knows he will be allowed the quantity needed for efficient accomplishment of his use. He knows whether or not he must share and, if he must, with how many. He knows that if he needs a firm supply and the source is variable, he must arrange for storage. He knows that, if the government takes back its grant of water, it will compensate him for the loss.

The Philippine Water Council and its staff are men of good will, public servants seeking to advance the best interests of the government and to wring the last benefit from water use. But since the intent is to accomplish much of the development of the Philippines through the private sector—by individuals, cooperatives, and businesses engaged in food production and processing, raw material extraction and processing, manufacturing, and mining—the question may be asked whether such tenuous rights may not frighten away such water users and actually prove counterproductive in achieving the government's objective. When the present crisis is over the interim regulations are to be replaced with a permanent water code. At that point, the Philippine government might well consider whether its interests may be better served and more benefits obtained by giving greater assurance to those whose energies must be enlisted in the effort to develop the nation's water resources.

V. CONCLUSION

I might close with an anecdote. On a mission to Jamaica for the Food and Agriculture Organization I recommended provisions similar to those suggested for Swaziland.[20] My charge in the assignment to Jamaica was to draft a law which would give aid and encouragement to the developing Jamaican economy—based largely on irrigated sugar cane with a more recent overlay of tourism, mining, and manufacturing—and to protect the island's cities and tropical environment. In submitting various drafts I encountered some resistance to American language and quietly shifted from "prior appropriation" to the British "protected right," with which the Jamaicans felt more comfortable. During the process a counterproposal was made for an "administrative system" of permits covering the "expected constant yield," and for the rationing of water in times of shortage based on "the value of the particular uses" and "the national interest." The supposed simplicity of this, compared to my allegedly complicated recommendations, had a certain appeal, but eventually my proposal won out. It has since received cabinet approval, although it has not yet been adopted by the Parliament.

---

20. Trelease, A Proposed Water Resources Act for Jamaica, FAO Doc. No. AGL:SF/JAM/12 (1973).

During the discussion, the Jamaican codirector of the project probed into how operations would actually be conducted. He was quick to see the type of pressures that could be brought and the difficult decisions that would have to be made in determining the size of the "expected constant yield" and whether one more permit could be squeezed into it. He also saw the ease with which he could issue permits that prohibited interference with previously issued protected rights. And he was enchanted with the notion of handling shortages by priority coupled with temporary transfers of water, as in New Mexico.

"I see—under the other system I might have to choose between shutting down a new hotel or starving some cane farmers. But one or two farmers' quota would supply the hotel, and under your law I could just notify the hotel manager to start negotiations. Why, I might even act as broker and help them get together."

I believe that man caught a glimpse of what water law is all about.

4

Allocation and Management of Interstate Water Resources: The Emergence of the Federal-Interstate Compact

Jerome C. Muys[*]

I. Introduction

It is appropriate in this bicentennial year that this conference is reexamining the mechanisms which the Founding Fathers built into the Constitution to deal with interstate water problems. They obviously anticipated that a variety of regional disputes might arise within the newly-created federal system which would be beyond the power of a single state to deal with and yet not within what were then thought to be the relatively narrow powers which the states had delegated to the National Congress. Hence the Constitution provided for the continued use of interstate agreements or "compacts" (a device which had been liberally used in Colonial America to resolve boundary disputes and had received acceptance in the Articles of Confederation), subject only to the requirement of Congressional consent to such agreements. Thus, article I, section 10, clause 3 provides that: "No state shall, without the consent of Congress . . . enter into any agreement or compact with another state or with a foreign power."[1]

The second mechanism provided for the settlement of interstate disputes was original action in the Supreme Court of the United States.[2] Both techniques have been frequently em-

---

[*] A.B., 1954, Princeton University; L.L.B., 1957, Stanford University; Adjunct Professor, George Washington University National Law Center. The author is a member of the firm of Debevoise & Liberman, Washington, D.C.

1. Although the compact clause seems to mandate Congressional consent for all interstate agreements, the Supreme Court has stated that such consent is required only where the compact threatens to impinge on national interests. Virginia v. Tennessee, 148 U.S. 503, 518-19 (1893); New Hampshire v. Maine, 96 S.Ct. 2113 (1976). Similarly, consent is not required prior to formal agreement, as the clause suggests, but may be evidenced either before or after agreement is reached. Virginia v. Tennessee, 148 U.S. 503, 521 (1893). The critical question is whether "Congress, by some positive act in relation to such agreement, [has] signified the consent of that body to its validity." Green v. Biddle, 21 U.S. (8 Wheat.) 1, 86 (1823).

2. U.S. Const., art. 3, §2.

ployed over the years, primarily in connection with interstate water resources matters. Some 35 compacts have been approved by Congress relating to water resources management, and a large number of Supreme Court decisions have been rendered on disputes over the consumptive use or pollution of the waters of 14 interstate river basins.[3]

It was not until its 1963 decision in *Arizona v. California,*[4] an interstate dispute over the allocation of the waters of the Lower Colorado River Basin, that the Supreme Court discovered that a third possibility for the solution of interstate water disputes existed, namely through Congressional exercise of some of its powers, particularly the power to regulate interstate commerce, the scope of which had gradually been expanded by the Supreme Court since the 1930s. I refer to the Court's "discovery" of such Congressional power advisedly, since in a 1907 interstate water decision, *Kansas v. Colorado,* the Court had explained that "[a]s Congress cannot make compacts between the States, as it cannot, in respect to certain matters, by legislation compel their separate action, disputes between them must be settled either by force or else by appeal to tribunals empowered to determine the right and wrong thereof."[5] However, half a century later in *Arizona v. California,* the Court concluded that Congress had in fact imposed a compact on several of the states of the Lower Colorado River Basin through the Boulder Canyon Project Act of 1928.[6] It held that Congress had effected a "statutary apportionment" of the waters of the mainstream of the Colorado River at Hoover Dam and below among the states of California, Arizona, and Nevada by conferring upon the Secretary of the Interior, as part of his

---

3. Compacts currently in effect are set out in Appendix A to this paper. For a scholarly compilation of most of the compacts as of 1968 dealing with consumptive use, pollution control, and flood control with respect to interstate waters as well as related legislation and the principal Supreme Court decisions in interstate water disputes, see Witmer, *Documents on the Use and Control of the Waters of Interstate and International Streams,* H.R. Doc. No. 319, 90th Cong., 2d Sess. (1968).

The Court's interstate water decisions as of April 1959 are also collected in a useful indexed compilation prepared by Professor Charles E. Corker and filed by the California defendants with the Special Master in Arizona v. California, 373 U.S. 546 (1963), as a supplement to their proposed findings of fact and conclusions of law.

4. 373 U.S. 546 (1963).

5. 206 U.S. 46, 97 (1907).

6. 373 U.S. 546 (1963); *see also* Boulder Canyon Project Act of 1928, 43 U.S.C. §§ 617-617t (1970).

authority to manage Hoover Dam and the other water conservation works authorized under that Act, the power to make a "contractual allocation" of those waters in the event that the three states were unable to agree to the terms of a tristate compact to which consent was given in the Act.[7]

Of these three means for allocating interstate waters, I have been asked to focus on interstate compacts. But before dealing with that subject, I want to review briefly Supreme Court litigation and Congressional allocation as a means of resolving interstate water disputes.

The guiding principle which the Supreme Court has applied in interstate water disputes is the doctrine of "equitable apportionment." In *Nebraska v. Wyoming,*[8] the Court enunciated the basic factors involved in determining the "equitable shares" of an interstate stream to which competing states are entitled:

[I]n determining whether one State is "using, or threatening to use, more than its equitable share of the benefits of a stream, all the factors which create equities in favor of one State or the other must be weighed as of the date when the controversy is mooted." 320 US p. 394. That case did not involve a controversy between two appropriation States. But if an allocation between appropriation States is to be just and equitable, strict adherence to the priority rule may not be possible. For example, the economy of a region may have been established on the basis of junior appropriations. So far as possible those established uses should be protected though strict application of the priority rule might jeopardize them. Apportionment calls for the exercise of an informed judgment on a consideration of many factors. Priority of appropriation is the guiding principle. But physical and climatic conditions, the consumptive use of water in the several sections of the river, the character and rate of return flows, the extent of established uses, the availability of storage water, the practical effect of wasteful uses on downstream areas, the damage to upstream areas as compared to the benefits to downstream areas, if a limitation is imposed on the former—these are all relevant factors. They are merely an illustrative, not an exhaustive catalogue. They indicate the nature of the problem of apportionment and the delicate adjustment of interests which must be made.[9]

---

7. 373 U.S. 546 (1963).
8. 325 U.S. 589 (1945).
9. *Id.* at 618.

With respect to "statutory apportionment" of interstate waters, there is no real guidance beyond the Supreme Court's analysis of the legislative history of the Boulder Canyon Project Act in *Arizona v. California.* One can only speculate whether some of the multitude of Congressional authorizations for multiple purpose projects under the federal reclamation and flood control programs may someday receive a similar interpretation. For example, did the Secretary of the Interior's recent execution of a contract with Montana for delivery of 300,000 acre-feet of water from the Fort Peck Reservoir to users in that state, referred to by Assistant Secretary Horton this morning,[10] accomplish a *pro tanto* "contractual allocation" of the waters of the Missouri Basin? Whether Congress will be inclined to legislatively direct the allocation of interstate waters among competing states in particular controversies in the future is also highly speculative. It would seem preferable for the affected states to determine their own water destiny by agreement, rather than to have it decided by a Congressional majority which may have little interest in the problems peculiar to a region, or whose votes may be influenced by political considerations wholly unrelated to the merits of a particular basin's water problems.

It is apparent that the determination of a state's equitable share in the waters of an interstate river basin is fraught with complex factual, legal, policy, and political considerations, and the Supreme Court has pointedly commented on several occasions that the difficulty of the task makes it one peculiarly appropriate for resolution by interstate agreement if at all possible. In *Nebraska v. Wyoming,* the Court characterized the problem as follows:

> There is some suggestion that if we undertake an apportionment of the waters of this interstate river, we embark upon an enterprise involving administrative functions beyond our province. . . . [T]hese controversies between States over the waters of interstate streams "involve the interests of quasi-sovereigns, present complicated and delicate questions, and, due to the possibility of future change of conditions, necessitate expert administration rather than judicial imposition of a hard and fast rule. Such controversies may appropriately be composed by negotia-

---

10. *See* Horton, *Water Issues in Perspective, infra,* at 405.

tion and agreement, pursuant to the compact clause of the Federal Constitution. We say of this case, as the court has said of interstate differences of like nature, that such mutual accomodation and agreement should, if possible, be the medium of settlement, instead of invocation of our adjudicatory power." But the efforts at settlement in this case have failed. A genuine controversy exists. The gravity and importance of the case are apparent. The difficulties of drafting and enforcing a decree are no justification for us to refuse to perform the important function entrusted to us by the Constitution.[11]

Similarly, in the New York Harbor pollution litigation, the Court admonished the party states as follows:

We cannot withhold the suggestion, inspired by the consideration of this case, that the grave problem of sewage disposal presented by the large and growing populations living on the shores of New York Bay is one more likely to be wisely solved by cooperative study and by conference and mutual concession on the part of the representatives of the States so vitally interested in it than by proceedings in any court, however constituted.[12]

The Court has always exercised its discretionary original jurisdiction cautiously, and there are some signals that it may apply even more rigorous standards in the future.[13]

II. COMPACTS

With respect to the use of interstate compacts for the resolution of interstate water disputes, I have dealt with that subject at length in a study for the National Water Commission in 1971[14] and in a briefer article in 1973[15] and do not intend to duplicate that detailed analysis here. Rather, I propose to survey briefly the use of interstate compacts in the water resources field, review the conclusions and recommendations contained in my study for the National Water Commission, and then amplify on my view that the federal-interstate compact offers the optimal permanent institutional arrangement for regional water resources management, particularly in the Western United States.

Water compacts (other than those relating to navigation

---

11. 325 U.S. 589, 616 (1945).

12. New York v. New Jersey, 256 U.S. 296, 313 (1921).

13. *See, e.g.,* Ohio v. Wyandotte Chemical Corp., 401 U.S. 493 (1971).

14. J. MUYS, INTERSTATE WATER COMPACTS (1971) (NTIS PB202 998).

15. Muys, *Interstate Compacts and Regional Water Resources Planning and Management,* 6 NAT. RES. LAW. 153 (1973).

and fishing) may be grouped into four categories relating generally to (1) water allocation, (2) pollution control, (3) flood control and planning, and (4) comprehensive water regulation and project development programs, *i.e.,* principally the federal-interstate compact.

The basic purpose of all 18 existing water allocation compacts is to accomplish an equitable apportionment of the waters of the affected interstate streams. They reflect a number of different approaches to allocating water rights to the signatory states, but whatever the allocation formula, existing uses and rights are usually protected. About half of them provide that the allocations are to include all federal uses, which can be significant in the western states because of the predominance of federally-owned land and federal water projects constructed by the Bureau of Reclamation under the Reclamation Act or by the Corps of Engineers under various Congressional authorizations.

The earliest compacts generally charged the chief water officials of the compacting states with obtaining and correlating necessary hydrologic data on supply and uses, and authorizing them to agree to such regulations as were necessary to implement the compact apportionment. More recent compacts, however, provide for the establishment of a permanent administrative entity to carry out the functions essential for achieving the compact's objectives.

Some 10 compacts deal with interstate water pollution control in a variety of ways. The older compacts are single purpose agreements concerned only with pollution, but the more recent compacts encompass a more comprehensive approach to water quality problems. All provide for an administrative agency to implement the compact purposes. The powers conferred on these commissions range from the Potomac River Basin Commission's rather limited authority to study and recommend remedial actions on pollution problems to the broader water quality standard-setting and enforcement powers of the Delaware and Susquehanna commissions.

A handful of flood control and planning compacts, created generally in response to the federal flood control program of the 1930s in order to promote cooperative state action in that effort, now largely appear to be dead letters.

The federal-interstate compacts on the Delaware and Susquehanna Rivers are what I have characterized as comprehensive regulatory and project development compacts. Under a general directive in the Delaware River Basin Compact to "adopt and promote uniform and coordinated policies for water conservation, control, use, and management in the basin [and to] encourage the planning, development, and financing of water resources projects according to such plans and policies." The Delaware River Basin Commission is charged with formulating a "comprehensive plan" for the development and use of the basin's waters, and is endowed with very broad planning, licensing, regulatory, and project construction powers to aid in implementing the basin plan. The Susquehanna River Basin Compact follows a similar format.

In my study for the National Water Commission I evaluated the effectiveness of existing water compacts and compared the compact mechanism to other institutional approaches to river basin management. With respect to compact commissions established to monitor or administer water allocations or to carry out limited functions associated with joint planning or certain aspects of the states' role in federal flood control programs, I concluded that the performance of most of them was generally adequate given their relatively modest objectives.

In the water quality area, efforts through interstate compact mechanisms to deal with water pollution problems generally appeared to have been no better or worse than the overall national effort, and I could draw no general conclusions as to the impact of the compact approach on particular rivers, although I was impressed with the efforts of ORSANCO on the Ohio River.[16]

As to the federal-interstate compact approach, it was, and is, my enthusiastic conclusion that the Delaware River Basin Commission (DRBC) has compiled an impressive record of accomplishment, much of which I am convinced would not have resulted but for the existence and efforts of DRBC.

---

16. For an analysis of operative and proposed compacts dealing primarily with water pollution control see Chambers, *Water Pollution Control Through Interstate Agreement*, 1 U. CAL. DAVIS L. REV. 43 (1969) and Curlin, *The Interstate Water Pollution Compact—Paper Tiger or Effective Regulatory Device*, 2 ECOL. L.Q. 333 (1972).

In addition to the evaluation of the record of various compacts, I also examined the potential of the compact as an institutional mechanism for future water resources management against six legal and political criteria:

1. The availability and adequacy of legal and administrative authority that may be exercised by compact to deal with problems deemed important by the compacting parties;

2. The degree of difficulty in creating, implementing, and altering a compact program, including the ability to match function and area and to respond expeditiously to changing needs and conditions;

3. The degree to which the compact affords meaningful public participation in planning and the formulation of decisions;

4. The ability to facilitate and achieve productive cooperation and coordination among federal, state, local, and private interests;

5. Political accountability and responsiveness; and

6. The ability to establish regional visibility and to attract adequate executive leadership and staff.

In addition I considered a number of traditional arguments sometimes advanced against interstate compacts and found them either to be unpersuasive or generally inapplicable to water compacts. In light of my study, I concluded that the compact mechanism, specifically the federal-interstate variety, affords the optimum permanent institutional approach to regional water problems.

Perhaps the chief advantage of the compact approach to river basin management is its adaptability to the particular needs of a basin. It is axiomatic that each river basin has its distinctive physical and political characteristics; such peculiarities demand specific legal approaches. Since a compact must be the product of agreement among the states, it can be shaped as the states desire, in accordance with their particular regional philosophy of appropriate intergovernmental relations. It can be targeted on a single problem, such as water quality management, or may seek comprehensive, multipurpose goals. Similarly, it may create a permanent administrative entity and endow that entity with such powers as the states consider appropriate to accomplish their regional objectives, provided they are consistent with broad national water resource goals.

Although the states generally possess ample authority to confer adequate powers on compact commissions, it is difficult to disagree with one characterization of most traditional water compacts as creatures of "states jealous of their prerogatives and niggardly in their grants of authority."[17] With the exception of the Delaware and Susquehanna compacts, and a few others, the authority granted to compact commissions has been extremely limited and their funding, accordingly, as anemic.

What this historic pattern unfortunately seems to reflect is a lack of commitment on the part of the states to any cooperative regional effort that would require a significant delegation of power to an interstate entity they may not be able to wholly control. The irony of this approach is that the more successful the states have been in hobbling compact agencies in order to protect their sovereign prerogatives, the more likely it has become that regional water problems will be dealt with by federal programs wholly superseding state or local authority. If the states, and particularly the western states, are truly determined to have a stronger role in regional water development, it seems clear to me that they must recognize and utilize the potential of the compact as a mechanism for positive action on regional water problems and confer adequate powers on compact agencies to deal with such problems effectively.

I find little substance to the argument sometimes advanced that the endowment of compact commissions with broad powers will simply add an unnecessary or undesirable layer of government between existing state and federal water agencies. Both state and federal water officials often appear apprehensive that some of their responsibilities might be usurped by a regional agency, a reaction which might be termed the bureaucratic version of the "territorial imperative." Federal agencies also contend that such regional entities should not be allowed to preempt federal agency responsibilities for national water programs allegedly requiring uniform, functional implementation throughout the Nation. This latter argument assumes that because the Congress has previously filled the gap left by the states, a point of no return has been reached. But the Bureau of Reclamation, the Corps of Engi-

---

17. H. ODUM & H. MOORE, AMERICAN REGIONALISM 206 (1938).

neers, and the other federal executive agencies and independent regulatory commissions involved in water matters were established by Congress to meet specific national needs at particular times. There is nothing to preclude Congress from now deciding that changed conditions or national sentiment—and I think that there is ample current evidence of both—dictate that other institutional arrangements, such as regional compact commissions, may be a more appropriate way to implement national water policies than is continued wholesale reliance on federal agencies.

To the extent that there may be a need for overall national policies on certain water resource matters, there arises a distinctly different issue from the question of the institutional means by which such policies should be carried out. It is clear that Congress may utilize any agent it chooses to implement national programs. Hence, if Congress should elect to have the national flood control program, or the reclamation program, or the licensing of nonfederal dams carried out by joint federal-state regional entities of some kind, there is no constitutional reason why that could not be done. The national policies would still be articulated in federal legislation binding on the regional entities, so there would be no subversion of the paramount national interest. However, if compacts are to be used in attacking regional water quality and other water resource management problems, it will be essential that Congress scrutinize each compact to determine whether it implements the national programs provided for in federal law or may serve only to impede them. For example, with regard to regional water quality control efforts, the Environmental Protection Agency has aptly recognized that although "compacts have already demonstrated their usefulness, and . . . have the potential for playing a more important role," nevertheless, "a compact which established dilatory procedures, or which provided an inadequate commitment of resources from the signatory states, could have the effect of delaying the establishment of enforceable standards or plans."[18]

---

18. *Hearings on S.907 Before the Senate Committee on the Judiciary,* 92d Cong., 1st Sess. 87, 91 (1971), in which the Senate Public Works Committee expressed similar concern in connection with the proposed Interstate Environment Compact Act. *See also* S. Rep. No. 92-643, 92d Cong., 2d Sess. (1972).

A major criticism of compacts is that they require an inordinately long time to negotiate and effectuate by state ratification and Congressional consent. Although the track record of the various kinds of water compacts is uneven on this score, there is substantial evidence to support a conclusion that the compact is not inherently more cumbersome and time-consuming in its creation and change than other institutional approaches to comparable water resource problems. Most delays appear to have been caused by specific policy controversies which are not unique to the use of the compact mechanism, but also plague efforts at problem solving through interagency committees, river basin planning commissions, and Congressional legislation. The fact that it took the Corps of Engineers and the Bureau of Reclamation 16 months to consummate a one-page power marketing agreement on the Missouri River is illustrative. I should also note that 12 years elapsed between the filing of Arizona's complaint in the Supreme Court in 1951 in *Arizona v. California* until the Court's decision in 1963,[19] and the post-decree proceedings to resolve the question of "present perfected rights" are still pending.

The recent experiences with the Delaware and Susquehanna compacts demonstrate that even relatively complex interstate agreements can be negotiated and approved with impressive swiftness, given proper incentive on the part of the states. An obvious problem, however, is that a compact must find acceptance in the legislatures of all the compacting states and Congress, thus affording multiple opportunities for delay or frustration of the compact plan. Similarly, the rigid constraints which have been placed on compact agencies by their creators in some cases have necessitated a return to the legislatures for additional authority with the concomitant delays associated with that process. Nevertheless, given the implementation of recommendations made to the National Water Commission for (1) a more explicit statement of Congressional policy on water compacts, (2) more constructive federal participation in compact negotiations, and (3) some liberalization of the state ratification and Congressional consent process, the potential for significantly expediting the compact negotiation and approval process appears excellent.

---

19. 373 U.S. 546, 550-51 (1963).

Finally, I want to emphasize why I recommended to the National Water Commission that the federal-interstate compact should be endorsed as the preferred permanent institutional arrangement for regional water resources planning and management.

The great goal of river basin planning and management over the last half-century has been to achieve meaningful coordination of federal and nonfederal water resources plans and actions. With respect to interstate waters, the search has also been for a mechanism to provide a regional perspective to the development and implementation of a comprehensive plan. The interstate compact always has provided a theoretical means for achieving those two objectives and, starting about 30 years ago, began to be used to provide the permanent administrative mechanism lacking in more informal approaches, such as interagency committees. However, the compact approach has traditionally evidenced important shortcomings. A major one relates to the role of the federal government. The broad constitutional powers of the federal government over the development, use, and management of the nation's water resources inevitably make it the controlling force in the success or failure of cooperative state efforts to deal with regional water problems. It is ever present, either as the provider of essential hydrologic data, as a de facto river master through its construction and control of reclamation and flood control projects or the Federal Power Commission's licensing of nonfederal hydroelectic projects, or as the ultimate regulator of activities affecting a river's quality through the Environmental Protection Agency's administration of the federal water pollution control program. Where its land ownership is significant, as in the West, its claims to water for consumptive use on its lands or for minimum streamflows to maintain important in-stream environmental values is a significant aspect of the regional water picture. Similarly, the activities carried out on federal lands by the land management agencies or their private licensees, lessees, and permittees have an important impact on water quality. Yet the federal government has neither been a party to the traditional compacts nor been formally committed in any way to support the compact programs.

Most of the water allocation compacts and several of the

older pollution control compacts merely invite the President to appoint a federal representative to sit as a neutral, nonvoting chairman of these commissions, occasionally granting him the right to cast decisive votes when the states cannot agree. But the federal government in those situations appears to be little more than an honored observer, without obligation to see that federal plans or programs in the region are coordinated to the maximum extent feasible with those of the states. Obviously, a compact plan for an interstate river basin cannot be "comprehensive" if it does not encompass federal water planning as an integral part of the effort, nor can it serve any meaningful function unless all interests in a basin, and particularly the federal government, are committed to carry out their respective programs in accordance with it.

A second major shortcoming is that the member states of the traditional interstate compacts do not appear to have been really committed to a regional approach to river basin problems. Their participation has been cautious and hesitant, concerned primarily with preservation or promotion of their individual interests. Thus, one commentator has concluded that "the interstate compact approach to river basin development therefore tends to accentuate state and local parochialism at the expense of regional and national goals in water use policy."[20] In short, the traditional interstate compact approach has been "regional" in name only.

It was against this generally discouraging backdrop of interstate compact performance that the federal-interstate compact on the Delaware emerged in 1961 to provide both (1) the long-sought linkage between federal and state planning and program implementation,[21] and (2) the regional emphasis lacking in earlier compact approaches. The Delaware River Basin Compact embodied two significant innovations in the compact approach to interstate river basin problems. First, it estab-

---

20. W. Barton, Interstate Compacts in the Political Process 177 (1965).

21. The Compact preamble states that its foundation rationale was that unified regional development and control were essential because of "the duplicating, overlapping, and uncoordinated administration of some forty-three State agencies, fourteen interstate agencies, and nineteen Federal agencies which exercise a multiplicity of powers and duties resulting in a splintering of authorities and responsibilities." Delaware River Basin Compact, Pub. L. No. 87-328, 75 Stat. 688 (1961) [hereinafter cited as DRBC].

lished a structure for meaningful comprehensive planning by including the United States as a signatory party and imposing significant coordinating constraints on both the states and the federal government. Second, it assured a more regionally-oriented approach through a generous grant of powers to the Delaware River Basin Commission (DRBC) and by providing for the injection of a broader perspective of basin problems through the federal government's active participation in the compact program.

To assure that development projects in the basin are in general conformity with the comprehensive plan developed by the DRBC, section 3.8 of the Compact confers a "licensing" power on the DRBC by providing that "no project having a substantial effect on the water resources of the basin shall hereafter be undertaken by any person, corporation or governmental authority unless it shall have been first submitted to and approved by the Commission."[22] The Commission must approve any project which it finds "would not substantially impair or conflict with the comprehensive plan," and a project not meeting that standard may be either disapproved or approved subject to modification to make it consistent with the plan.

In addition to its comprehensive licensing authority, the DRBC is granted broad regulatory and financing powers (other than the power to tax) and is even authorized to construct, develop, operate, and maintain "all projects, facilities, properties, activities and services, determined by the commission to be necessary, convenient or useful for the purposes of [the] compact."[23]

The DRBC's powers have been exercised in consonance with "the purpose of the signatory parties to preserve and utilize the functions, powers and duties of existing offices and agencies of government to the extent not inconsistent with the compact," and the Commission is "authorized and directed to utilize and employ such offices and agencies for the purpose of this compact to the fullest extent it finds feasible and advantageous."[24] Thus each state's authority is preserved to

22. *Id.*
23. DRBC at §3.6(a).
24. DRBC at §1.5.

the maximum extent compatible with the Compact's objectives.

One of the unique features of the Compact is the DRBC's power to allocate the waters of the basin among the signatory states in accordance with the doctrine of equitable apportionment,[25] a provision designed as an alternative to (1) what was considered to be the relatively inflexible apportionments made by the traditional water allocation compacts and (2) litigation in the United States Supreme Court. This allocation power, as well as all other DRBC authority, may not be used to adversely affect the rights and obligations of the states under a 1954 Supreme Court decree,[26] other than by unanimous agreement.[27] The DRBC's power to make interstate allocations of water is supplemented by its authority to regulate withdrawals and diversions of surface and groundwaters in certain situations.

The Compact mandates interstate and federal-state cooperation through the constraints which DRBC approval of the comprehensive plan places on the water resource programs of the signatory parties. All water projects in the basin are required to conform to the DRBC's comprehensive plan. Specifically, with respect to federal projects, a reservation of the consent legislation provides that "whenever a comprehensive plan, or any part or revision thereof, has been adopted with the concurrence of the member appointed by the President, the exercise of any powers conferred by law on any officer, agency, or instrumentality of the United States with regard to water and related land resources in the Delaware River Basin shall not substantially conflict with any such portion of such comprehensive plan."[28] Since the content of the comprehensive plan is determined by majority vote of the DRBC, on which the federal government has a single vote with each of the state representatives, Congress has provided an escape valve in its consent legislation which provides that the federal government

---

25. DRBC at §3.3.

26. New Jersey v. New York, 347 U.S. 995 (1954).

27. DRBC at § §3.3(a), 3.4, 3.5.

28. DRBC at §15.1(S)(2). "Concurrence" of the federal member is presumed unless he files a notice of nonconcurrence with the Commission within 60 days after notice of action with respect to the comprehensive plan.

need not shape its projects to a plan with which it is not in agreement, authorizing the President to "suspend, modify or delete" any provision of the comprehensive plan affecting federal interests when he "shall find . . . that the national interest so requires."

The Compact's procedural requirements are designed to afford maximum opportunity for the expression of public opinion on significant matters prior to DRBC decisions. Thus public hearings are required as a precondition to almost all important DRBC actions, and all meetings are required to be open to the public.[29] In addition, the Commission is authorized, but not directed, to establish advisory committees representing a broad spectrum of water resource interest groups.[30]

The DRBC has compiled an impressive record of accomplishments over the past 15 years[31] which are particularly noteworthy when viewed against the obstacles it has faced, particularly its role in breaking much new ground as the first federal-interstate compact, the broad responsibilities it has been delegated under the Compact in areas which all merit serious attention, its relatively modest financing, and the distraction of the 1965-1966 Northeast drought emergency which commanded much of its time and resources in those formative years. Nevertheless, it has moved forward in many areas. It played an important role in alleviating the 1965-1966 Northeast drought crisis. It has developed a comprehensive plan for the basin and has reviewed some 2500 proposed projects for their compatibility with that plan. A basin-wide water quality control program has been established, including regional sewage collection and treatment works. The DRBC has assumed responsibility for the cost of nonfederal water supply features in federal reservoirs in the basin, thus serving as a middleman between the Corps of Engineers and state and local ultimate users. As a corollary to that program it has instituted charges for basin-wide water withdrawals for consumptive use in excess

---

29. DRBC at § § 13.1, 14.2, 14.4(b).

30. DRBC at §3.10.

31. For a general review of DRBC operations, see Muys, *supra* note 14, at 157-92; *see also* U.S. Advisory Comm. on Intergovernmental Relations, Multi-State Regionalism 95-96, 99-108, 111-20 (1972). The DRBC publishes an excellent annual report detailing the highlights of its operations.

of 1971 levels. It has made studies of water supply and demand in the basin, a major component of which is a Commission-mandated master power plant siting study prepared by electric utilities in the basin. The DRBC has laid the groundwork for comprehensive flood plain regulation. In recent years, it has placed increasing emphasis on environmental values, and in 1975 it took the almost unprecedented step of recommending Congressional deauthorization of the major proposed reservoir project in the basin, the controversial Tocks Island Dam. It has been a useful mechanism for facilitating public participation in the planning of projects in the basin and is providing a basin-wide point of view for balancing diverse values and exploring various alternatives to proposed projects.

Both in theory and practice the Delaware River Basin Compact has shown that disparate federal, state, and local elements in water resources development can be forged into a comprehensive, cooperative, and consciously directed regional program. While it is too early to tell whether the similar compact on the Susquehanna will be as successful, at this point the framework for regional coordination under the federal-interstate compact mechanism appears unrivalled by any existing or proposed institutional arrangement.

Although some jurisdictional problems in the federal-interstate compact approach are still in the process of being resolved, this compact approach justifies serious and thoughtful consideration by other regions. It merits particular consideration in the western public land states where the federal government's dominant role as landowner and water master makes the goals of the federal-interstate compact particularly relevant. It is meaningless to talk of comprehensive planning and management of water and land resources in the West if the federal government is not to be an integral part of the effort. Effective water and land use planning requires a fully cooperative, coordinated effort among the federal government, the states and, perhaps most important, the Indian tribes who are probably holding the biggest and most secure water rights in the West. Almost all of the water allocation compacts were agreed to before the full impact of the so-called "reservation doctrine" of federal and Indian water rights was announced by the Supreme Court in *Arizona v. California* in 1963.[32] Consequently, I think it safe to assume that the estimated water requirements which undoubtedly formed the basis of the allocations to the compacting states were grossly understated for those states with substantial areas of reserved federal and Indian land. I know from my National Water Commission study that this was the case with respect to the Upper Colorado River Compact. Whether the conflicting equities in those situations can be fairly balanced remains to be seen. What is clear is that federal and Indian claims should be fully reflected in, and bound by, any future efforts at compact allocations or renegotiation of present allocations.

Similarly, future compact allocations or reallocations must reflect not only federal rights and obligations as landowner and trustee of Indian rights, but should be made with careful consideration, to the extent possible, of the impact of the national water pollution control program on consumptive use water rights. It would be idle to allocate quantities of water to a particular state or states if physical and geographic factors or use patterns, coupled with the limitation of water quality control standards under the Federal Water Pollution Control Act, would never permit those waters to be put to maximum beneficial use.

If the federal government were a signatory party to a compact and therefore bound by it the same as each of the states, to the extent constitutionally permissible, the federal representative would serve as the focal point for all federal interests, whether consumptive use rights, in-stream and other environmental values, water quality control, flood control, project construction and licensing, and the like. That kind of arrangement would compel coordination and sanity in comprehensive river basin development, and I would hope it would be embraced by both the states and the federal government.

However, in conversations with state water officials about the prospects of such an approach in the West I have sensed an attitude of mixed despair and hostility toward the concept, apparently a residual legacy of antipathy toward the federal dominance of land and water use policy in the West.

---

32. 373 U.S. 546 (1963).

While I can understand this attitude, I believe that it is shortsighted. The fact is that old "States' Rights" arguments are futile, since the federal government, both as a legal and practical matter, wields paramount power in the West in land and water (and now air)[33] resources. Although periodic gestures of comity and cooperation are made by various federal officials, they are only as substantial as the tenure of those officials. What is needed is a Congressionally approved regional institutional arrangement which will mandate cooperative, coordinated action by federal agencies in conformity with the views of the affected basin states, while necessarily reserving the federal government's right to assert the paramount national prerogative in appropriate situations. That vehicle, in my view, is the federal-interstate compact now operating so successfully on the Delaware.

III. CONCLUSION

Over 50 years ago Harvard law professor (later Supreme Court Justice) Felix Frankfurter collaborated with Harvard Dean James M. Landis in a classic article advocating the "imaginative adaptation of the compact idea" to regional problems. Their conclusion is appropriate to our times:

> The overwhelming difficulties confronting modern society must not be at the mercy of the false antithesis embodied in the shibboleths "States-Rights" and "National Supremacy." We must not deny ourselves new or unfamiliar modes in realizing national ideals. Our regions are realities. Political thinkers must respond to these realities. Instead of leading to parochialism, it will bring a fresh ferment of political thought whereby national aims may be achieved through various forms of political adjustments.[34]

---

33. Under the EPA's nondeterioration regulations promulgated under the Clean Air Act, as well as even more stringent statutory amendments which have been proposed, constraints on future development in the public land states are dependent in many cases on the impact of various activities on certain classes of federal lands. *See* 40 C.F.R. §52.21 (1976); H.R. 10498, §108 & S. 3219, §6, 94th Cong., 2d Sess. (1976) (House and Senate versions of the Clean Air Act Amendments of 1976). Although each body passed its version of the bill, the Conference Committee Report was not acted on before adjournment. H. REP. No. 94-1242, 94th Cong., 2d Sess. (1976).

34. Frankfurter & Landis, *The Compact Clause of the Constitution—A Study in Interstate Adjustments*, 34 YALE L.J. 685, 729 (1925).

Appendix:
Compacts Relating to the Planning and Management of Interstate Water Resources
I. WATER ALLOCATION COMPACTS

Arkansas River Compact, Pub. L. No. 81-82, 63 Stat. 145 (1949) (signed by the States 14 Dec. 1948).

Arkansas River Basin Compact, Pub. L. No. 89-789, §107(a), 80 Stat. 1409 (1966) (signed by the States 31 Mar. 1965).

Arkansas River Basin Compact, Pub. L. No. 93-152, 87 Stat. 569 (1973) (signed by the States 16 Mar. 1970).

Bear River Compact, Pub. L. No. 85-348, 72 Stat. 38 (1958) (signed by the States 4 Feb. 1955).

Belle Fourche River Compact, Pub. L. No. 78-236, 58 Stat. 94 (1944) (signed by the States 18 Feb. 1943).

Canadian River Compact, Pub. L. No. 82-345, 66 Stat. 74 (1952) (signed by the States 6 Dec. 1950).

Colorado River Compact, COLO. REV. STAT. ANN. § §37-61-101 *et seq.* (1973), approved by Congress, Pub. L. No. 70-642, §13, 45 Stat. 1057, 1059 (1928) (signed by the States 24 Nov. 1922). Text may be found at 70 Cong. Rec. 324 (1928).

Costilla Creek Compact, *as amended,* Pub. L. No. 88-198, 77 Stat. 350 (1963) (signed by the States 30 Sept. 1944).

Kansas-Nebraska Big Blue River Compact, Pub. L. No. 92-308, 86 Stat. 193 (1972) (signed by the States 25 Jan. 1971).

Klamath River Basin Compact, Pub. L. No. 85-222, 71 Stat. 497 (1957).

La Plata River Compact, Pub. L. No. 68-346, 43 Stat. 796 (1925) (signed by the States 27 Nov. 1922).

Pecos River Compact, Pub. L. No. 81-91, 63 Stat. 159 (1949) (signed by the States 3 Dec. 1948).

Republican River Compact, Pub. L. No. 78-60, 57 Stat. 86 (1943) (signed by the States 31 Dec. 1942).

Rio Grande Compact, Pub. L. No. 76-96, 53 Stat. 785 (1939) (signed by the States 18 Mar. 1938).

Sabine River Compact, Pub. L. No. 83-578, 68 Stat. 690 (1954) (signed by the States 26 Jan. 1953), *as amended,* Pub. L. No. 87-418, 76 Stat. 34 (1962).

Snake River Compact, Pub. L. No. 81-464, 64 Stat. 29 (1950) (signed by the States 10 Oct. 1949).

South Platte River Compact, Pub. L. No. 69-37, 44 Stat. 195 (1926) (signed by the States 3 May 1923).

Upper Colorado River Basin Compact, Pub. L. No. 81-37, 63 Stat. 31 (1949).

Upper Niobara Basin Compact, Pub. L. No. 91-52, 83 Stat. 86 (1969).

Yellowstone River Compact, Pub. L. No. 82-231, 65 Stat. 663 (1951) (signed by the States 8 Dec. 1950).

II. SINGLE PURPOSE POLLUTION CONTROL COMPACTS

New England Interstate Water Pollution Control Compact, Pub. L. No. 80-292, 61 Stat. 682 (1947).

New York Harbor (Tri-State) Interstate Sanitation Compact, Pub. L. No. 74-62, 49 Stat. 932 (1935).

Ohio River Valley Water Sanitation Compact, Pub. L. No. 76-739, 54 Stat. 752 (1940).

Potomac River Basin Compact, Pub. L. No. 76-93, 54 Stat. 748 (1940) (signed by the States 16 Apr. 1940), *as amended*, Pub. L. No. 91-407, 84 Stat. 856 (1970).

Tennessee River Basin Water Pollution Control Compact, Pub. L. No. 85-734, 72 Stat. 823 (1958).

III. PLANNING AND FLOOD CONTROL COMPACTS

Connecticut River Flood Control Compact, Pub. L. No. 83-52, 67 Stat. 45 (1953).

Great Lakes Basin Compact, Pub. L. No. 90-419, 82 Stat. 414 (1968).

Merrimack River Flood Control Compact, Pub. L. No. 85-23, 71 Stat. 18 (1957).

Red River of the North Compact, Pub. L. No. 75-456, 52 Stat. 151 (1938) (signed by the States 23 June 1937).

Thames River Flood Control Compact, Pub. L. No. 85-526, 72 Stat. 364 (1958).

Wabash Valley Compact, Pub. L. No. 86-375, 73 Stat. 695 (1959) (approved by Indiana on 26 Feb. 1959 and by Illinois on 20 Mar. 1959).

Wheeling Creek Watershed Protection and Flood Prevention District Compact, Pub. L. No. 90-181, 81 Stat. 553 (1967) (approved by Pennsylvania on 2 Aug. 1967 and by West Virginia on 1 Mar. 1967).

IV. MULTIPURPOSE REGULATORY COMPACTS

Delaware River Basin Compact, Pub. L. No. 87-328, 75 Stat. 689 (1961).

Missouri-Illinois Bi-State Compact, Pub. L. No. 81-743, 64 Stat. 569 (1950), *as amended,* Pub. L. No. 86-303, 73 Stat. 583 (1959).

Susquehanna River Basin Compact, Pub. L. No. 91-575, 84 Stat. 1509 (1970).

5
Transmountain Diversions of Water in Colorado

Raphael J. Moses[*]

Most of Colorado's internal water problems arise from the fact that Colorado is a rectangular state, established by Congress, in its infinite wisdom, without regard to river basin drainages.[1] Thus we find ourselves, on our Centennial anniversary, with most of the people living east of the Continental Divide, and most of the water running in streams on the western side of that same divide.

The exterior boundaries of Colorado may be great for cartographers, but they are a constant source of friction for water users. Not only does the western half of Colorado lie in the drainage of the Colorado River and its tributaries, but North Park should, geographically, be part of Wyoming; and the San

---

[*] A.B. (1935), LL.B. (1937), J.D. (1972), University of Colorado; Visiting Lecturer and Regent Emeritus at the University of Colorado; Consultant to Colorado Water Conservation Board. The author was the Special Assistant Attorney General for the Rio Grande Compact, 1957-58. Member of the firm, Moses, Wittemeyer, Harrison & Woodruff, Boulder, Colorado.

1. The writer became so fascinated with the background of Colorado's "rectilinearism," if a word may be coined, that a long detour in preparation occurred. Unfortunately, there appears to be little to indicate how Colorado's shape evolved. L.R. Hafen, in a 1926 article, mentions it only briefly. He said:

> The bill for creation of "Colorado Territory" introduced in the previous session (April 3, 1860) was brought up in the Senate January 30, 1861, and the name changed to "Idaho Territory." The original bill had designated the Green and the Colorado rivers as the western boundary of the Territory, while the other boundaries were identical with those of the present state. This western boundary was first changed (in the bill) to the 33d meridian and finally to the 32d (from Washington). The bill was again considered February 4th and Senator Wilson "at the request of the delegate from that Territory" proposed to substitute the name "Colorado" for "Idaho." The bill was so amended and immediately passed.
>
> The bill now went to the House and was considered on the 18th. The Delegate from New Mexico objected to having Colorado include that portion of New Mexico north of the 37th parallel, but his objections were disregarded. The bill with minor changes was passed by the House and now returned to the Senate. The Senate concurred in the amendment on the 26th and the President approved the measure two days later. . . .

Hafen, *Steps to Statehood in Colorado*, 3 THE COLORADO MAGAZINE 97,106 (1926). It should be noted that even if the western boundary of Colorado had been the Green and Colorado Rivers, the transmountain diversion problems would not have been eliminated. Only by making the Continental Divide the western boundary would the problem go away.

Luis Valley, ethnically, historically, and geographically should have been part of New Mexico.

Originally, no legal inhibitions barred transmountain diversions of water designed to overcome quirks of geography. The Colorado Constitution provides:

> The right to divert the unappropriated waters of any natural stream to beneficial uses shall never be denied. Priority of appropriation shall give the better right as between those using the water for the same purpose . . . .[2]

In *Coffin v. Left Hand Ditch Company*,[3] the landmark decision which resulted in what is now commonly known as the "Colorado Doctrine," our Supreme Court said:

> [W]e hold that, in the absence of express statutes to the contrary, the first appropriator of water from a natural stream for a beneficial purpose has , . . . a prior right thereto, to the extent of such appropriation.
>
> [T]he right to water acquired by priority of appropriation thereof is not in any way dependent upon the *locus* of its application to the beneficial use designed.

Coffin itself involved a transmountain diversion, albeit a very low mountain. The Left Hand Ditch Company had taken water out of the St. Vrain Creek across a divide into the watershed of Left Hand Creek, and Coffin, a downstream riparian owner on the St. Vrain, complained. The analogy applies to the Continental Divide as well. A prior appropriator from the Western Slope to the Eastern Slope retains his priority, and the place of use is not material.

Colorado has had many private transmountain diversions. Some of the most significant are the diversion from the Laramie River to the Poudre watershed, the substantial Twin Lakes Diversion from the headwaters of the Roaring Fork to Lake Creek—a tributary of the Arkansas, the Busk-Ivanhoe Tunnel in the same vicinity, and smaller ones from the Pine and Piedra, tributaries of the San Juan, into the headwaters of the Rio Grande.

By far the largest transmountain diversions have been made by cities and by water conservancy districts. The largest transmountain diversion in the state is that of the Northern

---

2. COLO. CONST. art 14, §6.
3. 6 Colo. 443, 19 P. 466 (1882).

Colorado Water Conservancy District, some 340,000 acre-feet diverted from the headwaters of the Colorado River into northeastern Colorado by way of the Adams Tunnel. This Bureau of Reclamation Project, commonly known as the Colorado-Big Thompson, is controlled by operating principles set out in United States Senate documents.[4] Plans are underway by the Municipal Subdistrict of the Northern Colorado Water Conservancy District to increase this amount by 30,000 acre-feet by means of the Six Cities Project.

Going south along the Continental Divide, we next encounter the transmountain diversions by the City and County of Denver, consisting of existing divisions through the Moffat and Roberts Tunnels diverting respectively from the Fraser River and the Blue River and their tributaries, and proposed diversions from the Piney and the Gore. The proposed diversions would utilize the existing Dillon Reservoir and Roberts Tunnel.

Colorado Springs and Aurora have joined together to construct the first phase of the Homestake Project, which takes water from Homestake Creek, a tributary of the Eagle, through a tunnel into the Upper Arkansas. The second phase of this project has been deferred because of the additional costs associated with additional restrictive environmental constraints.

The Frying Pan-Arkansas diversion will take 67,000 acre-feet of water from the upper tributaries of the Frying Pan River and Hunter Creek through the Boustead Tunnel into enlarged Turquoise Reservoir on the Upper Arkansas, there to enlarged Twin Lakes Reservoir on Lake Creek, a tributary of the Arkan-

---

4. In his excellent article entitled *Compensatory Storage*, 22 ROCKY MTN. L. REV. 452, 455 (1950), Charles J. Beise expresses it this way:

At the time the foregoing developments occurred, one individual representing the West Slope assumed an outstanding role as protector of that area. Congressman Edward T. Taylor, as Chairman of the Appropriations Committee of the House, was, by virtue of his position, able to enforce his edicts and to preclude the development of any publicly financed project which would divert water from his congressional district to the East Slope, unless the proponents of such project were willing to make such concessions as he deemed necessary. This is no criticism of Congressman Taylor, who was sincere in his belief that an area developing more slowly needed protection from one developing more rapidly. Thus, because of Congressman Taylor's political prominence, the West Slope was placed in an unusually strong bargaining position.

sas River, for irrigation and municipal use in the valley of the Arkansas and Fountain Creek.

In the 1930s, the sponsors of the Colorado-Big Thompson were pushing strongly for authorization. Concerned citizens of the Western Slope, visualizing the loss of their water to the Eastern Slope and buttressed by the fact that their representative, Congressman Ed Taylor, was chairman of the House Appropriations Committee, were able to accomplish two things: the establishment of the Colorado Water Conservation Board as the State's policymaking entity in water matters, and the formation of water conservancy districts.[5]

The act authorizing formation of conservancy districts contains the first area-of-origin protective legislation ever adopted in Colorado. The act provides:

> [A]ny works or facilities planned and designed for the exportation of water from the natural basin of the Colorado river and its tributaries in Colorado, by any district created under this article, shall be subject to the provisions of the Colorado river compact and the "Boulder Canyon Project Act." Any such works or facilities shall be designed, constructed, and operated in such manner that the present appropriations of water, and in addition thereto prospective uses of water for irrigation and other beneficial consumptive use purposes, including consumptive uses for domestic, mining, and industrial purposes, within the natural basin of the Colorado River in the State of Colorado, from which water is exported, will not be impaired nor increased in cost at the expense of the water users within the natural basin. The facilities and other means for the accomplishment of said purpose shall be incorporated in and made a part of any project plans for the exportation of water from said natural basin in Colorado.[6]

Sec. 1(c) of that same act provides:

> To have and to exercise the power of eminent domain and dominant eminent domain and in the manner provided by law for the condemnation of private property for public use to take any property necessary to the exercise of the powers granted in this article; except that such district shall not have or exercise the power of eminent domain over or by means thereof to acquire the title to or beneficial use of vested water rights for transmountain diversion, and in connection therewith such district shall not have the power to carry or transport water in transmountain diversion, the

5. COLO. REV. STAT. ANN. §37-45-118(1)(b)(iv) (1973).
6. *Id*.

title to which has been acquired by any municipality by virtue of eminent domain proceedings against any such vested rights.

As a result of these provisions, and the operating principles of the Colorado-Big Thompson Project,[7] Green Mountain Reservoir was constructed at Eastern Slope water users' expense, as a compensating reservoir for the Big Thompson Project.

Similarly, Ruedi Reservoir was constructed, under the provisions of the same statute and of the operating principles of the Frying Pan-Arkansas Project,[8] as a compensating reservoir for the Frying Pan-Arkansas Project.

Subsequently, the Colorado Water Conservation Board, responsive to continued Western Slope concerns, adopted a resolution that it would approve no further federally financed transmountain diversions until the total water requirements of the Watern Slope had been determined.[9] To date, such a determination has not been made.

The increased concern on the part of Western Slope residents about the inadequacy of water supplies for Western Slope development will be a major obstacle to future major transmountain diversions. However, increased environmental constraints pose an even greater threat to such diversions.

For example, the inclusion by the Congress of a substantial part of Denver's proposed Eagle-Piney watershed in the Gore Creek Wilderness Area[10] will, in the opinion of the Denver Water Board, increase the cost of that project by several hundred million dollars. Such environmental expenditures may render the project economically impracticable.

The necessity for the sponsor of a transmountain diverter to obtain federal rights of way across the federal forest lands that blanket the Continental Divide may further impede the construction of such projects. Colorado Springs and Aurora

7. S. Doc. No. 80, 75th Cong., 1st Sess. (1937).

8. H.R. Doc. No. 130, 87th Cong., 1st Sess. (1961).

9. *See* MINUTES, Colorado Water Conservation Board (April 1969).

10. Act of July 12, 1976, Pub. L. No. 94-352, 90 Stat. 870 (1976) (to be codified in 16 U.S.C. §§1131n., 1132n.).

11. Colorado Springs and Aurora have each acquired other water rights in lieu of presently developing the second stage of Homestake. *See, e.g.*, Preliminary Official Statement and Notice of Sale, $27,000,000 City of Colorado Springs Utilities Improvement Revenue Bonds, Series 1976A (released July 31, 1976).

have already been advised that materials, supplies, and equipment for the second phase of their Homestake Project will have to be helicoptered to the site. The additional costs, over the estimated cost, together with inflation, have combined to cause these cities to defer construction of the second phase. Instead, these cities are purchasing additional water rights formerly used for agriculture.[11] The problems which arise from this kind of a policy decision could be the subject of an entire additional paper.

In 1973, the Colorado legislature approved the instream appropriation of water by the Colorado Water Conservation Board, on behalf of the people:

> For the benefit and enjoyment of present and future generations, "beneficial use" shall also include the appropriation by the State of Colorado in the manner prescribed by law of such minimum flows between specific points or levels for and on natural streams and lakes as are required to preserve the natural environment to a reasonable degree.[12]

Although the constitutionality of this legislation is, as of the moment, untested, the Water Conservation Board has blanketed the Western Slope with applications for instream decrees which will effectively bar future filings for transmountain diversions.

What are the ethics of transmountain diversions? I suspect that most people, regardless of which side of the mountain they live on, sympathize with the Western Slope's desire to keep the water over there. This feeling undoubtedly permitted the passage of the area-of-origin legislation earlier referred to.[13]

It should be noted that such legislation refers only to transmountain diversions by water conservation districts, so that major cities are not restricted save by the environmental constraints which translate into costs which make the economics questionable.

We have always maintained that water seeks its own economic level, or as it is sometimes expressed, "water flows uphill to money." However, there is a limit to the money available, particularly where alternate choices exist, and they do exist.

---

12. COLO. REV. STAT. ANN. §37-92-103(4) (1973).
13. COLO. REV. STAT. ANN. §37-45-118(1)(b)(iv) (1973).

If one desired to be fanciful, he could resort to what I call the "reverse domino" scenario. That goes something like this: Western Colorado will agree to transmountain diversions the day that California agrees to forego its Colorado River entitlement. That will happen only when all of Southern California's needs are supplied from Northern California. Northern California will let its water go when Oregon agrees to replace it. Oregon will replace the water when Washington agrees to furnish the water Oregon gives up, and Washington will do this only if Canada foregoes its Columbia River rights. Canada will act only if the flow of the MacKenzie is reversed to supply the Columbia needs, and that will only happen when the United States supplies Canada with water from the Yukon.

Everyone who thinks any of these events will soon occur, please stand up.

In short, the day of major transmountain diversions of water in Colorado has passed, and we are unlikely to see built even those that have been on the drawing board for years. Politics, ethics, economics, and environmental concerns all raise obstacles. Any one is probably enough. The combination is overwhelming.

6
Water Law and the Public Interest: A Commentary

Robert Emmet Clark[*]

I was going to address you as "fellow students of water problems and fellow slaves of the mythical marketplace," but the two need not be equated. My place on this program is one that I enjoy, that of a gadfly and a critic.

Some of you know that I have been a member of the bar of Arizona and New Mexico for 30 years. Many of you know that I have been in Arizona for the last 12 years; I went there for one year to be a visiting professor, and we are still there! I found something I could really criticize—namely, the Arizona water law, which is terrible.

When I was in New Mexico, we always used to have something to say about Texas; now, in this gathering, I think I should say something about Arizona. And what I have to say is pretty bad. You may have read the last Arizona Supreme Court decision that emphasizes exactly what Mr. Ogilvie of the Denver Water Board has discussed—the plight of municipal water users. I am especially pleased that he discussed municipal suppliers, because I feel like a prophet on that subject. While the farmers are going to grow pecans—which take about seven acre-feet per year—the mines are theoretically going to be shut down for lack of sufficient water, and the city of Tucson is going to be left somewhere in the middle.[1] Obviously, some reevaluation of our water priorities will soon be necessary.

I should also like to make a disclaimer here. Some of the people on this panel represent particular interest groups. I do not represent any interest other than the critical ideas of a teacher and an opportunity to disagree with my long-time friend, Frank Trelease, about the role of public management—a concept that has been found in all systems that evolved from the primitive prior appropriation doctrine.

---

[*] Professor of Law, University of Arizona.
1. Farmers Inv. Co. v. Pima Mining Co., 111 Ariz. 56, 523 P.2d 482 (1974).

The comparative system outlined by Professor Trelease emphasizes what makes this subject both serious and interesting. Water law demonstrates that jurisprudential studies are not high-level, metaphysical, or theoretical. The law of necessity, or of utility, is evident in most water law systems around the world. Thus, ever since the time of Mesopotamia and Egypt, the visible sources of the rivers have been the sources used, and the parties using them acquired the right to continue their uses.

Three questions may be asked in this jurisprudential context:

(1) What are the sources of the law? Can a man with a shovel and some enterprise using the stream to grow some frijoles be one? Should he be one?

(2) How does the law change? How does it grow? How does it develop? The permit system and its many variations might be one instructive example in this regard.

(3) What is the purpose of the law? Is it the purpose of the law of Arizona to ensure that the farmers will have water when others do not? Clearly, that is not the purpose, and clearly the legislation in Arizona will have to be changed.

A review of these juridprudential concerns further demonstrates my point: we must have a better system of public management of all resources, not just water resources. Professor Trelease knows that the prior appropriation system is no longer in its pure form, that it has been modified by statute, and that the modifications are directed toward greater public management. In fact, the Wyoming Supreme Court, early in this century, made one of the strongest statements about public management in a case involving the permit system.

But, greater representation of the public's interest in water allocation is still necessary. We can no longer allow the pressures of special-interest groups to determine, one against the other, which interest shall prevail. This must be changed and is being changed. When I speak of the public management system I realize that Professor Trelease thinks that is a system of the God-damn bureaucrat and the wise administrator, which in his mind are the same thing.

But the marketplace is a wonderful thing to talk about; it is a wonderful myth. The economists have an objective standard that we in the law do not, since we deal in "weasel words" like "justice," "fairness," "equality," and "equity." The economists use "money" and they use it to measure love, and debt, and water rights. The economists cannot adequately measure the law's concerns, and the marketplace cannot be allowed to dictate the law's functions. Public participation and management is sorely needed in the water decisionmaking system.

7

Legal Restraints and Responses to the Allocation and Distribution of Water

Michael D. White[*]

The legal aspects of water allocation and distribution are governed by three variable factors:

1. The law being applied—which could be state, interstate, federal, or international;

2. The legal classification of the water involved—an artificial distinction between surface and underground stream waters on one hand and underground percolating water on the other; and

3. Whether one is dealing with the initial allocation or a second generation allocation of water.

I. THE LAW BEING APPLIED AND THE LEGAL CLASSIFICATION OF WATER

The first two factors, the law which is being applied and the legal classification of the water involved, are inextricably entangled. As will be explained below, the legal classifications of water depend on the jurisdiction involved. Similarly, how allocation and distribution of waters are made depends in turn on their legal classification. The best way to approach this briar patch is to address in turn each level of law involved: state, interstate, federal, and international.

A. *State Law*

There are at least 50 different systems of water law in the United States. Although certain jurisdictional types can be fairly easy to identify, no two states are exactly the same. As a starting point, however, most states classify water into two broad categories: stream water and groundwater. Many jurisdictions further divide groundwater into two types: underground streams and percolating water.

1. Stream Water

There are three general types of jurisdictions when it comes to the allocation and distribution of stream water: prior

---

* Member of the firm White & Burke, Denver, Colorado; lecturer at the University of Denver College of Law.

appropriation, riparian, and those that mix appropriation and riparian.

(a.) The Appropriation Doctrine

The appropriation doctrine has as its basic tenet the familiar maxim of "first-in-time, first-in-right." This simply means that the person who first uses water will always have the overriding or senior right to continue the use of that water. Similarly, the second person to use water from a stream has the second most senior right. Subsequent users (or "appropriators") are accorded increasingly junior water rights until there is no water available for anyone to use. The phenomenon of a large number of water rights having various degrees of relative seniority is called the priority system.

The prior appropriation doctrine is followed in those portions of the country where water is scarce and, like tax law, it is established primarily by statutes which are frequently interpreted by case law. Nine states recognize a pure prior appropriation doctrine: Alaska, Arizona, Colorado, Idaho, Montana, Nevada, New Mexico, Utah, and Wyoming. These nine states are further divided into two jurisdictional types: the mandate version of the prior appropriation doctrine (which now includes only Colorado, but formerly included Montana) and the permit version of the prior appropriation doctrine, which has been adopted by all the other western states.

Under the mandate version as it exists in Colorado, the Constitution establishes an individual right to appropriate water. While water rights may be created by individual acts, the priorities for those rights can be established only by court decree. The process of obtaining a decree or priority for a water right in Colorado is commonly referred to as "adjudication." Adjudications formerly took place in the district courts throughout the State of Colorado. Now, however, they are conducted only in seven "water courts," one for each of the major river basins in the state.

Under the permit version of the prior appropriation doctrine, water rights are not created by individual act but are, instead, awarded in the form of permits and/or certificates by various state administrative officials.

(b.) The Riparian Doctrine

Riparian water right systems exist in approximately thirty

states, most of which are the more humid states in the Midwest and East. In theory, at least, these states are divided into two jurisdictional versions of the riparian doctrine: the natural flow and the reasonable use versions.

The natural flow version, which is rapidly going out of style and may well be extinct in all states by now, embodies the older concept that an owner of land alongside the stream is entitled to the maintenance of that stream in its natural condition with respect to both the quantity and quality of the stream flow.

Since about the turn of the century, courts have acted to modify the harsh rule of the natural flow version which, by its very nature, discouraged or prohibited consumptive uses of water. This judicial tinkering resulted in what is now generally referred to as the reasonable use version of the riparian doctrine. Under the reasonable use version, which is probably applied in all of the riparian jurisdictions by now, each owner of land along a stream is entitled to the reasonable use of the water in the stream. While it does not actively discourage or prohibit consumptive uses of stream water, the reasonable use version does create a great deal of uncertainty, since what is a "reasonable use" is determined on an ad hoc basis and may vary from year to year, depending on the amount of water in the stream as well as the social value of the uses by other riparian owners.

Regardless of the jurisdictional type involved, there are several issues which affect water allocation and distribution in the riparian states. Most of these issues revolve around the question of what is "riparian land." Riparian water rights, of course, are owned only by those persons who own "riparian land," that land which touches a stream. Whether a severed portion of a riparian parcel continues to be considered riparian land regardless of the fact that it no longer touches the stream is a question that is resolved differently in different jurisdictions. In addition, whether water may be used on land which is not riparian is also treated differently among the jurisdictions.

(c.) Mixed Jurisdictions

A number of states mix the prior appropriation doctrine and the riparian doctrine. In the West, riparian rights are still recognized in Kansas, Mississippi, North Dakota, Oklahoma, Oregon, South Dakota, Texas, and Washington. In those states, however, all new water rights are established under the permit version of the prior appropriation doctrine. It appears that in only two western states, California and Nebraska, are new rights perfected under the riparian doctrine.

Finally, many of the states normally thought of as riparian states have recently begun to establish new water rights under some permit system which may incorporate principles from the prior appropriation doctrine. These states include, to some degree, Delaware, Florida, Iowa, Kentucky, Maryland, Minnesota, New Jersey, North Carolina, and Wisconsin.

2. Underground Water

In very general terms, underground water is divided into two classifications: underground stream water and percolating water. Underground stream water is generally thought of as that underground water which has discernible flow within ascertainable boundaries. Percolating water is that underground water which oozes through the ground, without perceptible velocity. The presumption in most states, but not in Colorado, is that underground water is presumed to be percolating.

In Colorado, however, all water, including underground water, is presumed to be tributary to a natural stream. The burden of showing the water as nontributary falls on the person who makes that assertion.

In very general terms, underground stream water is treated in most jurisdictions under the same rules that apply to those streams that are on the surface of the earth.

With respect to underground water that is classified as percolating water, however, there are five distinct jurisdictional types which should be considered: the absolute privilege doctrine, the American reasonable use doctrine, the Restatement of Torts reasonable use doctrine, the correlative rights doctrine, and the appropriation doctrine.

The absolute privilege doctrine is the oldest groundwater doctrine in the United States, and appears to provide that the owner of land has an absolute right to pump all the water he can find underneath his land for any purpose whatsoever, whether on or off his overlying land.

The American reasonable use version is similar, but provides that uses off the overlying land may be unreasonable and unlawful if the pumping for those off-site uses injures a neighbor of the overlying landowner.

The Restatement of Torts version of the reasonable use doctrine incorporates a process of balancing between competing uses—regardless of whether or not those uses are on or off overlying land.

The correlative rights doctrine, found primarily in California, involves the concept of sharing in times of shortage, based on the amount of land owned by the competing overlying owners.

The appropriation doctrine as applied to underground water is found in most of the western states which have adopted the appropriation doctrine for surface streams. In most of the appropriation doctrine states, however, there are differences between the way the appropriation doctrine is applied to surface streams and underground waters. For example, in Colorado there are three distinct and different applications of the appropriation doctrine to groundwater. First, most Colorado underground water is presumed to be tributary and is treated exactly the same way as the waters of a natural surface stream. Second, in what are called designated groundwater basins located on the eastern plains of the state, Colorado uses the permit rather than the mandate version of the prior appropriation doctrine, requiring that permits for rights to use underground water be obtained from the Colorado Groundwater Commission. Third, there is also a requirement that permits to construct all wells be obtained from the State Engineer. He will issue such permits to construct wells (the permits not giving any right to use water) only when there is unappropriated groundwater available and when the proposed well would not injure the rights of other water right owners. There are numerous exceptions to the standards for the issuance of well construction permits, including those for smaller wells, those for aquifers which are wholly confined, and those for groundwater which will take more than one hundred years to reach a natural stream.

B. *Interstate Allocation and Distribution*

Because so many of our country's major streams or rivers

cross state boundaries, it is necessary to allocate the water of those streams among the various states which they cross. Without such allocation, the old rule of "highority is priority" would apply, with the upper states taking the lion's share, if not all, of the water in the interstate streams. By and large, there are two ways in which water is allocated among those states which happen to be on an interstate stream: interstate compact or a decree of the United States Supreme Court exercising its original jurisdiction in suits among states.

Compacts are essentially treaties or contracts among the states on interstate streams, which take a variety of approaches to the allocation of water among those states. Although those approaches have been skillfully described by Jerome Muys, it may be of interest to know that Colorado is a party to compacts which affect the allocation of water of the Colorado River, the LaPlata River, the Animas-LaPlata Project, the South Platte River, the Rio Grande, the Republican River, Costilla Creek, and the Arkansas River.

When it is impossible for states to agree among themselves, disputes over interstate streams inevitably find their way to the United States Supreme Court. When that happens, the United States Supreme Court acts as a trial court when the litigation is among states and eventually issues a decree allocating the waters of the interstate stream involved. In Colorado, there are two such decrees which affect two of our rivers: the Laramie River and the North Platte River.

There are two significant problems with the interstate allocation of water, whether it be by an interstate compact or a court decree. The terms of those documents often are ambiguous, yet very difficult to change. In addition, interstate allocation generally ignores groundwater, which is a very important component of the hydrologic cycle. Perhaps the most prominent example of this omission today is the Madison formation, which underlies both Wyoming and South Dakota. And yet there is no interstate mechanism at present to resolve the problem.

C. *Federal*

Although federal law affects water allocation and distribution in a number of ways, there are four principal areas in which the impact of federal law is most strongly felt: the navigation servitude, reserved rights, water pollution control, and reclamation and flood control projects.

1. Navigation Servitude

The navigation servitude applies to streams which are classically navigable, those which could support commerce, as well as the tributaries which support them. The servitude is a paramount right in the United States government to the use for purposes of commerce of the waters of navigable streams. This means that water rights under state law which interfere with the use of water for navigation are potentially and alarmingly unstable. Parenthetically, it should be noted that it has been suggested that states have a navigation easement or a navigation servitude that is remarkably similar to that of the federal government.

2. U.S. Reserved Rights

Reserved water rights of the United States are associated with all withdrawals and reservations of land from the public domain. The general theory is that at one time the United States owned all the land in the western United States, particularly in those states, such as Colorado, that have come to be known as public domain states. As settlement and development of those public lands increased, the United States began to withdraw or reserve large portions of the public domain for such uses as national forests, national parks, Indian reservations, etc. At the time that these large tracts of land were withdrawn or reserved, little thought was given to where the water would come from to be used to promote the purposes of the reservations. As a result, around the turn of the century the federal courts began to remedy this oversight through the legislative and executive branches of the federal government.

Beginning with Indian reservations, the courts began to enunciate a doctrine which has come to be known as the Federal Reserved Right Doctrine. Under that doctrine, the courts have found an implied reservation of water which necessarily accompanies the reservation or withdrawal of land by the United States. The water so reserved is in that amount which is necessary to effectuate the purposes of the land reservation or withdrawal. In addition, the reserved water right bears a priority as of the date that the land was reserved or withdrawn.

Needless to say, the concept of reserved rights has been in almost continual litigation since the federal courts began to establish the doctrine. Not only is there continued opposition to the general concept of reserved rights, but there also is a growing realization that those reserved rights associated with very old reservations will be senior to those private rights which have been perfected under state law. Presently, there is litigation in progress throughout the Western Slope of Colorado as well as on the North Platte and the South Platte Rivers on the Eastern Slope. That litigation is in fairly early stages in all the trial courts involved.

3. Water Pollution Control

In the area of water pollution control, the 1972 Federal Water Pollution Control Act Amendments established two programs which affect water resorces. First, the National Pollutant Discharge Elimination System (NPDES) was established to control the discharge of pollutants from point sources through a permit program which can be run either by the U.S. Environmental Protection Agency or those particular states which have obtained federal approval of their own permit program (as is the case in Colorado). Second, with respect to nonpoint sources of pollution, water quality planning efforts under Section 208 of the 1972 Amendments will eventually result in significant controls on nonpoint sources of pollution. Not only is §208 planning taking place on the state level in all states, it is also taking place at the designated regional planning agency level, of which there are six in Colorado:

> 1. The greater Denver metropolitan area, comprised of the City and County of Denver, and Adams, Arapahoe, Jefferson, and Boulder Counties, for which the Denver Regional Council of Governments is a designated planning agency.
> 2. Teller and El Paso Counties (Colorado Springs), for which the Pikes Peak Area COG is a designated planning agency.
> 3. Pueblo County, for which the Pueblo Area COG is a designated planning agency.
> 4. Larimer and Weld Counties, for which the Larimer-Weld COG is a designated planning agency.
> 5. Routt, Jackson, Grand, Summit, Eagle, and Pit-

kin Counties, for which the Northwest Colorado COG is a designated planning agency.

6. Moffat, Rio Blanco, Garfield, and Mesa Counties, for which the Colorado West Area COG is a designated planning agency.

Both the NPDES and the §208 programs raise severe water allocation questions. For example, with respect to those effluent guidelines, standards, and limitations which apply to point sources under the NPDES program, as effluent limitations grow more severe there is an inherent requirement that consumption or evaporation of wastewater increases. As that consumption increases, the amount of available water decreases. For example, for each 500-megawatt coal-fired power plant, we can expect that eight to ten thousand acres of irrigated land will either be dried up or forced to go without water. In addition, under most prior appropriation doctrines, downstream junior owners are entitled to the maintenance of stream conditions as they were at the time of their appropriations. If consumption is increased in order to meet the requirements of the NPDES program, those downstream owners will have legally-recognizable tort claims against the holders of NPDES permits. This situation causes a significant and as yet unresolved conflict between the effluent limitations under federal law and the water rights of downstream owners under state law.

With respect to nonpoint sources regulated under §208, there are also difficulties. The primary problem is that §208 requires land use controls to deal with the nonpoint sources of pollution, such as irrigation return flow. The new irrigation management practices which will be necessary to control the irrigation return flow under §208 may drastically alter the course of western agricultural economics. If, however, irrigators should be required to use more efficient means of irrigation (such as a switch from flood to sprinkler irrigation), less water *may* be consumed by evapotranspiration, increasing the availability of water.

4. Federal Projects

Finally, we are all aware of the pervasive and oftentimes beneficial effects of federal projects throughout the West. The problem with those projects is that their operation usually blithely ignores water right allocations under state law. As a result, these projects may throw any state allocation plans into a tailspin.

D. *International Allocation*

Waters of international rivers are allocated by international treaties which enjoy the benefit of the supremacy clause of the United States Constitution, taking precedence over state and interstate allocations of water. In Colorado, we are primarily concerned with the treaty between the United States and Mexico, which has an effect on both the Colorado River and the Rio Grande.

II. Problems of Initial Allocation

Although other levels of government play an important role in water allocation, the primary focus today is still on state levels of government and how they distribute water. The various state agencies raise a number of problems, the most important of which are discussed below.

A. *Riparian Jurisdictions*

In riparian jurisdictions, problems are found on either end of the spectrum. Under the natural flow version of the riparian doctrine, water allocation is very inflexible because of the need to maintain the natural flow and quality of the water. As a result, industrial development is not encouraged except through rather extraordinary means.

Under the reasonable use version of the riparian doctrine, where riparian owners share in the use of water based on the relative social value of their particular use, allocations are made on a case-by-case, ad hoc basis which ignores the need for certainty, an essential prerequisite for major capital investment.

B. *Appropriation Jurisdictions*

Under the appropriation doctrines, water users enjoy a certain amount of certainty because of the rather absolute nature of initial allocations of water. As will be pointed out later, however, the rational readjustment or secondary allocation following the initial allocation is somewhat difficult.

More specifically, in the jurisdictions which follow the permit version of the prior appropriation doctrine, the initial allocation is generally based on three factors: the availability of unappropriated water, the possibility of injury to other water rights, and the "public interest." The "public interest" is a fertile field for the wise allocation of water resources. Unfortunately, however, the meaning of "public interest" is usually restricted to economic or utilitarian concerns. Although recent legislation has begun to emphasize environmental concerns in the public interest, the "public interest" still does not generally include other broad concerns, such as the preservation of agricultural lands.

In Colorado, which adheres to the mandate version of the prior appropriation doctrine, the initial allocation of water, at least for a conditional water right, requires only a showing that the water right owner intends to appropriate water and that he actually conduct some first step on the land which is indicative of that intent. There is absolutely no concern with the public interest when priorities are awarded by the water courts. In addition, the water right is essentially a hunting license because the water courts also are not at all concerned with the availability of unappropriated water.

III.   PROBLEMS OF SECOND GENERATION ALLOCATION

In riparian jurisdictions, even those which have adopted the reasonable use version of the doctrine, it is very difficult to make rational allocations of water to new uses. What again is involved is an ad hoc determination of the relative social value of the new competing use. This, of course, has the same infirmity of uncertainty suffered by the first generation allocation.

In those prior appropriation states which have adopted the permit version of the doctrine, it is still usually possible to take advantage of the "public interest" in the administrative approval of change of water rights. The "public interest" concept still must be refined and developed as was true in the first generation allocation of water. In addition to the "public interest" test, the permit states generally do have yet another limitation on reallocation of water: that the change of the water right cannot injure other water rights.

In Colorado, the sole remaining mandate jurisdiction of all the prior appropriation states, the traditional test is that no reallocation or change of water right may be allowed if it will injure other water rights. There is, at least on the face of the statute, no provision for consideration of the "public interest" by the water court when it approves a reallocation or change.

In 1969, however, the Colorado General Assembly recodified the State's water law. With respect to change proceedings and plans of augmentation, the General Assembly did a curious thing. A literal reading of the new statute indicates that the injury prohibited in a change proceeding is injury to the owners or users of water rights rather than the water rights themselves. This, of course, suggests a back-door approach to insertion of the "public interest" in the Colorado water court proceedings involving change of water rights and approval of plans of augmentation. If the proscribed injury is to "owners or users," then that injury might be considered to include such things as environmental, economic, social, aesthetic, and similar considerations. At the present, we have no case law on this new interpretation, and its impact on the course of future Colorado water law remains to be seen.

IV. MISCELLANEOUS ASPECTS OF WATER RESOURCE ALLOCATION AND DISTRIBUTION

Although there are innumerable other factors which influence water resource allocation and distribution, there are seven of them which are of particular importance today, especially in Colorado: minimum stream flows, use of developed water, anti-export statutes, basin of origin protection statutes, constitutional preferences for the use of water, condemnation of water rights, and the relationship between water allocation and land use control.

A. *Minimum Stream Flows*

The federal government as well as various state governments throughout the West have begun to assert minimum stream flows which are applicable to water heretofore unallocated by the prior appropriation system. The minimum stream flows, in addition to designation of wilderness areas by the federal government, as well as wild and scenic rivers by both state and federal governments, essentially foreclose any future allocation or reallocation of water.

B. *Developed Water*

In many of the state courts in the West, concepts of maximization or efficient utilization of water have been growing alongside a strict interpretation of the prior appropriation or priority doctrine. Courts have been under significant pressure to recognize a benefit for those persons who do make more efficient use of water. When push comes to shove, however, the old prohibition against "extended use" often precludes the enjoyment of such benefit. For example, a recent Colorado case provided that water salvaged by phreatophyte removal could not be used by the person who removed the phreatophytes but instead must be relinquished to the stream for the use of senior water right owners. While the opinion in this case is undoubtedly a victory for environmental values, the decision can probably not be justified from the standpoint of agriculture. With a yearly loss of irrigated agricultural land in Colorado, it might be prudent to encourage the replacement of trees with crops.

C. *Anti-Export Statutes*

Roughly one-third of our states have what are called "anti-export statutes," which prohibit or severely restrict the diversion of water from its state of origin to another state. The anti-export statutes are hot topics at this time if for no other reason than their application to coal slurry pipelines. Not only are the statutes of doubtful constitutionality (on the theory that they place an unreasonable burden on interstate commerce), they also do not seem to promote the rational allocation of water resources, without consideration to state lines.

D. *Basin of Origin Protection*

Even within states, there is competition between different regions for available water supplies. Several states try to control inter-basin transfers of water by what are called "basin of origin protection statutes," which may prohibit or severely regulate the transfer of water from one river basin to another. In Colorado, we have only one such provision, which is applicable only to water conservancy districts.

E. *Constitutional Preferences*

Many state constitutions create preferences among different types of uses. For example, in Colorado, preference is given to domestic use of water over agricultural and to agricultural uses over manufacturing uses. The effect of such preferences varies among different jurisdictions. In some jurisdictions, those preferences mean what they say—essentially establishing a parallel allocation system which, in times of shortage, may override the priority system. In other jurisdictions, the preferences simply provide guidance to the state administrative official who is forced to choose between otherwise identical but competing applications for the same water. Other states, such as Colorado, simply give to the preferred right the power of private condemnation over water rights for less preferred uses. Even in Colorado, the preference is somewhat of a joke, since it is difficult to imagine that any agricultural user, for example, could come up with enough money to condemn a manufacturing water right.

F. *Condemnation of Water Rights*

When money is available for that purpose, condemnation of water rights is a powerful tool. In recognition of the almost unlimited power which has been vested in municipalities in Colorado to condemn water rights, Colorado's General Assembly recently adopted House Bill 1555 (1974), which limits municipal condemnation to the satisfaction of only those needs anticipated within the next fifteen years and which requires that condemnation be preceded by an environmental impact statement as well as substantial community planning. As of yet, unfortunately, House Bill 1555 has not been the subject of recorded litigation. Its effect remains uncertain, and it has become a thorn in the side of those persons who are attempting to plan for municipal water supplies.

G. *Relationship Between Water Allocation and Land Use Controls*

We are gradually learning that the manipulation of water resources may be a valuable aspect of any land use control program. By and large, local governments, political subdivisions of their states, are tending to take a lead in this regard. For example, the following solutions have been proposed by local governments to deal with the interrelationship between land and water:

1. Prohibiting the construction of water facilities in certain areas by traditional zoning regulations.
2. Refusing to issue a building permit for construction of any water facilities until the water court makes certain findings, *e.g.*, that water quality and minimum stream flows will not be impaired.
3. Zoning of water rights as an interest in real property similar to land.
4. By adoption of a comprehensive plan, restricting the location of all pipeline facilities to federal lands.

While local governments seem to be the most active in this area, states are also starting to get on the water/land use relationship. For example, in Colorado, House Bill 1041 (1974), which is administered by the state Land Use Commission, included the following two matters of state interest:

> 1. "Site selection and construction of major new domestic water and sewage treatment systems and major extension of existing domestic water and sewage treatment systems."
> 2. "Efficient utilization of municipal and industrial water projects."

V. CONCLUSION

Today's water law is like an incredibly complicated machine that is held together and added to by odd assortments of baling wire. This means that, to lay persons, water law is an inscrutable system. If it takes a specialist to understand and use the law, have not members of the general public been denied the opportunity to become meaningfully involved in water allocation and distribution decisions?

Part of the confusion, of course, may defy clarification because of the numerous levels of government involved. On the other hand, it should be possible for each level of government (including the State of Colorado) to make the law more understandable and more responsive. In Colorado, it probably would not be advisable to conduct a massive overhaul of our water law—after all, we have built an entire economy on it. On the other hand, there are a number of small ways in which the water law can be greatly simplified from a procedural standpoint. In addition, as a matter of substance, we clearly do need some mechanism by which the water courts, as well as the State Engineer, are required to take into consideration the "public interest," whatever that may be. Until that is done, we will continue to make water allocation decisions in this state without any rational basis except for the energy and foresight of individual appropriators.

Part 2
Political and Economic

8
Emerging Values in Water Resource Management

Gary Hart[*]

I want to comment on an important phenomenon for consideration by people who are experts in resource management: that is, a national awareness just beginning to develop which recognizes that our natural resources are limited and must be intelligently allocated if they are going to serve the general welfare of this country. This is particularly true of those resources which are owned and managed by the federal government. It is also true of water.

The traditional exploitation of public resources for private gain is being replaced by a new emphasis on a stewardship of these resources for the public benefit. That water resources fall within the focus of this new awareness has put tremendous pressure on the traditional process under which water policies and priorities are determined. At the outset it must be remembered that water is a unique resource. It is self-renewing, like timber, but it is also a fixed and limited resource like a mineral in that once it is allocated for a specific use, it is almost always available only for that use.

In the western states the ordeal of questioning traditional assumptions, which is going on and must continue to go on, will be enhanced because the exploited character of water resources development will have to change dramatically. Development of water resources in the West has always been regarded as a critical component in economic development, and this has been magnified by the relative, and often extreme, scarcity of water throughout the western region. Western water resource development has grown through first simple then complex rules based on a doctrine of appropriative water rights and beneficial use, which have in turn justified some of civilization's most awesome technical undertakings designed to put water to use. Water has been the tool of economic development and often the

---
[*] United States Senator, Colorado.

key to that development. Economic growth under the old rules paid little attention to social and environmental values. As long as the principle objective of fostering economic growth was justified, water projects were deemed to be in the general welfare. And, with this justification came enormous amounts of federal financial and technical assistance.

Water projects, and of course other public works projects, were funded to satisfy what amounted to a circular demand to exploit available resources and promote economic growth. The basic equation for justifying water resource projects, both in general and with regard to specific projects, was the cost-benefit ratio. Balance sheets for developing this analysis were based on the old prerequisites for growth, quantifiable financial and economic factors, such as the initial capital outlays and the return on investments. Reliance on these quantifiable factors neglected assessment of non-quantifiable environmental and social considerations. These values have always been present, but our economic priorities, until recently, discounted them to the point where they were never really taken seriously. The emergence of new social and environmental values is forcing reevaluation of this whole equation, using concepts which are entirely different from those of water policy decisions in the past. But, because no formula incorporating these present values has emerged, in some cases the only avenue open to those questioning a specific water project is to totally oppose its construction.

Apart from the emerging resource management ethic, there are other variables which have come into the equation. There are increasing fiscal limitations on the economic efficiency and effectiveness of water projects. Competition for the federal dollar has, of course, intensified and will continue to do so, even more than we have seen in recent years. Water available for irrigation, the vast bulk of consumptive use, is beginning to reach its practical limits. New demands for water for urban growth, for recreational use, for water quality restoration, and for energy development are beginning to be strong competitors with traditional agricultural uses. One expert in resource management observed that "culmination of new environmental constraints and the relentless mathematics of exponential growth have brought us to the grim reality of physical shortage. In several regions, we are dividing up the last canteen." He continues to say that the essential character of water resource management in the future will not be the development of new supplies, but rather the more intensive management of relatively fixed supplies and reallocation of supplies among competitive uses.

And that is the point I am trying to make. Water resource management has shifted from the development of new supplies to this kind of prudent management of existing supplies and the allocation of these supplies among competing uses. Technological innovation must achieve the balance between the traditional demand that we are all familiar with and these new uses. The planning process that has served until recently will have to be overhauled; the planners and policy makers will have to reorder water priorities in their states and local regions to accommodate the new facts of resource life. As a part of this new focus, engineers and technicians must devise means to manage water resources more efficiently and effectively. They will be the ones who will present the alternatives to the politicians who have the ultimate responsibility to determine what needs must be met.

Competing pressures are manifest in this decisionmaking process. As a member of the Senate Public Works Committee, the pressures—as well as responsibilities to integrate the new resource management awareness into the development of a traditional resource—are evident to me. However, this responsibility has not been fully accepted. I think that those of us in the public arena have to acknowledge that. The old equations that I have mentioned still hold firm, and at the base of our application of those equations is the advice that those of us in the public arena get from those in the sciences and engineering. It is the responsibility of the engineer or of the scientist who is involved in the process of policymaking to provide the technical analysis of alternatives, not merely to say why or why not a particular project can or cannot be developed.

Alternatives are still available to us. We just have not focused on what those alternatives may be. Rather we have taken projects on an "up" or "down" basis as I have indicated. This is particularly the fault of the politicians who have not pressed for inclusion of other factors. The reason for this is simple: traditional water projects result in jobs and economic stimulus for the home constituency. I believe this situation is changing.

Gradually, awareness by those in policymaking positions is moving us away from the traditional premises upon which projects were evaluated. The cost-benefit ratio is being dissected, not always by the politicians, but by interested individuals or organizations who are tuned into new and emerging values. As is too often the case, the people become aware of the changes that have to be made, but political judgment is slow to adapt to those changes.

Looking forward to the future of water resource management, development of new rules can only be accomplished by evaluating the multiple demands that are placed on this critical and increasingly limited resource. Demands obviously include traditional needs, but policymakers must also look to new needs such as recreation, fish and wildlife conservation, energy development, assertion of Indian water rights, and enhanced water quality. The technological skills of engineers and scientists will have to focus on meeting these demands. Water resource management will have to move away from a public works orientation to a more literal reclamation such as recycling, desalination, reducing losses from conveyance systems, and increasing the efficiency of water use in all regards.

But, maximizing water values cannot be achieved by new technology alone. It will find its ultimate solution in more sophisticated management at every level. And, as a result, the rule that we use to guide our decisions will also have to change. Ways must be found to adapt appropriate rights and beneficial use doctrines to multiple-use priorities; cost-benefit analyses will have to incorporate the unquantifiable variables I have already mentioned. The goals of water management will have to correspond to what is newly perceived as the public welfare. Procedures recently incorporated into the policymaking area require and demand broader public participation, a forum for the discussion of alternatives which will force politicians to take a more active role in changing the rules themselves. The pressure on political figures to come up with alternatives hand-in-hand with the scientists and technicians will lead to broader options to recognize new demands.

The old process for determining priorities for the use of water has become obsolete, and emerging public values support change. No longer will the decisions be made by a specialized few who base their decisions on outmoded concepts; the process has been opened up to integrate new concepts. To some the costs will be high. Sacred cows will undoubtedly be sacrificed. But this reassessment must come about if water resource management is to be brought in line with modern national goals.

9

The Market for Property Rights in Water

*Timothy D. Tregarthen**

The market for any good or service will operate more or less efficiently depending on the structural characteristics of the market, the adequacy of the definition of the property rights being exchanged, the availability of information, and the cost of bargaining and reaching agreements among interested parties. Water, despite frequent allegations that it is somehow wholly unlike all other goods, is no exception. The oft-cited complaint that water flows uphill toward money not only fails to reflect the gravity of the situation, but raises what is in many cases a non-problem. Under certain conditions, the flow of water toward money is a perfectly desirable result. This paper examines those conditions and suggests changes in existing legal approaches to the problem of water allocation.

I. THE ROLE OF PROPERTY RIGHTS IN THE MARKETPLACE

The function of defined rights in property is perhaps best understood by considering the consequences of their absence. All the goods would, in effect, be "owned" in common. As a result, there would be no incentive to economize on the use of any good, to maintain the condition of the good, or to engage in investment to improve it or increase its quantity. The benefits of productive activity could not be appropriated by any agent in the economy; little productive activity would result. The absence of clearly defined property rights would assure a large scale and continuing tragedy of the commons.

The economic problem is fundamentally one of choice; alternative uses exist for virtually all goods and services, requiring that decisions be made to select from among these alternatives. Well defined rights give decision makers in the economy a guide as to what they can reasonably expect of others. If rights to the use of a particular asset clearly rest with an individual, then the results of that individual's use of the asset are internalized, forcing him or her to bear the costs and benefits of decisions made concerning that use. Property rights

* B.A., 1967, California State University; M.A., 1970, Ph.D., 1972, University of California at Davis. Associate Professor of Economics, University of Colorado, Colorado Springs. I am grateful to participants of the Water Needs for the Future Conference for helpful suggestions.

thus seek to internalize what would otherwise be externalities.[1] To be complete, this internalization must involve the exclusion of all other parties from the use of the right, and these parties must be unaffected by that individual's use. Where the use is collective in nature, as in the enjoyment of a beautiful stream, it may be appropriate to define exclusive ownership to some collection of individuals, represented perhaps by a government agency. Thus exclusive ownership may rest with a single individual or with an agent representing several individuals. The important thing is that rights to the use of a good or service rest exclusively with agents affected by that use.[2]

Once defined, property rights to the use of a good or service must be enforceable; owners must have the ability to seek relief for any violation of the rights owned.[3] Finally, ownership of the rights to the use of any good or service should include the rights to appropriate returns from this and to transfer ownership rights for a price.[4]

The marketplace in which rights are to be exchanged should ideally be characterized by large numbers of buyers and sellers for rights to each good and service. Potential sellers should have ready access to each market, and information should be readily available concerning the terms at which rights are being sought and offered for sale. Bargaining costs should be low enough to assure that all parties with an interest in an exchange can participate in it. The satisfaction of these conditions should assure an efficient allocation of resources. Unhappily, one or more of these conditions is typically not met; the marketplace of the real world is an imperfect mechanism for allocating society's goods and services.

The market, whatever its imperfections, should serve in a rough way to face decision makers with the full costs and benefits of their decisions. Bids by buyers of a good generate price information about the benefits of using resources for the pro-

---

1. Demsetz, *Toward a Theory of Property Rights,* 57 AM. ECON. REV. 347, 350 (1967).

2. Cheung, *The Structure of a Contract and the Theory of a Non-Exclusive Resource,* in THE ECONOMICS OF PROPERTY RIGHTS 27 (E. Furubotn & S. Pejovich eds. 1974).

3. C. STONE, SHOULD TREES HAVE STANDING? TOWARD LEGAL RIGHTS FOR NATURAL OBJECTS 11 (1974).

4. Cheung, *supra* note 2.

duction of that good; bids by producers of other goods for those same resources generate price information about its cost. Where exclusion is not complete, the information provided by prices will be incorrect. If, for example, all beneficiaries of a beautiful stream are not excluded from enjoying it if they do not pay for it, prices will not reflect the value of the stream as an aesthetic or recreational resource. If potential bidders are left out of the exchange process because of inadequate information, prices will again provide incorrect signals. Markets dominated by a single seller (monopoly) or by a single buyer (monopsony) will generate prices which give, respectively, artificially high and low signals via the price mechanism. But if the market is working well, it will continuously generate valuable information in the form of prices, information which should guide resources toward their fabled "best use."

This notion of the ideal solution of a market model requires some cautions. First, the notion of "best" rests on each individual's perception of his or her own welfare. It is an axiom of economic analysis that individuals can and do make choices that they assume will make them better off. The added assertion that these individuals are the best judges of what is best for each of them is itself a value judgment for which there is no scientific foundation.[5] It is, however, a value judgment to which most economists, including this one, subscribe. If one assumes that individuals are incapable of making choices in their own interest, then one is left with the perplexing problem of deciding who is able to make such choices for them.

The second problem of this model is the role of uncertainty. All choices must be made on the basis of expectations about the future; the benefits of an activity can only be guessed at before it is undertaken. The benefits of activities foregone for the activity chosen will never be known. It is not surprising that individuals often make choices that seem, in retrospect, to have been wrong. This problem is solved in much of economic analysis by assuming perfect certainty and, thus, the absence of error. It is a useful assumption; uncertainty is a mathematically messy addition to most economic analyses. The fact that uncertainty cannot be assumed away in the real

---

5. *See, e.g.,* J. Quirk, Intermediate Microeconomics 59-60 (1976).

world does not by itself prove that individual choice must be abandoned; one would have to demonstrate that other mechanisms deal better with uncertainty. An important feature of a reasonably well-working marketplace is that it at least provides the incentive to make correct decisions. Mistakes will be made, but decision makers will presumably learn from such errors and attempt to avoid them in the future.

The notion of a "best," or "optimal" allocation of goods and services is thus more the stuff of mathematical models than of the real world. A more useful consideration by which one might test the market's usefulness is to inquire whether it, relative to other mechanisms for resource allocation that might be considered, tends more consistently to provide incentives that nudge decision makers along in the direction of improved resource allocation. Competitive markets with well-defined property rights, reasonably complete exclusion, and ready access to the exchange process should serve this more modest cause well.

II. THE INITIAL ALLOCATION OF RIGHTS IN WATER

A theory of the process by which rights are created has not been developed.[6] In general, one would expect that those individuals who first needed a resource would simply start using it; other users could be expected to do the same. As the demand for the use of a resource increased to the point at which the use of any one individual conflicted with that of another, *i.e.*, the resource was no longer a free good, exclusive property rights would be defined. Riparian doctrine, which defines a sort of collective ownership to rivers by owners of adjacent lands, represents a half step in this process. On the one hand, it imposes exclusion of those who do not own adjacent land, but does not define individual ownership of the water itself. It is an odd sort of compromise, one that implies that water has become a scarce good, but that treats it essentially as a free one.[7]

A clearer definition of rights has been achieved under the doctrine of prior appropriation. This was simply the granting

---

6. One preliminary effort to assess the creation of rights in land is given in Anderson & Hill, *The Evolution of Property Rights: A Study of the American West*, 18 J. LAW & ECON. 163 (1975).

7. G. RADOSEVICH, K. NOBE, D. ALLARDICE & C. KIRKWOOD, EVOLUTION AND ADMINISTRATION OF COLORADO WATER LAW: 1876-1976 at 16 (1976).

of specific titles to rights in water on a first-come, first-served basis. From the point of view of economic efficiency, this is an adequate way to initiate a market in rights for water. A lottery would also suffice. In either case, the initial allocation defines a starting point from which exchange can take place. Rights will, over time, be allocated to those users who place the highest value on them, providing that exchange is possible.[8]

Equity is also a relevant concern in the selection of a method by which the initial allocation of water rights is to be determined. The initial assignment of property rights, together with initial endowments of abilities and interests, determines the distribution of wealth in the economy. Rights to water use represent valuable assets; it would not be unreasonable to base their initial allocation on social goals with respect to the distribution of wealth. On this criterion, it is not obvious that the first-come, first-served approach of prior appropriation is of particular merit.

But another form of definition of rights preceded most grants to appropriators. States using prior appropriation doctrine typically asserted that the waters of the state were the property of the state, or of the people of the state.[9] These rights were then given to appropriators as they claimed them. This public largesse was impressive as well as surprising; it is not at all clear that gifts to first takers represent the most equitable means of transferring property from the public to the private sector.[10] The question is of more than historical interest. The public sector, by transferring wealth from itself on behalf of all individuals to a few individuals, has weakened its ability to reenter the market for water rights to buy back rights needed

---

8. Costly transactions may suggest an advantage for prior appropriations because this approach may reduce the number of future transactions needed to allocate the water rights. *See* R. POSNER, ECONOMIC ANALYSIS OF LAW (1973).

9. COLO. CONST., art. 16, §5 states:
> The water of every natural stream, not heretofore appropriated, within the state of Colorado, is hereby declared to be the property of the public, and the same is dedicated to the use of the people of the state, subject to appropriation as hereinafter provided.

10. N. Wollman argues that states should make use of the price mechanism by selling rights to the highest bidder. *See* Wollman, *Economic Factors in the Study of Water Use*, in THE LAW OF WATER ALLOCATION IN THE EASTERN UNITED STATES 565 (D. Haber & S. Bergen eds. 1958); for a differing view see Trelease, *Policies for Water Law: Property Rights, Economic Forces, and Public Regulation*, 5 NAT. RES. J. 1, 10 (1965).

for public use, as discussed below. To the extent that unappropriated rights remain, states should consider selling them rather than giving them away. The question is one of equity rather than efficiency, but equity is not an unimportant consideration in the allocation of goods and services.

III.   BENEFICIAL USE AND THE SECURITY OF RIGHTS IN WATER

. Status as the first claimant of a right under prior appropriation is (usually) a necessary but not sufficient condition to assure title to a right to use water.[11] The water claimed must be put to a beneficial use, a curious qualification that suggests all manner of limitations on rights in water. Some of these are indicated in the following excerpt from a Nevada case, *Union Mill & Mining Co. v. Dangberg*:[12]

> Under the principles of prior appropriation, the law is well settled that the right to water flowing in the public streams may be acquired by an actual appropriation of the water for a beneficial use; that, if it is used for irrigation, the appropriator is only entitled to the amount of water that is necessary to irrigate his land, by making a reasonable use of the water; that the object had in view at the time of the appropriation and diversion of the water is to be considered in connection with the extent and right of appropriation; that if the capacity of the flume, ditch, canal, or other aqueduct, by means of which the water is conducted, is of greater capacity than is necessary to irrigate the lands of the appropriator, he will be restricted to the quantity of water needed for the purposes of irrigation, for watering his stock, and for domestic use; that the same rule applies to an appropriation made for any other beneficial use or purpose; that no person can, by virtue of his appropriation, acquire a right to any more water than is necessary for the purpose of his appropriation; that, if the water is used for the purpose of irrigating lands owned by the appropriator, the right is not confined to the amount of water used at the time the appropriation is made; the appropriator is entitled, not only to his needs and necessities at that time, but to such other and further amount of water, within the capacity of his ditch, as would be required for the future improvement and extended cultivation of his lands, if the right is otherwise kept up
> . . . .

A water right must thus be used for purposes that are beneficial in nature and suitable for the purpose in amount. The right can

---

11. *See* G. RADOSEVICH, *supra* note 7, at 20.

12. 81 F. 73, 94 (C.C. Nev. 1897); quoted in G. RADOSEVICH, *supra* note 7, at 22-23.

exceed present use if justified by the prospect of expanded operations, at least in agriculture. While the general nature of non-beneficial uses is unclear, rights can be forfeited in the event of non-use.[13] Existing legislation provides for the discontinuance of any diversion within a designated groundwater basin if the rights are no longer necessary for a beneficial use.[14]

In a world of freely exchanging rights in water, the doctrine of beneficial use would, of course, be unnecessary. Water use would be allocated to uses judged beneficial by the market. Non-use would not be a problem; owners of rights would have nothing to gain by holding them idle when they could be sold.[15] To be sure, the market's estimate of beneficial use might differ from that of the public, or its legislature. Some might, for example, object to the use of water in the washroom of a pornographic theatre. But the solution to such a problem is surely to regulate the theatre rather than shutting off its water.

If the beneficial use doctrine were merely unnecessary, there would be no particular cause for concern. It would serve as an amusing example of an eccentricity in the law, and nothing more. But the doctrine of beneficial use may be harmful, and thus warrants further examination. As noted above, rights in property must be enforceable if the market is to work properly; the absence of enforcement would destroy the market for rights. One usually thinks of this requirement in terms of protection from thieves and frauds. But, as Ciriacy-Wantrup has pointed out, security of rights requires more than the protection against unlawful use by others. It also requires tenure certainty, *i.e.,* protection from encroachment by the legal acts of others.[16] The doctrine of beneficial use, with its implications of judicial determination of need and non-use, in effect increases the uncertainty of title to rights in water, and therefore reduces their marketability. As Trelease has noted, the flexibil-

---

13. *See* Wheeler v. Northern Colo. Irrigation Co., 10 Colo. 582, 17 P. 487 (1887).

14. *See, e.g.,* Water Rights Determination and Administration Act of 1969, COLO. REV. STAT. ANN. §§ 37-92-101 *et seq.* (1973); especially §37-92-502(2).

15. An appropriator might find it desirable to hold rights idle temporarily; an efficient market would provide such an owner the opportunity to rent out rights not currently needed, as suggested below.

16. Ciriacy-Wantrup, *Concepts used as Economic Criteria for a System of Water Rights,* 32 LAND ECON. 295, 297 (1956).

ity of use in water rights is best assured by making those rights as rigid and clear as possible, thus making exchange easier.[17]

A classic example of the judicial mischief to which the doctrine of beneficial use can lead is the ruling in *Young v. Hinderlider*.[18] Hinderlider had made first application for certain water rights in New Mexico, intending to market the water to a number of farms. Young and Norton filed an application for the same water two months later, proposing to use the water to irrigate their own farm at a substantially lower cost per acre than that anticipated by Hinderlider. The District Court awarded the rights to Hindelider on grounds that he had applied first. The Supreme Court, however, developed an interest in the economics of the problem, ruling that "[t]he mere fact that the irrigation under the [Hinderlider] project would cost more per acre than under the [Young and Norton] project is not conclusive that the former project should be rejected. But the attempt to cover too much land may have gone so far that the cost of irrigation under that project would be so excessive that the owners of land under the project could not pay the water rights and farm the lands at a profit."[19] It ordered the District Court to reconsider which proposal suggested the more beneficial use on this basis. It is an intriguing exercise to consider the effects of such reasoning were it applied to the acquisition of property rights for all other forms of investment.

The doctrine of preferential use is similar in spirit to the beneficial use doctrine in that it imposes a non-market test of priorities in rights. In its most common form, the doctrine holds that domestic uses of water have priority over agricultural uses, which in turn have priority over manufacturing uses. The notion is quite silly. All economic activity is ultimately for domestic use, that is, consumption. The eating of food off of a manufactured plate does not seem greatly less domestic than washing the plate afterwards. The purpose of the priority structure imposed by this doctrine is to permit preferred uses to exercise powers of eminent domain in the

---

17. Trelease, *A Model State Water Code for River Basin Development*, 22 Law & Contemp. Prob. 301, 314 (1957); *see also* J. Hirschleifer, J. Dehaven & J. Milliman, Water Supply (1969).

18. 15 N.M. 666, 110 P. 1045 (1910).

19. 110 P. 1045, 1050 (1910).

acquisition of water rights.[20] The justification for such a provision is not apparent. As noted below, monopoly power is more likely to rest with municipal buyers than with sellers in the market for water; granting buyers additional power does not seem necessary.

IV. LIMITS ON THE TRANSFERABILITY OF WATER RIGHTS

Rights to water are typically expressed in terms of a rate of diversion at a specific point. Holders of rights do not own water that they return to the stream after they have used the rights. This definition results in two major sets of difficulties. First, it reduces the ability of the market to generate incentives to economize on the consumptive use of water.[21] Second, it reduces the marketability of the rights.

If rights to divert water implied full ownership of the water, then holders of these rights could sell "leftover" water to other users. This would force these owners to face the opportunity cost of wasting water. Users of irrigation water would, for example, have a greater incentive to line and cover ditches if water not consumed could be resold. The concern of the National Water Commission, that "[u]sers of water, public or private, are now typically awarded the right to divert and use water free of charge and need to give no heed to values that some other use of the water might yield," would be eliminated.[22] Some incentive to economize exists now, given that conservation measures can reduce the amount of water a user needs to divert, and thus allows that owner to sell some of his rights. Increasing the marketability of these rights by providing for a resale market for water recharged to the stream would increase the force of this incentive.

Because water rights are really rights to divert water for some use, the courts have imposed limitations on their sale when that sale involves a change in use. Agricultural rights in water, for example, involve a decreed right to divert a specific volume of water per unit of time. The citation from the *Union Mill & Mining* case quoted above suggests that the decreed right can exceed present use to the extent that expanded agri-

---

20. G. RADOSEVICH, *supra* note 7, at 64-65.
21. Trelease, *supra* note 10, at 27.
22. NATIONAL WATER COMMISSION, WATER POLICIES FOR THE FUTURE 251 (1973).

cultural operations are planned for the future. The greater the volume of water decreed, the greater the value of the right. When such rights are sold for domestic use, however, the nature of the right is changed. Because domestic use typically involves a continuous diversion of water and a greater degree of consumptive use, the full amount of water decreed to agricultural users cannot generally be sold. Instead, sales are limited to the amount of historical use, which must in addition be reasonable.[23] These rulings suggest that the volume of water implied by the right changes if the use changes, thus limiting the incentive for rights to transfer to what may be a more efficient use. Recognizing rights as decreed, and permitting the resale of water not used, would take care of the problem of incentives to conserve water as well as providing for the easy exchange of water among users.

Another legal limitation on the transferability of rights is the ban on the sale of rights to waters in one state to agents in other states.[24] This ban reduces the market's ability to communicate, through the price system, alternative needs for water. It also exacerbates a structural difficulty noted above. Interbasin transfers of water are characterized by the enormity of the scale with which they are carried out.[25] It is unlikely that within a state like Colorado there would be very many buyers able to build a large interbasin diversion project. This limits the number of domestic bidders for water in remote areas, thus resulting in possible monopoly power on the buyer's side, or monopsony. Monopsony power permits buyers to pay a price below the price that would exist in a competitive market. Eliminating competing purchasers from other states strengthens the bargaining power of local domestic buyers. As noted above, granting them powers of eminent domain makes things even worse.

---

23. In Farmers' Highline Canal & Reservoir Co. v. City of Golden, 129 Colo. 575, 272 P.2d 629 (1954), the court held that the amount of water claimed as historical agricultural use was excessive, and noted that the testimony of "any capable experienced farmer" could be used to determine a reasonable amount, which, in turn, would define the amount that could be sold for domestic use. *See also* Enlarged Southside Irrigation Ditch Co. v. John's Flood Ditch Co., 116 Colo. 580, 183 P.2d 552 (1947); City of Westminster v. Church, 167 Colo. 1, 445 P.2d 52 (1968).

24. J. HIRCHLEIFER, *supra* note 17, at 242.

25. C. HOWE & K. EASTER, INTERBASIN TRANSFERS OF WATER 4-5 (1971).

V. Market Failure and Water Rights

The discussion to this point has dealt with market problems in the exchange of water rights that result from public policy. But there are other difficulties inherent in the market process itself, difficulties that emerge when it is not possible to define property rights in a way that forces the market to incorporate all of the costs and benefits of decisions into the choice perspectives of the individuals making those decisions.

Some uses of water are not susceptible to easy exclusion of individuals that do not pay for them; a beautiful stream may be a difficult thing to price in the market. The benefits derived from the stream are no less economic as a result; the prices generated in the market will simply fail to reflect them adequately. The result will be too few unspoiled streams. In such cases, public purchase of water rights to preserve the streams may be justified. If the rights are already held by the public, the decision would involve a comparison of the public benefits of leaving the stream in its natural state with the bids offered for private purchase of the rights. The problem is the classic one of the public good.

A related objection to the market's allocation of water is the prospect that domestic users would be able to buy up all of the rights in water for irrigated agriculture. The fear is rather fanciful; water for irrigation accounts for such a high percentage of all water used that a relatively small percentage reduction in agricultural use would provide for a tremendous increase in residential or industrial use. In any event, if some diversion of water from agricultural use is expected, the problem is to determine whether such a market-induced diversion is undesirable. Food is not a public good; there is no problem there. But agricultural operations provide another service that has value; fields devoted to crops provide open space, which yields aesthetic benefits as well as flood control and reduced air pollution. The field that produces food thus produces other benefits at the same time. These other benefits are not characterized by exclusion; the price system therefore fails to reflect them. Farmers are thus forced to bid for factors of production, like water, with the deck stacked somewhat against them. If these public benefits are to be recognized, however, they suggest a payment to farmers for the open space benefits of their agricultural operations, not the provision of cheap water. The latter approach makes no more sense than decreeing that farm workers should receive a low wage to encourage agricultural operations. Keeping the price of any factor artificially low results in the waste and inefficient allocation of that factor.[26]

VI. TOWARD GREATER EFFICIENCY IN WATER MARKETS

A smoothly functioning market for rights in water would result in the easy exchange of water among agents and among uses, resulting in greater efficiency. Owners of water rights would continually be faced with bids reflecting the cost of their use of the rights; they would be induced in their own interest to economize on their use of water, and to sell their rights if some other agent placed a higher value on them. But observers of the water market commonly note that it does not work that way. The fact that water rights for agricultural uses sell for prices much lower than equivalent rights for other uses is evidence that the market does not work as smoothly as suggested here. This essay has explored some of the reasons for those rigidities; many of them can be eliminated by changing public policy.

But an added difficulty arises from the rather complex nature of water as a fluid resource. Rights in water are harder to define and to observe than, say, rights in basketballs. Purchasers and sellers of water rights face high information costs in determining which rights are available for sale and who may be buying them. Tracing the title to a water right is a complicated business. The authority of state water engineers and water allocation boards can be of great significance in dealing with these problems. If these agencies were to focus all their efforts on the problem of providing information about the rights owned in water, they would be providing a great service. Investment in information and the smooth functioning of the marketplace in water may yield benefits far greater than those of new water projects.[27]

As information systems in water allocation improve, there is reason to believe that a variety of new methods of exchanging

---

26. Nancy L. Sidener has suggested that provision of cheap agricultural water could even be construed as a violation of the prohibition of subsidies to export industries in the General Agreement on Tariffs and Trade.

27. *See* Null, *Water Use as a Property Right,* 22 THE COLORADO QUARTERLY 317, 326 (1974).

rights might emerge. Rights could be leased from owners for short periods. Problems of temporary shortage, such as drought, could be dealt with through such lease arrangements. Associated problems of uncertainty might generate the same response in the water market that they have in other markets, the creation of futures markets. It may become commonplace in the future to hear December quotes on July South Platte water. Water brokers might increase in number.

The market is no panacea. As has been noted above, public intervention will be required to deal with public goods—and public bads, such as pollution. But the market for any good has the enormous virtue of generating large amounts of information, transmitting this information in the form of prices, and through these prices prodding decision makers in the direction of more efficient use of scarce resources. It has been insufficiently used in the allocation of water; investment in its increased use should be a high priority of water policy.

10
A Social Well-Being Framework for Assessing Resource Management Alternatives

*David M. Freeman**

Alternative water projects and policies are central social and political phenomena because any one will impact unevenly on society. Some social groups are advantaged at costs to others. While economic techniques for determining the general magnitudes of dollar "costs" and "benefits" of alternative water programs are relatively well developed, the assumption has been generally accepted that the entire population will be affected in a roughly equal manner. This assumption is rarely tenable. The well-being of some groups is almost always damaged more than others—esthetically, politically, and socially. Many significant social costs are not reflected in marketplace exchange—dollar values simply fail to reflect true costs—and most such non-market costs have not been amenable to systematic analysis. It is the purpose of this paper to:

    A. Briefly state some of the most significant problems which must be confronted when attempting to address non-market social well-being considerations;

    B. Present an analytical approach to the definition of social well-being that copes with the problems;

    C. Illustrate the approach by presenting an analysis of four resource management alternatives conducted on a U.S. Forest Service planning unit identified here as "Big Vista Divide."[2]

II. THE PROBLEMS OF ANALYZING SOCIAL WELL-BEING

The problems of defining and measuring social well-being have been complex, intractable, and, for the most part, skirted by the social scientist who leaves the value judgments up to the public or other responsible authorities. Yet, it is impossible to sort out alternative natural resource program impacts except in the context of some value criterion defining what is meant by social well-being. Analysis of social well-being presents problems because:

A. Solutions for some groups are problems for others. To enhance social well-being of wilderness buffs undercuts the social well-being of snowmobilers, loggers, and other special-interest groups.

B. There is the problem of intensity of gains and losses among groups. One alternative may spread small benefits to many people while imparting a large cost to a very few people. How much pleasure of the many gainers should it take to balance off the pain of the fewer losers? Although marginal economic analysis can suggest something with regard to this problem, there is no known methodology which can net-out pleasure over pain when all important values are not adequately reflected in the marketplaces—as is the case with much natural resource planning.

C. People change their minds. Values and associated preferences are not permanent but can be fluid and unstable under changing circumstances. One's pattern of recreational preferences can be altered significantly by changing gasoline availability, real income levels, etc. Trying to predict what patterns of preference will hold in future decades for social groups in a rapidly changing society is a loose and hazardous exercise subject to great error.

D. Social well-being is, in any case, not defined by what the majority of affected publics claims to prefer.

As Kenneth Arrow has demonstrated, where there are at least two choosing parties and three or more alternatives from which to choose, it is not possible to construct a decision rule which will yield stable results that can be identified with the peoples' maximal or optimal welfare.[3] For example, assume that the decision maker is faced with choosing among three alternative ways of using the land base and that each of the alternatives distributed some value differentially to affected parties as shown below:

3. K. ARROW, SOCIAL CHOICE AND INDIVIDUAL VALUES (2d ed. 1963); see also Arrow, A Difficulty in the Concept of Social Welfare, 58 J. OF POL. ECON. 328 (1950).

Alternative	Payoff To		
	A	B	C
1	3	1	2
2	2	3	1
3	1	2	3

If no side payments are allowed by which the parties might agree on an alternative and compensate the losers, thereby making everything come out equally, there is nothing in the structure of the situation that makes the social well-being mix represented by any one alternative more preferable than any other.

Furthermore, if we let parties A, B, and C choose the preferred alternatives by a majority vote, taking two at a time, we see that they end up selecting different alternatives as the best, simply as a function of the order in which pairs are compared. If alternatives 2 and 3 are first compared, 2 will obtain the majority vote; 2 when compared to 1 will be defeated leaving alternative 1 as the best choice. Yet, if the first pair compared is that of alternatives 1 and 3, then 3 will defeat alternative 1, and 2 will then be chosen over 3, resulting in a different definition of what the same group ends up choosing as best.

Thus, there can be nothing but despair for someone seeking to serve social well-being by learning what people prefer and then investing in those management alternatives which secure majority support. Serving majority preferences might be politically wise, but it has no necessary connection to social well-being. What is politically acceptable at any given time may undercut social well-being.

III. APPROACH TO THE DEFINITION OF SOCIAL WELL-BEING

Productive and useful analysis of social well-being must be approached by distinguishing between two levels of choice:

A. *Prescriptive Choice*: At which level does one encounter all the problems mentioned above? Prescriptive choice has to do with people prescribing choices for themselves and/or others. It is simply impossible to do a useful and defensible analysis by tapping into individual preference patterns of particular persons, groups, or organizations. There are no methodologies for determining that dollars spent to produce X acre-feet of water for agricultural use will generate more net social well-being than the same dollars spent to make Y acre-feet of water available for municipal use.

B. *Context of Choice*: At which level is it possible and useful to determine whether a given management alternative will shrink, sustain, or expand the context of choice opportunities from which the publics may pursue and prescribe for themselves their particular and noncommensurable preferences? Decision makers are asked to view their land and water resources as setting contexts from which particular preferences can be met. The problem is to sustain and even increase the choice opportunities yielded by the land/water base. To broaden the context of choice is to serve social well-being—to undercut the context of choice is to damage social well-being. The decision maker is viewed as custodian and manager of choice opportunities. To get at the problem of analyzing what is happening to choice contexts as a consequence of implementing management alternatives, several analytical dimensions can be employed. One of these dimensions, the analysis of Futures Foregone, will be presented here.[4]

A. *Social Well-Being and The Analysis of Futures Foregone*

In sum, promoting social well-being is equivalent to promoting the context of choice which the planning area can afford to the diverse interested publics. One dimension of choice context is presented to measure whether the choice contexts will shrink more or less as a consequence of implementing different management alternatives. Who will be hurt and who will be advantaged if natural resource decision makers would choose to implement different management alternatives in designated planning areas? One key way to help and hurt people is to support or undercut futures for their activities on the land base. The part of social well-being which I wish to address here is that which has to do with who loses out on opportunities to act out their choices. A foregone future is an implementation of a management alternative that cancels out futures for incompatible choices or activities.

The idea of Futures Foregone is broken down into three measurable dimensions:

A. *The scope of loss*: What proportion of people or things will lose a future for their activities on the land base if the designated management alternative is implemented?

---

4. Analyses of other dimensions of the choice context are also under development and testing. They are presented in Freeman, Procedures to Display Effects of Land Management Alternatives on Social Well-Being, Dec. 1976 (prepared for the Division of State & Private Forestry, Area Planning & Development Branch, U.S. Forest Service).

B. *The intensity of loss*: How much will the lost future be missed in the planning area?

C. *The duration of loss*: What will be the length of time in years before the land base can sustain the foregone activities in their present condition after the proposed management alternative has been terminated?

A management alternative which foregoes futures for choice opportunities to a greater scope, with a greater intensity, and for a longer duration is a management alternative which is estimated to undercut social well-being, more than another management alternative which has lower futures foregone values associated with it.

B. The Meaning of Scope of Futures Foregone

Scope values indicate how much a choice opportunity for a future inside a given planning unit will be foregone if the designated management alternative is implemented. Scope values indicate the proportion of people or things affected by removing a future for a choice opportunity. (See **Figure 1** for illustration of the scope concept.)

A. Scope values of (-)1.00 indicate that a future for some group or activity will be totally eliminated or foregone in the particular Planning Unit. For all practical purposes no group member can pursue a future for his activity on the Unit.

B. Scope values of (-).50 indicate that the future for some group or activity will be one-half foregone in the particular Planning Unit. This means that one-half of the hunters, elk, timber cut, etc., present can be sustained on that Unit if the designated management strategy is implemented.

C. Scope values of 0 indicate that the future for some group or activity will be totally unaffected on a given Unit if the designated management strategy is implemented.

C. The Meaning of Intensity of Futures Foregone

Intensity values indicate the degree to which a foregone or lost future will be missed. Intensity values indicate the significance of loss. The key question for intensity is: Out of all the possible Resource Capability Units (RCU's) for sustaining a given future in the overall forest, how much will the lost future on the affected RCU's be missed if the designated management strategy is implemented? (See **Figure 2** for illustration of the intensity concept.)

FIGURE 1

MANAGEMENT ALTERNATIVE—
SCOPE OF IMPACT

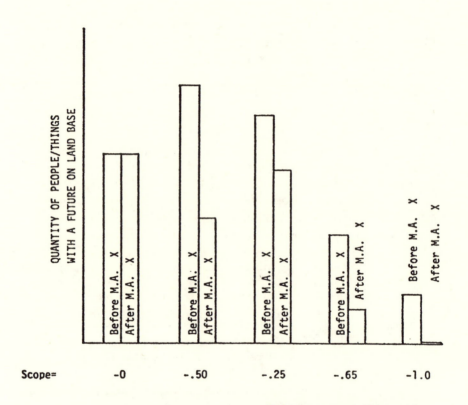

M.A.=Management Alternative

A. If the designed management alternative will undercut the possibility of a future for some group or activity, but that future is being sustained on many other RCU's, then the intensity of losing a future for that activity or group on the impacted Unit is low.

B. If the designated management alternative will eliminate the possibility of a future for some group or activity on a given RCU or set of units, but that future is being, or has been, foregone on many other units, the intensity of losing a future for that activity or group on the impacted unit is high.

C. People will miss a lost future choice opportunity more when that choice cannot be exercised elsewhere in accessible places.

FIGURE 2
MANAGEMENT ALTERNATIVE
INTENSITY OF FUTURES FOREGONE LOSS

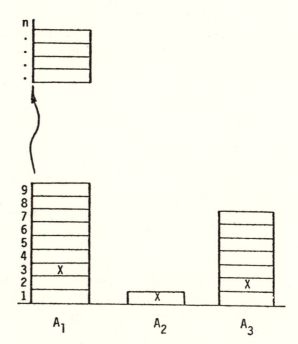

Number of Resource Capability Units on Which a Future For an Activity Can Be Sustained In Accessible Locations In The Forest.

Activities

To lose a future for group/activity "A_1" on one of many units would be a loss of low intensity.

To lose a future for activity "A_2" on the only unit left capable of sustaining it would be a loss of highest intensity.

To lose a future for activity "A_3" on one unit when only a few other units can sustain it would be a loss of moderate intensity.

D. The Meaning of Duration of Futures Foregone

Duration values indicate the length of time, in years, before the lost choice opportunity can be restored to its present condition after the proposed management alternative has been terminated. In other words, if decision makers should decide to terminate a given program, project, or policy, duration values indicate the number of years it is estimated to take to restore the land/water base to a point at which the previously foregone future for a choice opportunity can be exercised at present levels.

IV. THE METHOD AND PROCEDURE

A. The Source of the Data

Judgment is necessary as a source of data. However, since any given judge may start with a base of hidden biases, distorted information, fear of ridicule from peers, or reluctance to press views against strong personalities, it is important that the process of obtaining estimates minimize distortion factors and maximize the flow of information to the individual participant. To do this the Delphi technique is used.[5] The following steps are involved in the technique's operation:

A. The list of items is presented to each participant who remains separate and anonymous from the rest of the group.

B. Each participant writes down a judgment anonymously and passes it back to the coordinator.

C. The coordinator, in turn, sets aside those areas on which substantial agreement occurs and passes back the items on which disagreement has been revealed.

D. Keeping anonymity protected, each contributor gets to see any comments given as reasons for judgments made by the others and then proceeds to render once again a judgment, possibly revised, based on the anonymous inputs of the others.

E. Within the course of three or four rounds, there typically is a convergence of judgment, and where judgments fail to converge, reasons for the differences emerge.

---

5. For a detailed background in and discussion of the Delphi technique and its applications, the reader should refer to the following publications: N. DALKEY, D. ROURKE, R. LEWIS & D. SNYDER, STUDIES IN THE QUALITY OF LIFE: DELPHI AND DECISION-MAKING (1972); Pyke, A Practical Approach to Delphi, 2 FUTURES 143 (1970); Dalkey & Helmer, An Experimental Application of the Delphi Method to the Use of Experts, 9 MANAGEMENT SCI. 458 (1963); Pill, The Delphi Method—Substance, Context, a Critique and Annotated Bibliography, 5 SOCIO-ECONOMIC PLANNING SCI. (1969); Hill & Fowles, The Methodological Worth of the Delphi Forecasting Techniques, 7 TECHNOLOGICAL FORECASTING AND SOCIAL CHANGE 179 (1975).

The Delphi exercise is, therefore, a series of sequential interrogations based on opinion feedback at each step and focusing on areas of contention. It is an attempt to keep communication of informed judgments free from the biases of personality factors and social status, keeping the environment of judgment and communication as objective as possible.

A set of specific procedures has been developed for the purpose of obtaining data for the Futures Foregone portion of the analysis. These procedures have evolved out of extensive discussion and trials by the River Basin staff and limited field testing.

B. Interpreting the Data

The quantifications for Futures Foregone consist of ordinal values. Such values express the idea of "greater than" or "lesser than;" there is no standard unit underlying such scores. This means that when summing up all scope scores, for example, a value of -10 is not exactly two units greater than a value of -8; a score of -10 is merely somewhat greater than the value of -8. Ordinal measures only indicate the direction of social well-being impacts on each dimension, and alternative scores must be viewed as providing "greater than . . ." or "lesser than . . ." statements.

C. Panel Members and Their Characteristics

The group of judges participating in the exercise is small, not randomly selected, and is unrepresentative of the diverse affected publics in important ways. Participants were selected because:

A. Each has a background of experience with the Big Vista Divide Planning Area and a familiarity with the kinds of activities which take place on the unit.

B. Three Forest Service participants were selected not only because of their familiarity with the planning area but also because they possess technical backgrounds appropriate to the kinds of management issues being confronted.

C. Six citizen participants were selected from volunteers who had served as a Big Vista Divide land use study group —a group of private citizens who participated in a series of public involvement meetings conducted by the National Forest Service over the ten months preceding the Futures Foregone analysis.

It is important to note the hypothesis that participants need not be fully representative of all possible values or interests.[6] It is essential that participants be sufficiently knowledgeable about the planning area and the kinds of management strategies under consideration so that they can identify an impact on an activity or group even if they do not represent those interests. Similarly, it is reasonable to expect that knowledgeable judges can identify an impact on an activity or group even if they do not personally engage in that activity and are not members of that group. In fact, most judges quickly agreed on the nature of management alternative impacts on most items under consideration. In those cases where disagreement occurred, it was frequently reduced in succeeding rounds of the exercise and, when differences persisted after three rounds, discussion was carried out to uncover the nature of the outstanding differences of judgment.

The demographic characteristics of the judges are summarized in Table 1. Three foresters serving on the panel were joined by a real estate broker, a land-use planner, a city director of development, a resort owner-operator, and two county planners.

V. Illustrating the Futures Foregone Analysis on Big Vista Divide

A. *The Nature of the Management Alternatives Under Investigation*

The Management Alternatives evaluated for their impacts on social well-being are as follows:

> *Alternative A — Continue Present Management*
> Management emphasis is directed toward long term continuation of present uses and activities. Primary emphasis will be placed on maintaining endangered and threatened fish and wildlife habitats along with maintenance of historic and cultural sites. Dispersed recreational activities in a natural environment, protection and use of unique natural areas, and primitive types of recreation will also receive emphasis along with improve-

---

6. It is recognized that this is a major point and one on which specific empirical support has not been adequately developed. Discussions of this problem can be found in: G. Wills, Technological Forecasting (1972); Pyke, *A Practical Approach to Delphi*, 2 Futures 143 (1970); Hill & Fowles, *The Methodological Worth of the Delpi Forecasting Techniques*, 7 Technological Forecasting Techniques 179 (1975); Helmer & Rescher, *On the Epistemology of Inexact Sciences*, 6 Management Sci. 25 (1959).

Table 1

Demographic Characteristics of the
Panel Members

			Panel
I.	Age:	Under 25	0
		25-34	3
		35-44	4
		45-54	2
		55-64	0
		65+	0
II.	Sex:	Male	8
		Female	1
III.	Ethnic Group Status:		
		Anglo	9
		Chicano	0
		Black	0
		Indian	0
IV.	Education:		
		Professional (M.A., M.S., M.E., M.D., Ph.D., LL.B., etc.)	2
		Four Year College Graduate (A.B., B.S., B.M., etc.)	6
		1 - 3 Years College	1
V.	Gross Family Annual Income:		
		10,000-12,499	0
		12,500-14,999	2
		15,000-17,499	1
		17,500-19,999	2
		20,000-24,999	1
		25,000-29,999	2
		30,000+	1

ment of fish and wildlife habitats. Other resource uses and activities would be directed toward the protection of recreation and wildlife values.

On the west side of the Continental Divide emphasis is directed toward providing more intensive recreation and silvicultural opportunities which will contribute toward local economic and community stability. Thus, Alternative A would provide for a primitive, though non-wilderness area accomodating some forms of non-motorized recreation.

Alternative B — Maximum Wilderness

Protection and enhancement of amenity value will receive the primary emphasis. These amenities or intangible products and uses include: maximizing wilderness acreage within the definition of the Wilderness Act and Forest Service policy, fish and wildlife habitats, and protection of scenic and cultural features. Other resource uses and activities would be subordinated to the goals of environmental protection and maximizing wilderness. The maximum amount of wilderness within the definition of the Wilderness Act would be provided.

Alternative C — Recreational Diversity

Outdoor recreation would be optimized with primary emphasis on providing diversity of opportunities. Protection and enhancement of amenities and intangible values will receive emphasis. Fish and wildlife habitats will be protected and enhanced in support of optimizing recreation diversity. Alternative C would lie between alternatives B and D in the amount of wilderness provided.

Alternative D — Economic Development

Production of tangible forest products and resources would be optimized. Major emphasis will be placed on assisting local and regional economic growth and stability through development of high intensity recreation sites and utilization of renewable surface resources which include timber, forage, wildlife, and water. Resource utilization activities will emphasize maintaining compatibility of other resources, such as silvicultural practices, to improve water yields. Management emphasis will provide for maximizing economic values at minimal environmental costs. This alternative would provide the least amount of wilderness.

B. *The Overall Approach to Social Well-Being*

In sum, the approach to the analysis of social well-being is as follows:

A. to employ panels of judges selected for their knowledge and experience with the planning area under consideration;

B. to make estimates about the impacts of four different management alternatives on one dimension of social well-being —future choice opportunities foregone under each management alternative: Management alternatives which eliminate the fewest futures-for-choice opportunities and are judged to be superior from a social well-being standpoint.

What follows is the presentation of the data for each dimension of Futures Foregone.

C. *The Futures Foregone Data*

The Futures Foregone data is displayed in Table 2. Looking down the page the reader will see the estimates of the panel for scope. Where the scope of a loss is a non-zero value, one will see accompanying estimates for intensity and duration values. The overall Futures Foregone summary score is computed as follows:

TABLE 2

FUTURES FOREGONE

Social Group Category	ALTERNATIVE A Cont. Pres. Mgt.			ALTERNATIVE B Max. Wilderness			ALTERNATIVE C Rec. Diversity			ALTERNATIVE D Econ. Dev.		
	Scope	Int.	Dur.	Scope	Int.	Dur.	Scope	Int.	Dur.	Scope	Int.	Dur.
Sawmills/Planing Mills	-.3	2	5	-1	6	4	-.5	4	5	0		
Logging Contractors	-.3	2	3	-1	6	2	-.5	4	5	0		
Cattle/Sheep Grazing	0			0			-.2	4	3	0		
Other Livestock	0			0			-.3	4	1	0		
Food Processing	0			-1	2	3	-.3	2	3	0		
Wilderness Recreation	-.3	7	100	0			-.3	6	50	-.7	8	100
Dispersed Recreation	0			0			0			-.5	8	3
Wildlife Recreation	0			0			0			-.3	6	1
Developed Recreation	-.3	4	2	-.8	6	5	-.3	2	5	0		
Minerals/Mining	-.2	3	1	-.9	7	3	-.5	4	5	0		
Watershed	-.2	6	5	-.4	6	3	-.3	6	5	-.3	4	5
Gas Stations/Auto Dlrs.	-.2	2	1	-.6	2	1	-.3	2	1	0		
Eating/Drinking Estab.	-.2	2	1	-.4	4	1	-.3	2	1	0		
Transport/Warehousing	0			-.5	4	2	-.3	2	3	0		
Personal Services/Repair	0			-.5	4	2	0			0		
Other/Retail	0			-.4	4	2	-.3	2	1	0		
Hunting - Game Birds	0			0			0			-.4	3	2
Hunting - Small Animals	0			-.5	4	1	0			-.4	3	2
Hunting - Large Animals	0			-.3	4	1	0			-.3	4	5
Camping - Remote	0			0			0			-.7	7	2
Camping - Developed	-.2	4	4	-.5	6	2	0			0		
Hiking	0			0			0			0		
Auto Sightseeing	-.3	4	5	-.5	4	5	-.4	2	1	0		
Skiing/Snow-Downhill	0			-.5			0			0		
Skiing/Snow, Cross Ctry.	0			0			0			-.4	4	1
Skiing/Water	0			0			0			0		
Swimming	0			0			0			0		
Fishing	0			0			0			-.3	4	1
Boating - Power	-.5	2	1	-1.0	1	0	-.3	1	1	0		
Boating - Non-Power	0			0			0			-.2	2	0
Housing	-.3	2	2	-1.0	4	2	-.5	3	1	0		
Business - Industrial	-.3	2	5	-.8	2	3	-.8	2	5	0		
Business - Agricultural	0			0			-.5	3	5	0		
Σ =	-3.6	42	135	-12.6	76	42	-6.9	55	101	-5.0	57	123

FF = (S) (I)+(-D) =   -286.2   -999.6   -480.5   -408.0

Futures Foregone Ranking: A-Cont. Pres. Mgt.   -286.2
                           D-Econ. Dev.   -408.0
                           C-Rec. Diversity   -480.5
                           B-Maximum Wilderness -999.6

Note: Scores are outcome of Delphi Estimation Procedure. In those cases where there was not total consensus, the median score is employed.

FF = (ΣS) (ΣI) + (Σ-D)
Where:
FF = Futures Foregone for any single Management Alternative
S = Estimated Scope of Loss
I = Estimated Intensity of Loss
D = Estimated Duration of Loss (and where both scope and duration are entered as minus numbers).

In effect, this formula for computation of the FF score weights intensity as the single most important variable in the equation because scope can vary only between 0 and -1 while intensity can vary from 0 to 16. Duration, by adding it to the product of scope and intensity, has an important impact but not nearly as much as if the number of impact years were also used as a multiplier.

The logic is that higher scope and duration of losses can be tolerated where intensity of the loss is low, but when intensity of losses rises—because few or no alternative Resource Capability Units exist to support the activity in the surrounding area—then the foregone choice opportunity will be severely missed on the land base and that fact should be highlighted by an equation that makes intensity of loss a most significant determinant of the FF score.

The results of the Futures Foregone analysis are as follows:

Management Alternative	Futures Foregone Score	Rank Order
A. Continue Present Management	—286.2	1
B. Maximum Wilderness	—999.6	4
C. Recreational Diversity	—480.5	3
D. Economic Development	—408.0	2

Why do we find this pattern of outcomes? There are several points to be made:

A. Economic Development shows a second place finish in the Futures Foregone analysis because economic development in the Planning Unit is heavily recreation oriented as opposed to industrial, agricultural, or forest product oriented. In other words, economic development in this Planning Unit does not carry with it as much in the way of negative side effects, which would sound the deathknell of futures for many other activities, as one might think if one has the image of economic development as associated with intense industrial, agricultural, or forest product (timber) development.

B. Economic Development looks good as compared to Maximum Wilderness, not because of any inherent bias in the procedure against environmental quality and a wilderness management strategy, but because of the provisions of the separate alternatives. The Economic Development alternative provided for some wilderness area in the northern portion of the Planning Unit. The Maximum Wilderness alternative, on the other hand, provided for a much enlarged wilderness area to extend southward across the Planning Unit. Therefore, the management alternatives were constructed in such a manner that the Economic Development alternative provided for some wilderness while the Maximum Wilderness alternative failed to provide for many of the diverse activities which necessarily results in the loss of futures for many non-wilderness opportunities.

In other words, the Maximum Wilderness alternative emphasizing wilderness did not leave room for the diversity of activities which each of the other management strategies allowed for, and this fact is clearly reflected in the high Futures Foregone scores. Each of the other three alternatives provided for varying portions of wilderness in primitive recreation areas—thereby holding the wilderness losses down—whereas the Maximum Wilderness alternative did not provide as many opportunities for the other activities which the affected publics act out on the Planning Unit.

In sum, there is no inherent bias in the procedure against wilderness uses of the land base. The results obtained are an outcome of the manner in which the management alternatives were constructed. Had the Economic Development alternative not been so recreation oriented and had it not provided for a wilderness area in the northern portion of the Planning Unit, it would have drawn much higher Futures Foregone scores.

VI. Conclusions

Since demand for water and land resources is outstripping available supplies, it is critical that careful analysis of resource management alternatives be pursued before making irreversible commitments. Tool kits have been developed for constructing analyses of technical and economic aspects of such alternatives, but the toolbox labelled "Social Well-Being" has remained notably empty. This is no mere happenstance—the emptiness reflects the existence of tough conceptual problems which are outlined in Part II of this paper. No one knows how to solve these problems in any ultimate sense, but it is possible to construct a definition of social well-being which is subject to systematic analysis and measurement. The problems are sidestepped by moving away from the analysis of choices at the prescriptive level and by focusing on attributes of the context of choice offered by a given land/water planning unit. Whereas it is impossible to prescribe that there is any more net human well-being in a municipal use of X units of water than in a recreational or agricultural use, it is possible to examine the effects of the alternative uses on the choice context which would be available to present and future generations of affected groups. Those mixes of water/land use which expand the choice context, or which reduce the choice context the least, contribute more to social well-being than those which foreclose more futures for choice opportunities. The Futures Foregone analysis has potential because:

A. It makes possible the quantitative comparison of natural resource alternatives before highly irreversible commitments are made. Too often social well-being implications have been discovered only in retrospect. By the time the negative impacts are felt, and groups are mobilized, the investments in an alternative have been so high as to make remedial action costly, difficult, time-consuming, and peripheral to the damages sustained by negatively affected groups.

B. The Futures Foregone analysis can be performed at low cost. Given the current state of the art, it is possible to conduct a Futures Foregone analysis at a small fraction of the costs of technical and economic analysis, and it has been established that the procedures can be phased into natural resource planning processes without creating disruption of existing technical and economic procedures of analysis.

C. The analysis can provide a framework for the coherent structuring of public involvement. Much current public involvement is diffuse, unfocused, and difficult to analyze. Before systematic analysis of public involvement information can be accomplished, it is important to have a set of well-formulated questions. It is insufficient to have found that some groups support and oppose given projects or policies. The questions to be answered always have to do with trade-offs among different mixes of advantages and disadvantages. The analysis of Futures Foregone has the potential of providing a framework within which each set of proponents and opponents can begin to systematically comprehend the social effects of a given land/water use alternative and begin to visualize the overall pattern of those effects on other affected parties. The systematic display of such information might operate to increase the meaningfulness of participation in public involvement sessions, and it should result in more constructive consideration of trade-offs among opposing groups who otherwise tend to make public involvement sessions a forum for non-negotiable conflict.

D. The Futures Foregone analysis of social well-being can supplement more traditional technical and economic analysis in a complementary fashion. The social well-being analysis of Futures Foregone does not replace other technical and economic analysis, but it does open up new aspects of the resource allocation problem which have great significance to the quality of life. Alternative futures are a precious resource. Decision makers must husband, conserve, and expand them with as much consideration as any material resource.

It is impossible to prescribe particular choices in the name of social well-being today and for coming generations, but it is possible to think of serving others, including future generations, by retaining and expanding the context of choice as much as possible. To leave a legacy of expanded choice opportunities for others is to leave the greatest gift of all—it is what progress in social life is all about.

11

Let's Dismantle (Largely but Not Fully) the Federal Water Resource Development Establishment: The Apostasy of a Longstanding Water Development Federalist[*]

Henry P. Caulfield, Jr.[**]

I now live in Fort Collins, Colorado, a rapidly expanding city of some 50,000 people, and I serve as a member of the Fort Collins Water Board, in addition to teaching and doing research with respect to water and related land resource uses at Colorado State University. Thus, in recent years, I have been observing federal-state-local relations with regard to water from a diametrically opposite perspective than that provided by my many, previous years of federal service in Washington, D.C. The views which follow endeavor to reconcile my research findings, observations, and experiences from both perspectives.

I. SUPPORT FOR FEDERAL DEVELOPMENT DYING

To begin, I will make this general observation, with which others may want to strongly differ: The federal water development program is politically dying, if not already dead. In recent years, federal development programs have doubled (not even keeping pace with inflation in construction costs) while federally-assisted state and local programs, largely for wastewater management, have increased 16-fold. Clearly, national value priorities have changed.

The recent emergence of major federal responsibility for water quality was accomplished by the Water Pollution Control Acts of the last decade. With hardly a dissenting Congressional vote, the primary force in water pollution control was removed during the 1960s from the state to the federal level. This new federal responsibility was strongly supported by pub-

---

[*] Paper originally delivered as a Panel Member, Panel on the Role of Federal, State and Local Governments, National Conference on Water, sponsored by the U.S. Water Resources Council, Washington, D.C., April 22-24, 1975.

[**] Professor of Political Science, Colorado State University; former Director, U.S. Water Resources Council.

lic opinion, as indicated by many opinion polls. No such public opinion, or even solid interest group enthusiasm, calls loudly enough to be heard these days for federal water and related land development.

The last really big authorizations to the Bureau of Reclamation for federal water development in the West were those for the Central Arizona Project in 1968 and, earlier in the 1960s, for the Garrison Diversion and Oahe projects in North Dakota and South Dakota, respectively. These three big projects stemmed from implicit political understandings of decades before. They appear now as being pursued with something less than ecstatic political enthusiasm, even within the areas which they are presumed to benefit directly.

Similar observations could be made, generally, with respect to the water development programs of the Corps of Engineers and the Soil Conservation Service.

How might one explain this decline in national political support for federal water development projects? Let us discuss a number of possible interrelated explanations.

A. *Opposition of Office of Management and Budget*

There is no question that the institutional position of the Office of Management and Budget and its predecessor, the Bureau of the Budget, has been to oppose somehow all federal water development projects. Regardless of the political party of the President, this has been the institutional position for over 20 years. Many arguments and devices have been used over the years to implement this position. These include diversionary tactics such as encouragement of the establishment of national water commissions, suggesting unfeasible cost-sharing or reimbursement schemes, and insisting upon politically untenable benefit-cost standards. I can recall no federal water development project (including federally-assisted watershed projects of the Soil Conservation Service) that these budget agencies have strongly supported. This institutional position of this well-entrenched professional staff-arm of the President has undoubtedly helped to bring about political malaise, but cannot really explain it.

B. *Environmental Movement*

The rise in political legitimacy during the 1960s of wild and scenic rivers as an alternative use of rivers, along with other environmental concerns with rivers and lakes, has openly, forcefully, and successfully challenged the traditional federal water development programs. But the environmentalists would have been forced to compromise with federal water development much more than they have, if national political vitality in support of development were still abroad in the land. The environmentalists have contributed to this loss in vitality, but their strength does not fully explain it.

C. *Decline of Federal Role in the Development of the West*

The United States was developed from East to West. The origins of the water development functions of both the Corps of Engineers in the early 19th century and the Bureau of Reclamation at the end of the 19th century stem from national concern for development of the West, first to the Mississippi River and then through the arid West to the Pacific. Both programs stemmed politically from the desire to support agriculture: the interests of what were seen as pioneering, reliable, individualist farmers and ranchers. This support was given by the federalist Republican Party of Abraham Lincoln to the navigation program of the Corps of Engineers and by the federalist Republican Party of Theodore Roosevelt to irrigation development by the Bureau of Reclamation. The federalist Democratic Party of Franklin Roosevelt put a largely bipartisan federalist stamp upon water resources development, except with respect to federal public power development.

Quite apart from political response to the interests of our former national agricultural and rural majority, these federal programs could be justified more generally by the substantial failure (except for the early Erie Canal) of state navigational promotion efforts with federal land-grant support during the Canal Era, 1817-1838, and by the great difficulties encountered in nonfederal public and private irrigation development in the arid West in the latter part of the 19th century. Federal responsibility for planning, financing, constructing, operating, and maintaining navigation and irrigation projects was justified at the times of their origins by: (a) the superior financial capability of the federal government to finance projects whose benefits would accrue over a long period of time; and (b) the ability of the federal government to utilize most effectively the very scarce engineering and other scientific talent available to the Nation until more recent times.

Both of these justifications for federal direct responsibility are no longer valid. To the extent federal financial help is needed for nonfederal water development agencies, grants and loans can be made as is now the common practice in other areas of governmental concern. With the plethora of expert consulting engineering firms now available to states and local governments, to say nothing of their own increased professional personnel aided by financial grants under Title III of the Water Resources Planning Act since 1966 and expanded expertise in state land-grant universities by use of funds provided under the Water Resources Planning Research Act since 1965, federal professional expertise is no longer as essential as it once was.

All of this adds up to the fact that Western development no longer lights fires of political imagination, even in the West. The West is now as developed in large part as the East. And the Western states no longer provide a bloc within the Congress unequivocably dedicated to federally-promoted Western development.

D. *Needed Federal Development Largely Accomplished*

Among the interrelated factors that help to explain the decline in political support for federal water development projects is also the fact that the federal job has largely been accomplished. Probably this fact is generally perceived by many public leaders as well as by people generally.

The main stems of the Columbia, Colorado, Missouri, Ohio, Tennessee, Mississippi, Arkansas, Rio Grande rivers, and probably some others, have already been developed, more or less fully. Moreover, except for engineering dreams of large-scale continental water transfer, the potential large-scale irrigation schemes of the West have been, or are now being, accomplished.

E. *Emergence of the National Urban Majority*

Finally, among the interrelated factors that help to explain the decline in political support of water resource development projects is the political emergence of a national urban majority. Agriculture and other resource development concerns are not a major interest of this relatively new national majority; they are foreign to it.

In the area of domestic policy, the urban majority is primarily concerned with urban problems: housing, transportation, health, welfare, air and water pollution, urban open space and recreation areas, energy, etc. Its concern with the rural and natural hinterland, expressed effectively now for some 10 or more years, is that of the environmental movement. Urban people, not rural people, strongly support establishment of wilderness areas, national parks, wild and scenic rivers, and fish and wildlife enhancement.

The federal response to urban problems has not been a federalist response of direct public service such as that of the Corps of Engineers and the Bureau of Reclamation. The federal response has been categorical financial grants-in-aid to state and local governments and, more recently, block grants and general revenue sharing. Grantsmanship is now the dominant mode of federal-state-local relations.

Comprehensive major river basin plans for federal development of water and related land resources are foreign to "urban and regional plans" of urban professionals (both in and out of universities) and most of the urban public. They are two worlds apart. The emergence of the urban majority, nationally, and increasingly in each state (*e.g.,* recently in Colorado), indicates that this anachronism needs to be faced frontally and overcome at the level of national policy. But, in so facing this problem, it needs to be remembered that water resource development is still needed in this nation, particularly that which is intrastate.

II. Water Development Still Needed

Urban water management is clearly a need for the long-term future. Such management includes for many urban areas development of new domestic and industrial water supplies. For all areas it includes wastewater management and reuse of water to the greatest practicable extent. Urban flood plain management, including development of flood protection works in appropriate circumstances, is also a clear need for the future. Both urban water management and urban flood plain management are major urban public concerns.

The extent to which these needs and public concerns will require assumption by states of direct state responsibilities, as a service to two or more urban communities or for river basin management, will vary from state to state.

North Dakota, South Dakota, Nebraska, and Idaho are, possibly, the only states in the West with the economic need for new irrigation projects and with the agricultural-rural majorities which would support state planning, financing, construction, and operation and maintenance of state or special public-district irrigation works.

The longrun viability of rural watershed protection schemes of the Soil Conservation Service is not clear. No doubt it varies substantially from state to state. If this financial-assistance program were converted by the Congress to the more usual grant-in-aid form, with the technical personnel being state, rather than federal, employees, then the response of each state would correlate, presumably, with the degree of agricultural-rural political power in each state.

Not only are intrastate water developments needed in the future, some interstate water developments will also be needed. Continued federal responsibility for such new interstate navigation developments as are needed and politically viable is clear. Major elements of flood management on interstate rivers is also clearly federal.

What is not clear is the need and political viability of major federal urban water management schemes for interstate areas. The Corps of Engineers has tried valiantly to explore whether it has a viable role in urban water management in its Northeast Water Supply Study and other such studies. A hard question, for example, is this: Would a federally planned, financed, constructed, and operated wholesale water supply and pollution treatment scheme for multistate Metropolitan New York be politically viable? If not there, then where? Certainly not Denver or San Francisco.

Other relevant questions regarding interstate situations are these:

1. Is the responsibility that the federal government has recently assumed for water quality enhancement on the Colorado River unique? It could be.

2. Are the federal-interstate compact commissions on the Delaware and Susquehanna Rivers really viable as agencies to plan, finance, construct, and operate needed management works? They are not as yet.

3. Are the future domestic and foreign demands for American agricultural products such as to require development by the federal government of large water-transfer schemes for new irrigation development or for rescue of agricultural areas

that are mining their groundwaters, for example, West Texas? I doubt it.

III. NEW FEDERAL-STATE-LOCAL SYSTEM

If the foregoing analysis is basically accepted, then obviously fundamental changes are needed in the authorization of federal, state, and local responsibilities with respect to water.

The most important strategic action that the Congress needs to take is to repeal the authorizations of the Corps of Engineers and Bureau of Reclamation to plan, finance, construct, operate, and maintain further intrastate projects. This action should include deauthorization of the intrastate projects within the $30 billion and $8 billion of authorized, but unfunded projects that the Corps of Engineers and the Bureau of Reclamation, respectively, are said to have at the present time. The Congress should also repeal the authorization of the Soil Conservation Service to plan and supervise construction, etc., of small watershed protection projects. Finally, the Congress should repeal the Small Reclamation Projects Act.

These Congressional actions would clearly place basic decisional responsibility for intrastate water development upon state governments. State governments would then have to reappraise the division of responsibility for action between state governments and local governments. To make this change practicable, the Congress should authorize a program of block grants and loans to aid states in undertaking the types of projects formerly undertaken by the federal agencies.

Though the operational clarity of the distinction between intrastate and interstate is obviously critical to the working out of this proposal, working out this distinction in careful detail cannot be attempted here. Suffice it to say that in my judgment it is capable of being operationally made.

Under this proposal the federal government would have responsibility for planning, financing, constructing, operating, and maintaining interstate projects, except for those undertaken by federal-interstate compact commissions. Because federal, interstate, and intrastate concerns with water and related land use will continue, mechanisms for federal-state coordination and comprehensive planning will be needed in the future. The Congress, therefore, should study the present roles of federal-state river basin commissions created under Title II of the Water Resources Planning Act of 1965, the federal-interstate compact commissions on the Delaware and Susquehanna, the several federal regional commissions modelled on the Appalachian Regional Commission, and the federal executive councils created by the Executive Branch. In addition, it should study the basic procedures involved in federal-state-local relations embodied in Office of Management and Budget Circular A-95 as well as those directly in the water field. The upshot of such study should be Congressional reconciliation of these mechanisms and procedures in law.

These proposals could overcome the very substantial frustration that exists today in meeting water development needs. State people who have made a career of promoting federal projects at federal expense, and opposing (implicitly if not explicitly) state assumption of responsibility including financing, will need to shift their activities. The need for carrying out these proposals is sufficiently great to justify Congressional consideration as soon as this may be practicable.

IV. CONCLUSION

These proposals are radical. They involve radical changes in major institutions of government, and for people in them with whom I have long been associated. However, the importance to society of academic freedom (including tenure) is not just that an incumbent professor possess it but that he use it as he sees the need. I have now used it as I see the need.

I expect that from many quarters my apostasy in this paper will not be well-received—to say the least. Long-standing friendships that I value may be broken up. Nevertheless, I believe these proposals are worthy of real debate. If my present views can be successfully refuted and buried, so much the better. My own original faith in water development federalism will be vindicated. But if my views are not successfully refuted, or better proposals are not forthcoming, then let us get on with the task of further designing a new system of federal-state-local water and related land jurisdictions that makes professional sense and has political vitality for the future.

12
Water Issues in Perspective

*Jack O. Horton**

Instead of the legal framework addressed by many of the speakers I will discuss the actions of the government—particularly of the Department of the Interior—which address the problems of allocation, supply, and distribution of water. I will take a common man's approach to this framework (how to make government work) while looking at the complex legal array of problems, such as the problem of federal-state relations. I hope to provide at least a status report of the Department's progress with the law and with the operating units in the field.

Let me address four different areas very quickly: (1) the study and analysis of the supply of the upper Colorado River; (2) an analysis of the Missouri-Yellowstone; (3) state water rights and the relationship between state and federal government; and (4) the very difficult subject of Indian water rights.

In 1973, when I joined the Department of the Interior, it appeared that we had no overall study of projected water demands on the upper Colorado River; indeed, the areas of agreement and the areas of dispute as far as the supply was concerned were unclear. We have what now is regarded as a professional group of federal employees, assisted by state and private individuals, preparing a report entitled *Water for Energy in the Upper Colorado.* The report does not argue for diversion or use of more water for energy, but simply recognizes that within this country and this region there are increasing demands for the use of water from the upper Colorado. The figures were used in alternative scenarios; the Bureau of Reclamation uses a conservative estimate of supply of 5.8 million acre-feet, while many of the state authorities would argue that there is 6.5 million acre-feet available. In our presentation and in our analysis we subtracted from the 5.8 million acre-foot estimate the present uses, totalling 3.7 million acre-feet—leaving, of course,

---

* Assistant Secretary of the Interior, Land and Water Resources.

2.1 million acre-feet. We then tried to determine a reasonable estimate of future uses for irrigation, agriculture, recreation, and fish and wildlife flows. We came up with the following results, estimating the predicted demands on the Colorado basin by the year 2000. We found that, despite many opinions to the contrary, there was less than 1 million acre-feet needed for energy uses; in fact, the amount was only 870,000 acre-feet. We projected another 800,000 acre-feet for new agricultural uses, and 150,000 for required fish and wildlife flows. Thus, we predicted a possible "pinch-point," supply no longer exceeding demand, occurring between 1995 and the year 2000. Of course this will vary depending upon what assumptions are placed in the equation.

The same calculations were performed for the upper Missouri; in fact, there were two studies—one done by the Bureau of Reclamation, and one being an outstanding federal-state study called the Northern Great Plains Resource Program. As in the upper Colorado, we found that a considerably lesser volume of water would be required for energy than had previously been thought. The Missouri-Yellowstone system is far larger than the Colorado, containing 28 million acre-feet. Of that average historic flow, 6.5 million acre-feet are now being used and depleted. Taking into account future demands placed by energy, agriculture, mining and industry, Indian water, and fish and wildlife flows, there will still remain 15 million unused acre-feet of water by the year 2000.

The above figures and studies were intended to provide a framework for planning and discussion of water management needs. Within this general mathematical framework the Department has tried to come up with a coordinating mechanism involving the state governors that will make possible more sophisticated planning systems between the federal and state levels of government than we have had before.

Starting in 1973, we realized that one of the paramount difficulties in water planning and use in the Missouri was the lack of coordination between the Corps of Engineers, who had built the reservoirs for flood control and for navigation, and the Bureau of Reclamation, who had diverted and used the water for irrigation and who had the authority to market water for industrial purposes. The Department spent almost 16 months negotiating a memorandum of understanding between these two parties. This was a major first step in effective water management, being the first time there had ever been an agreement between the two proud and professional federal water agencies.

The next step in 1973, was to inform the western governors of the procedural results of this agreement, and to emphasize that a greater decisionmaking role should be assumed by the states. The professional state water agencies and officials should have that responsibility. Accordingly we have given them in every instance the first right to contract or process any application that comes to the federal government for use of Missouri water for industrial purposes. Additionally, we offered them the opportunity to contract for significant single blocks of water behind the federal reservoirs in the Missouri system. And, on Oct. 1, 1976, in what is truly an historic step forward, the Department signed a contract with the Governor of Montana which gives to the State the right to handle all applications to the first 300,000 acre-feet from Fort Peck at no cost to the State, until they should subcontract that water for industrial or industrial-related uses.

The reason this arrangement was successful is because we have found new ways to solve old problems, and we are not now looking at the historic dispute that has aggravated the water situation for so long on these two river systems. Another reason this agreement was successful was because there were very important agricultural spin-offs for the use of Fort Peck water. The first known state water application will be for what conceptually is called a gasification plant. Once operational, the plant will produce ammonia fertilizer, which means that nitrogen ammonium fertilizer will be much cheaper in Montana than it has been before.

The toughest problem we face, however, is not the supply question or water for energy, nor is it the difficulties between the federal agencies and the state agencies. In my opinion, without question, the most pressing and demanding problem that we have yet to address, let alone resolve, is the problem of Indian water rights. As the state looks towards future irrigation and energy demands, and as we look at our responsibilities on the Colorado and on the Missouri, we realize that we have not yet come up with a well-defined understanding of what Indian water rights are and what they involve.

In the first instance, those waters which fall on or flow across an Indian reservation are available to them for agricultural purposes. But can they also use that water for non-agricultural purposes? Do they have to use it only on the reservation? Can they sell water to energy companies? Indeed, can they sell it for future irrigation development or to cities? These questions remained unanswered, but we have not progressed even that far. We have not defined what these water rights are. Moreover, there is a standing dispute between the federal agencies and the Bureau concerning what formulates an economic understanding of what it means to produce practicably irrigable developments on an Indian reservation.

I am pleased to say that modest progress has been made within the Department of the Interior. Specifically, we have had a task force working on the problem for about a year, and it is my hope that there will soon be an announcement that will initiate progress toward an administrative solution of Indian water rights problems. We believe that practical solutions can be found and negotiated with the Indians and the states that will recognize that, by law, certain amounts of water are due to the Indians; and it is time that we started to recognize those rights, to quantify those rights, and to assist the various Indian reservations in making these waters useful to their reservations and to their people. This, I hope, will be a new way to solve a long-standing problem.

These issues evidence that we cannot rely on old formulae to answer new questions. We are, I believe, going to build reclamation projects, not to settle family farmers on their quarter-sections but: (1) because this country is going to need food for both domestic and international consumption; (2) because irrigation remains the most economic and sound use of a great deal of water in the American West; (3) because we will have mastered the technique of economic analysis of water problems; and (4) because we will have mastered the techniques of more efficient irrigation and be willing to end wasteful practices.

13
The Role of Water in the History and Development of Colorado

*David Lavender**

Any account of the role filled by water in the growth of Colorado must begin with yet another description of the implacable circumstances of geography. From the standpoint of persons whose culture is rooted in more humid climes, both rainfall and, as a consequence, streamflow are deficient west of the 100th meridian. Moreover, and this is also important to our tale, such streams as do exist are perverse, deceptive, and difficult to control. Arroyos either have no water in them at all or else roar with destructive flash floods laden with sand. Sand is also an eternal part of the freight even of rivers that do not dry up every summer.

The consequences are different on the different sides of the Rockies. To the east the rivers lack volume enough to cut firm channels through the gently sloping plains. Thus, the settling sand aggrades the streambed. The water wanders, and the braided flow that results is, in the folk cliche of the early settlers, a mile wide and an inch deep, too thick to drink but too thin to plow, the biggest rivers with the least water in the land. A significant portion of the flow, moreover, is completely underground. Obviously such a river presents grave problems to men endeavoring to build permanent headgates or seeking to determine ownership of the buried portions of the flow.

West of the Rockies, by contrast, the land lacks the flat sameness of the Plains. There the loads of sand have helped the water scour out canyons that are things of beauty but hardly joys forever to the frustrated settlers who want to use them for either transportation or diversion.

The point is that in the midst of a dry land of enormous extent—almost two-fifths of the area of the coterminous United States—a few cantankerous streams do exist. They exist because of the echelons of the mountains, most of them running north and south, that wrinkle the sun-smitten spaces between

---

* Thacher School, Ojai, California; Guggenheim Fellowship Recipient, 1961, 1969.

the Sierra Nevada and the Rockies. Although these uplifts occupy only 15 percent of the West's total area, they drain from passing clouds 90 percent of the moisture that reaches the ground between the 100th meridian and the western slopes of the Sierra Nevada-Cascade chain.

Because Colorado possesses the highest average elevation of any state in the Union, it captures a disproportionate share of this moisture. Of all the major streams that flow to the ocean from the interior of the American West, the Columbia River is the only one that does not receive appreciable augmentation from the Colorado Rockies.

Because water promotes prosperity, particularly when used in connection with booming new industrial and cybernetic pursuits, Coloradans are inclined to be possessive about "their" streams and to become embroiled with neighboring states that cast covetous eyes upon the same rivers. These many controversies, particularly those involving the Colorado River, are an integral part of the story of the state—a story not yet ended.

The beginnings of the state's water story are likewise shrouded in obscurity. We do know, however, that long before the documentation of ordinary events seemed necessary, the Indians of the American Southwest had learned to grow crops. Some of their maize and squash they dry-farmed, some they planted on terraces where run-off water from storms could be collected, and some they irrigated with diversion canals that tapped the streams at a few easily approachable spots.

Canal irrigation was the system adopted by the first whites to encounter America's aridity. In fact, some early settlers in Arizona actually resurrected many miles of the prehistoric ditches of the Gila River area, just as the Bureau of Land Management today occasionally utilizes ancient Pueblo Indian check dams to distribute the run-off of storm waters sluicing across the exposed slickrock of southwestern Colorado. More generally, however, the ditches were dug by those who used them—by the Spanish colonists of New Mexico, the fur traders at their posts on the high plains, and the Mormons of Utah. By 1856, well before Colorado Territory had been created, Mexican settlers in the San Luis Valley had built at least a dozen short ditches for bringing water to their croplands.

There is a paradox here. Agriculture accounted for the first water development in the intermountain West, and agriculture today remains the single greatest consumer of mountain water. The basic law of water diversion, however, did not come from agriculture but from mining.

Western water law is a California invention. When the argonauts of 1848 and 1849 descended on the foothills of the Sierra Nevada, they were trespassers on the public domain. The United States, which had just acquired the land from Mexico, had codified no laws concerning the acquisition of placer mining claims. In order to fill the vacuum, the California miners drew up, at local meetings, some 500 sets of district laws designed to legalize their extralegal position.

The men—there were very few women miners—did not want title to the ground. Titles would have resulted in taxes, and besides, the great majority intended to abandon their small plots as soon as the gold had been extracted. All they wanted was a usufructuary right. The point to recall is this: as soon as use ceased, so did the right to mine, at least until 1866 when Congress finally got around to promulgating laws whereby title to mining ground could be perfected.[1]

Methods for acquiring the water needed in the mining process followed an analogous course. A claimant—either an individual, a partnership, or a corporation—posted a notice of intent and began a survey for a ditch. That was enough to establish a right, and the right continued for as long as the water was used.

Inevitably the volume of water in the foothill streams diminished as the dry summer advanced. No attempt was made, however, to equitably apportion the shrinking supplies among different claimants. Instead it was decreed that whoever first put water to use was entitled to his full quota before later diverters could take a drop. This procedure was the basis of what later became known as the doctrine of prior appropriation for beneficial use, or, to resort to the catch phrase used in all water discussions, "first in time is first in right."

Significantly, the three gold strikes that launched the Col-

---

1. 30 U.S.C. § 32 (1970).

orado mining stampede were made by men experienced in California customs—William Green Russell, George Jackson, and John Gregory. Russell, it is worth noting, soon turned from mining to promoting a ditch company that supplied water to placer claims. Nor was his example unique. When water decrees were adjudicated in Colorado the number one right on Clear Creek went to David K. Wall, also a California veteran, who had used his diverted water during the summer of 1859 to grow potatoes on two acres of soil now embraced within the city limits of Golden. California practice thus became Colorado custom.

The first ditches, like the first placer claims and truck gardens, were simple. Complexity and conflict did not develop until the advent of the Kansas Pacific and Denver Pacific railroads in 1870. At that point a mania for cooperative colonies seized the area. One of the earliest and most successful of those ventures was Union Colony, precursor of Greeley. An early rival was the Fort Collins Agricultural Colony, founded on the site of an abandoned military reservation beside the Cache La Poudre River. The word "colony" contained such magic connotations, indeed, that General William Palmer of the Denver & Rio Grande Railroad used the term to lend glamor to his speculative townsites of Colorado Springs and South Pueblo.

Because the colonies depended for life on ditch water, interest in irrigation swelled high. In October 1873, territorial Governor Samuel Elbert convened here in Denver the Nation's first symposium on the subject. Delegates attended from Utah, Wyoming, New Mexico, Kansas, Nebraska, and Colorado. In 1873 Colorado was not yet a state, but already the delegates knew that the rivers of the West were too difficult to be handled by individual effort. Fervently they recommended federal aid for the construction of reservoirs and distribution systems. Congress, however, paid no heed.

Meanwhile accelerating demands for irrigation water led to conflict, notably an acrimonious dispute between Greeley and Fort Collins over the drought-shrunken waters of the Cache La Poudre. Their troubles forced the 1876 convention charged with preparing a state constitution to devote part of its attention to water problems. As a result, the legality of prior appropriation of water was written into the State's organic law;[2] a trail-blazing step of such importance that prior appropriation, the basic law of all Rocky Mountain States, is often called the Colorado Doctrine.

The codification of firm laws regarding water, a growing population, and favorable climatic conditions during the 1880s touched off a burst of competitive ditch and reservoir building throughout the South Platte watershed, and somewhat later, the Arkansas Valley. Several of the projects were carried to completion by the cooperative effort of the farmers who would benefit; others were the fruit of private corporations financed by capital from the East and from Great Britain. About 1900, mutual companies legally capable of selling bonds to finance their work became as great a rage as colonies had been a quarter of a century earlier.

Geography played its inescapable part in these new developments. Water-seekers from the northern tributaries of the South Platte Valley discovered that by running canals across relatively low passes in the Continental Divide they could move Pacific water to overappropriated streams on the Eastern Slope. During the slack farm season between planting and harvest, whole families would sometimes camp in the high country while working on community ditches. Although these were the Nation's first transmountain diversion projects, it is unlikely that the participants realized even faintly the consequences that would follow from their activity.

The ditch building enthusiasm of the 1880s was temporarily chilled by the economic depression of the 1890s. Seeking relief, fervent Populists filled the Western air with demands that the federal government extend aid to suffering communities. Free silver was one such burning issue. Another revolved around federally sponsored conservation and reclamation measures. The latter drive came to fruition with the National Reclamation Act of 1902,[3] which put the United States Government into the business of building dams and distribution systems on rivers too cantankerous for local agencies to handle. Those who like to use hindsight for finding omens can discover

---

2. COLO. CONST., art. 16, § 6.
3. Act of June 17, 1902, Pub. L. No. 57-161, 32 Stat. 388 (1902).

one in the fact that Colorado's first two federal projects, the Uncompahgre and the Grand Valley systems, both involved the waters of the Colorado River.

First, however, we need to glance at Colorado's disputes with Wyoming over the Laramie River,[4] a tributary of the North Platte. In that situation, Colorado wanted to "have its cake and eat it too." Because the Laramie River originates in Colorado, the state maintained that diversions within Colorado were legitimate even when they interfered with prior appropriations in Wyoming. The United States Supreme Court struck down the contention on the grounds that both states subscribed to the doctrine of prior appropriation and that both must follow it regardless of political boundaries.[5]

The decision came at a time when Californians were pressing Congress to authorize a project on the lower Colorado River that, among other things, would facilitate the diversion of large amounts of water into the fabulously rich Imperial Valley. If approved, the Imperial project would almost certainly lead to other diversions and hence enable Southern California to establish priorities capable of retarding industrial and agricultural developments in the states higher up the River.

The upper states, still smarting from the Laramie River decision, took alarm. Denver, for instance, was already dreaming of a water tunnel through the Continental Divide—the pioneer bore of the Moffat Railroad eventually opened the way—and Utah was studying means for augmenting its Strawberry Project, which even then was moving water out of the Uintah foothills to the Wasatch Front. If such dreams were to be realized, California would have to be forestalled.

The vigorous opposition of the mountain states led California to subscribe to the famed Colorado River Compact of 1922,[6] which divided the waters of the River not among the states involved—jealousies were too intense for that—but between the upper and lower basins. This allocation, whose impact on the State of Colorado can hardly be exaggerated, vitiated the right of appropriation insofar as interstate streams are con-

---

4. Wyoming v. Colorado, 259 U.S. 419 (1921).
5. *Id.* at 466.
6. COLO. REV. STAT. ANN. §§ 37-61-102 *et seq.* (1973).

cerned, and the precedent was reaffirmed in 1948 when Colorado, New Mexico, Utah, and Wyoming at last agreed to divide the upper basin's allotment of water among themselves.[7] Nearly 52 percent of the River's water was assigned to Colorado.

All of that 52 percent originates on the Western Slope, which is the wettest part of Colorado's mountain oasis. Historically, however, not much of that western water has been beneficially used. Except in favored spots near the Utah border, the growing season is too short for large-scale agriculture, and isolation discouraged most industry. As a result, only one-fifth of Colorado's residents live in the western two-fifths of the state, and so Eastern Slope dwellers thought it quite permissible to reach across the mountains to satisfy their water needs. After all, does not the state constitution declare that water anywhere within the boundaries belongs to *all* the people, subject only to the limits of prior appropriation?

Even the barest mention of three of the Eastern Slope's increasingly mammoth transversions will indicate the shifting direction of Colorado affairs. First is the traditional Colorado-Big Thompson Project; traditional in that it was designed to supply agricultural water to the overextended South Platte. But as a marked sign of the times the Colorado-Big Thompson also generated hydroelectric power for industrial use. A second project is the great mixing bowl of the Arkansas Valley—Turquoise Lake. In that expanding reservoir near Leadville, the waters of the Homestake Project, designed for the urban centers of Colorado Springs and Aurora, intrude into water intended ultimately for the melon and sugar beet farmers of the lower Arkansas—agricultural and urban uses mingling more or less on equal terms. Then, finally, there are Denver's Roberts Tunnel and lovely Dillon Lake, in which agricultural considerations play scant part. The thought is sobering. Industrial growth has made Denver, like Los Angeles, so powerful politically and financially that the city can complete, unaided, projects of a magnitude that agricultural districts can handle only with federal help.

The implications are not lost on the residents of the Western Slope. They feel, as the people of Colorado's northwestern

---

7. COLO. REV. STAT. ANN. §§ 37-62-101 *et seq.* (1973).

counties felt during the Laramie River disputes with Wyoming, that they ought to have some control over water originating in their area. They echo suspicions similar to those that all Colorado turned on California before the signing of the Colorado River Compact, namely, a dread that prior appropriation by strongly muscled adversaries can strangle their own hopes of prosperity.

The possibility of profitable development on the Western Slope looms larger now than ever before. The area contains enormous reserves of energy currently locked out of reach in the form of coal and oil shale. Releasing that energy will take large quantities of water, both for the processes themselves and for the new towns that may be built. In addition, the potentials for water-based recreation are high on the Western Slope, and the savants tell us that recreation will become increasingly important as the nation grows increasingly urbanized. But will the necessary water be available beyond the Divide if the momentum of history keeps it flowing east?

My murky crystal ball does not show clear answers. But the examples of the past will inevitably play their part during the discussions and compromises that must precede final decisions about the future welfare of both halves of this mountain-divided state.

14
Interstate River Compacts: Impact on Colorado

*Ival V. Goslin**

I. INTRODUCTION

The first interstate water compacts[1] predated the Constitution itself, originating under the Articles of Confederation.[2] The earliest compacts were interstate agreements dealing with boundary problems, navigation, and fishing rights in interstate waters. Increasing population in the American colonies and competition for agricultural lands, navigation, and fishing privileges led to the negotiation of agreements that permitted these activities to continue under equitable limitations. Recognizing the value of such agreements, the colonists specifically created a "compact clause" in article I, section 10, clause 3, of the Constitution of the United States. The pioneers followed the same pattern.

As large numbers of peoples moved westward in search of economic and social opportunities, problems moved with them. When the number of people in a given area increased to the point that water resources became short in relation to the demands placed upon them, agreements were negotiated under which the resources could be equitably used by members of society. These agreements between and among sovereign states developed into interstate river compacts.

Today there are 20 major interstate river compacts in the United States that allocate water between and among states. The State of Colorado is a party to nine of them and to three interstate agreements that can be designated as subcompacts inasmuch as they are important segments of one of the nine major compacts.[3] A quick review of the geography of the area and history of water development in Colorado illustrates the importance of these compacts to the state.

---

* B.S., Utah State University; B.A., M.A., University of Utah. Mr. Goslin has been the Executive Director of the Upper Colorado River Commission since 1955.
1. WEBSTER'S THIRD NEW INTERNATIONAL DICTIONARY (unabridged 1961) defines a compact as "an interstate agreement entered into to handle a particular problem or task."
2. J. MUYS, INTERSTATE WATER COMPACTS 5 (1971) (NTIS 202 998).
3. A chronological list of water allocation compacts and subcompacts involving the State of Colorado is found in the appendix to this article.

II. Significant Geography

Geographic and orographic conditions play major roles in the distribution and amounts of precipitation that fall upon Colorado. The location and arrangement of the mountains and valleys through their influence upon air movements determine to a great extent the nature of the runoff of the various stream systems. Precipitation varies annually from 40-50 inches on the high mountain ranges to about 8-10 inches in the more arid regions of the state.

Water has acted as an important catalyst for both agriculture and industry in the economic development of Colorado from the time the first white settlers arrived. As in most western states, the distribution of population shows no direct correlation to the availability of surface water. As an example, about two-thirds of the Colorado people live within the South Platte River basin that produces less than 10 percent of the state's average annual surface water. The Colorado River Basin contains about 10 percent of the population, but its average annual surface runoff comprises about 70 percent of the total.

Colorado, in relation to its neighboring states, is a high-altitude region having in excess of 50 mountain peaks reaching over 14,000 feet. Reference is often made to Colorado as the "roof of the nation." Five major stream systems, the Arkansas, Colorado, Platte, and Republican Rivers, and the Rio Grande, deliver water to nine other states under compact terms.[4] Thus, despite its arid regions, Colorado is a water-producing state from the standpoint that precipitation falls upon it, and much of the runoff flows beyond its borders.[5]

III. A Capsule of Early Colorado Water History

Construction of the earliest recorded continuous water development by white settlers was started as early as 1852 on

---

4. Arizona, California, Kansas, Nebraska, Nevada, New Mexico, Texas, Utah, and Wyoming.

5. An interesting statement in United States Bureau of Reclamation & Colorado Dep't of Natural Resources, Water For Tomorrow, Colorado State Water Plan 2-14 (1974), says:

> With few exceptions, waters originating in other states are not available for use in Colorado. On the other hand, all the surface flows of the State, except natural losses, are available by gravity to 18 other states.

This statement appears to be a slight exaggeration of the actual facts, but it does indicate the nature of the problem.

the People's Ditch, a diversion from the Rio Grande in the San Luis Valley in southeastern Colorado. This ditch has been used since its completion and has the earliest decreed priority (1852) in Colorado. About this same time other water developments were initiated, the largest of which was on the Purgatory River near Trinidad.

In the 1860s and 1870s many new immigrants constructed more extensive irrigation facilities in the valleys of the Rio Grande, Purgatory, and South Platte Rivers. Irrigation development was very rapid, especially in the warmer climate of southern Colorado where by 1864 in the Purgatory River basin the summer base flows were completely appropriated.

Later in the 19th century and in the early years of the 20th century larger irrigation systems were constructed in the Rio Grande Valley and in the South Platte, Arkansas, and Colorado River basins. Where it has been physically and economically possible these irrigation enterprises have been expanded. Irrigation systems in these basins still constitute the foundation for a substantial portion of the economy of the state.

It should not be overlooked that some of the earliest water usage in Colorado was for mining and mineral processing. Exportation of water from the West Slope to eastern Colorado commenced in 1880 when the small Ewing Ditch for placer mining was constructed from the headwaters of the Eagle River to the Arkansas River watershed. Today 25 transmountain diversions transport approximately one-half million acre-feet of Colorado River system water per year to eastern Colorado for domestic, municipal, agricultural, electric energy generation, and industrial purposes.

Since 1900 settlement of the West has been very rapid. Passage by the Congress of the Reclamation Act in 1902, together with the increasing demands for more lands for agricultural and industrial expansion, accelerated the development of water resources and hydroelectric energy generation.

IV. NEED FOR INTERSTATE RIVER AGREEMENTS

Colorado and her sister states became deeply involved in the western migrations of people. Conditions were right for settlement, for acquisition of mineral and agricultural lands, and for the development of the related water resources with the blessing and encouragement of federal and state governments. Water supplies of western streams at first appeared to be limitless. By the beginning of the 20th century it was realized that the water supplies of these same streams were far from ample in proportion to the other natural resources—such as land, minerals, oil, and gas—that required water for their exploitation and processing.

With the State of Colorado as a nucleus at the headwaters of important water sources, formal legal processes evolved from pressures of increasing populations claiming the use of more and more waters from streams that flowed by gravity to other states.

Aside from the unique position of Colorado at the "roof of the nation," Colorado also found herself in a vulnerable political situation with respect to other states using water from the same river systems. Colorado officials soon became aware of the fact that water users in these other states were staking claims to the consumptive use of large quantities of water from what they believed should be Colorado rivers. There was real apprehension that these claims might develop into permanent legal rights under the doctrine of prior appropriation. There was some irony in the situation, too, because this doctrine, also known as the "Colorado doctrine," had been perfected in Colorado in earlier days to establish valid water rights for mining enterprises.

It was inevitable that the requirements for more and more water would collide with the limited supply. This collision led to disagreements among users of waters of interstate streams and, consequently, to actual or potential disputes between and among states. The result had to be either interstate litigation, an adversary approach, or use of the interstate compact, a cooperative, constitutionally approved approach through mutual understandings of the disputants.[6] Colorado has been a leader with respect to both approaches in the field of water resources.

V. STATE OF COLORADO—INTERSTATE RIVER COMPACTS

Compacts were not generally used for the apportionment

---

6. U.S. CONST. art. I, §10, clause 3 provides:
   No State shall, without the consent of Congress . . . enter into any agreement or compact with another State or with a foreign power.

of water between and among states until 1922. With Colorado as one of the paramount leaders, the Colorado River Compact of 1922 was negotiated by commissioners representing the seven states of the Colorado River Basin—Arizona, California, Colorado, Nevada, New Mexico, Utah, and Wyoming — and a federal representative, Mr. Herbert Hoover. Among the various factors that precipitated action on the part of Colorado and her neighboring upstream states, the following appear to have had a major influence:

(a) In 1907 the Supreme Court had encouraged the use of interstate agreement or litigation in the settlement of a dispute between Colorado and Kansas involving the Arkansas River.[7]

(b) The other states of the basin had for years viewed with trepidation the apparent efforts of California to dominate water usage from the Colorado River. In August 1920 the League of the Southwest, an organization for the promotion of western development, adopted a resolution stating that the rights of the Colorado River Basin states and of the United States should be settled and determined by compact. By January 1922 each of the seven states and the United States had appointed commissioners to negotiate an agreement. Simultaneously, California was pressing Congress vigorously for authorization of construction of a federally-financed regulating reservoir on the lower reaches of the river to provide flood control, electric power, and irrigation benefits.

(c) In June 1922 the U.S. Supreme Court handed down its decision in *Wyoming v. Colorado*,[8] which upheld the doctrine of prior appropriation of water without regard to state lines. The final negotiation of the compact took place in the atmosphere created by the Court's decision.

---

7. In Kansas v. Colorado, 206 U.S. 46, 97 (1907) the Supreme Court said:
   As Congress cannot make compacts between the States, as it cannot, in respect to certain matters, by legislation compel their separate action, disputes between them must be settled either by force or else by appeal to tribunals empowered to determine the right and wrong thereof.

8. In Wyoming v. Colorado, 259 U.S. 419, 496 (1922), the Supreme Court, in its opinion, said:
   As the available supply is 288,000 acre-feet and the amount covered by senior appropriations in Wyoming is 272,500 acre-feet, there remain 15,500 acre-feet which are subject to this junior appropriation in Colorado.

The decision in *Wyoming v. Colorado* confirmed the fears of Colorado and the other states of the Colorado River Basin that the already rapidly growing State of California was in an opportune position to appropriate the lion's share of Colorado River waters. The upriver states openly opposed the construction of storage or diversion works on the lower reach of the river that would place that area in a position to monopolize the use of the waters through prior appropriation. Delph E. Carpenter, Commissioner for the State of Colorado, effectively summarized the situation:

> The upper state has but one alternative, that of using every means to retard development in the lower state until the uses within the upper state have reached their maximum. The states may avoid this unfortunate situation by determining their respective rights by interstate compact before further development in either state, thus permitting freedom of development in the lower state without injury to future growth in the upper.[9]

The decision in *Wyoming v. Colorado* became the stimulus which consummated the Colorado River Compact, signed on November 24, 1922.

A. *Colorado River Compact*[10]

In the 1920s, laws with respect to rights to use water from interstate streams were not firmly established. Each state claimed the exclusive authority to regulate the appropriation of all water within its borders. The federal government claimed jurisdiction of interstate streams. The lower reach of the Colorado River was considered navigable and subject to federal laws. At the same time people of the Southwest were promoting the idea that there should be federal financing of the construction of a large multiple-purpose water development in the lower basin, principally for the benefit of California.

If a stalemate of long duration were to be avoided, some type of agreement allocating the use of the river's waters among the seven basin states was necessary. The lower basin states wanted an interstate agreement because they needed the political support of the upper basin states for passage of authorizing

---

9. R. WILBUR & N. ELY, THE HOOVER DAM DOCUMENTS, H.R. DOC. No. 717, 80th Cong., 2d Sess. A84 (1948).

10. Colorado River Compact, Pub. L. No. 70-642, §§12-19, 43 Stat. 1057 (1928) (signed by the States 24 Nov. 1922) [hereinafter Colorado River Compact].

legislation by the Congress. The upper basin states, like Colorado, favored a compact in order to protect their deferred water use against prior appropriations in the lower basin.

The State of Colorado's main concern was to effectuate an equitable apportionment of the waters of the Colorado River system in perpetuity in order to assure that, in the future when it was needed, her water resource development would not be impaired or precluded. The purpose of the Colorado River Compact, as stated in Article I, adequately expresses the objectives being sought and has become representative of similar statements of purpose in other compacts that followed.

ARTICLE I

The major purposes of this compact are to provide for the equitable division and apportionment of the use of the waters of the Colorado River System; to establish the relative importance of different beneficial uses of water; to promote interstate comity; to remove causes of present and future controversies; and to secure the expeditious agricultural and industrial development of the Colorado River Basin, the storage of its waters, and the protection of life and property from floods. To these ends the Colorado River Basin is divided into two Basins, and an apportionment of the use of part of the water of the Colorado River System is made to each of them with the provision that further equitable apportionments may be made.

The Colorado River Compact is regarded as the grandfather of water allocation compacts in the United States. Among some of its more important provisions are the following:

1. The Colorado River Basin was divided into two subbasins—the upper basin and the lower basin—with the line of demarcation located at Lee Ferry, Arizona, which was defined as a point one mile below the mouth of the Paria River which is located a few miles south of the Utah-Arizona boundary. Here the waters of the entire upper basin system, including the Paria River and return flows from the upper basin projects, converge into one stream.

2. The annual beneficial consumptive use of 7,500,000 acre-feet of water was apportioned to each subbasin—to the upper basin and to the lower basin—with the lower basin granted the right to consumptively use another million acre-feet annually if it is available.

3. States of the basin were aligned into two divisions. The states of the upper division include Colorado, New Mexico, Utah, and Wyoming; the states of the lower division are Arizona, California, and Nevada.

4. Rights of Mexico to use water under a future treaty were recognized.

5. The states of the upper division are not to cause the flow of the Colorado River at Lee Ferry to be less than 75,000,000 acre-feet in any period of ten consecutive years.

6. The Colorado River Basin is defined to include "all of the drainage area of the Colorado River system and all other territory within the United States of America to which the waters of the Colorado River System shall be beneficially applied."

7. A term which is very important to the State of Colorado is, "Colorado River System," which means "that portion of the Colorado River and its tributaries within the United States of America."

8. The Compact negotiators, believing they were dividing the use of only a part of the river's flow, provided that at any time after October 1, 1963, if and when either basin had reached its total consumptive use as apportioned, the use of the remaining waters could be further apportioned between the two basins.

9. The Colorado was recognized as a navigable river, but "the use of its waters for purposes of navigation shall be subservient to the uses of such waters for domestic, agricultural, and power purposes."

10. Consumption of water for agricultural and domestic purposes was made dominant over impoundment and use of water for generation of electric energy.

11. Each state was permited to regulate and control the appropriation, use, and distribution of water within its boundaries, subject to other provisions of the Compact.

12. The Compact may be terminated at any time by the unanimous agreement of the signatory states,

but all rights established under it shall be perpetu-
ated.

13. The compact is not to be construed as affecting
the obligations of the federal government to the
Indian tribes.

It should be noted that water quality is not mentioned in
the Colorado River Compact. Also, the apportionments of
water are to two defined subbasins and not to individual states.

B. *La Plata River Compact*[11]

Colorado and New Mexico executed this Compact in 1922
to provide for the division of waters of the La Plata River. An
allocation formula limits the use of water by each state on the
basis of magnitudes of the streamflow during specified periods
of time. Rotation of the use of the waters between the two
states during low flow periods is permitted if the respective
state engineers concur that the most beneficial use of the waters can be accomplished in this manner.

C. *South Platte River Compact*[12]

This Compact between Colorado and Nebraska divides the
waters of the South Platte River. During certain periods, such
as from October 15 to April 1, Colorado has full use of the
waters of the South Platte River within Colorado with Nebraska entitled to divert surplus waters under certain conditions. Between April 1 and October 15, if the flow at the state
line is less than 120 cubic feet per second, Colorado cannot
permit diversions from the lower reaches of the river to water
users whose dates of priority are later than June 14, 1897.

D. *Rio Grande Compact*[13]

The Rio Grande Compact involves apportionments of the
waters of the Rio Grande among three states: Colorado, New
Mexico, and Texas. Colorado's obligation to deliver water at
the New Mexico state line is based on runoff measurements at
four "index" stream-gauging stations on the headwater

---

11. La Plata River Compact, Pub. L. No. 68-346, 43 Stat. 796 (1925) (signed by
the States 27 Nov. 1922).

12. South Platte River Compact, Pub. L. No. 69-37, 44 Stat. 195 (1926) (signed
by the States 27 Apr. 1923).

13. Rio Grande Compact, Pub. L. No. 76-96, 53 Stat. 785 (1939) (signed by the
States 18 Mar. 1938).

streams. This Compact includes schedules of required deliveries of water, for an accrual system of debits and credits in annual deliveries, and control of reservoir storage waters.

This Compact has a water quality element in it. If water is delivered from the closed basin portion of the San Luis Valley after 1937, Colorado shall not be credited with the amount of such water delivered, unless the proportion of sodium ions is less than 45 percent of the total positive ions when the salinity concentration exceeds 350 parts per million.

E. *Republican River Compact*[14]

Colorado, Kansas, and Nebraska negotiated this Compact apportioning the waters of the Republican River and its tributaries.

The State of Colorado's share of the water amounts to 43,100 acre-feet per year based upon the average virgin flow[15] from six specified tributaries of the Republican River. Provision is also made for adjusting the allocations if the computed virgin flow for a given year varies more than ten percent from the average annual virgin flow.

F. *Upper Colorado River Basin Compact*[16]

The federal government informed the states of the Colorado River Basin that no water development projects could be constructed in those states until the states had agreed upon their respective rights to deplete the water supply of the Colorado River, or the courts had apportioned available water among them.[17] The five states (Arizona, Colorado, New Mexico, Utah, and Wyoming) having interests in the upper basin negotiated and executed the Upper Colorado River Basin Compact in 1948. After each state's legislature had ratified this Compact, Congress gave its consent to it in 1949. The consumptive use of water apportioned to the upper basin by the Colorado River Compact of 1922[18] was allocated on an annual

---

14. Republican River Compact, Pub. L. No. 78-60, 57 Stat. 86 (1943) (signed by the States 31 Dec. 1942).

15. "Virgin flow" is the flow of a stream undepleted by the activities of man.

16. Upper Colorado River Basin Compact, Pub. L. No. 81-37, 63 Stat. 31 (1949) (signed by the States 11 Oct. 1948) [hereinafter Upper Colorado River Basin Compact].

17. Letter from the Director, Bureau of the Budget to the Secretary of the Interior, H.R. Doc. No. 419, 80th Cong., 1st Sess. (1947).

18. Colorado River Compact, art. III.

basis by the Upper Colorado River Basin Compact to the upper basin states as follows:[19]

| Arizona | 50,000 acre-feet |

and of the remainder:

Colorado	51.75 percent
New Mexico	11.25 percent
Utah	23.00 percent
Wyoming	14.00 percent

The Compact created the Upper Colorado River Commission as an administrative agency for the four upper division states: Colorado, New Mexico, Utah, and Wyoming. Arizona with its fixed amount of consumptive use of water and minor interests in the upper basin is not a member of the Commission. The President appoints a federal representative who has the same vote as each state's commissioner and who serves as chairman. Rules and regulations are described under which the Commission can order curtailment of water uses within a state or states when deemed necessary to meet delivery requirements by the upper division states to the lower basin under the terms of the Colorado River Compact. Three agreements or subcompacts between Colorado and other signatory states[20] pertaining to the use of water of interstate tributaries are included within the Compact. Recognition is given and more definitive terms are applied to the La Plata River Compact of 1922.[21] Consumptive use of water in the upper basin and in each state thereof is to be measured in terms of manmade depletions of the virgin flow of the Colorado River at Lee Ferry[22] instead of by the method of diversions of water minus return flows as used in other portions of the basin.

---

19. Upper Colorado River Basin Compact, art. III.

20. Subcompacts within the Upper Colorado River Basin Compact are: Little Snake River (art. XI) between Colorado and Wyoming; Yampa River (art. XIII) between Colorado and Utah; and San Juan River (art. XIV) between Colorado and New Mexico.

21. Upper Colorado River Basin Compact, art. X.

22. Upper Colorado River Basin Compact, art. II(e) states that Lee Ferry means a point in the Colorado River one mile below the mouth of the Paria River. This point is about 13 miles downstream from the Utah-Arizona state line and is the division point between the Upper and Lower Basins.

G. *Arkansas River Compact*[23]

The Arkansas River Compact provides operating criteria for John Martin Reservoir constructed by the Corps of Engineers in 1943. The Compact provides that during the winter storage season (November 1 - March 31) Colorado may demand releases of water from the reservoir equivalent to the river flow but not to exceed 100 cubic feet per second.

During the summer (April 1 - October 31) Colorado may demand releases of storage water equivalent to the river flow up to 500 cubic feet per second. Kansas may demand releases of water equal to the portion of the river flow between 500 and 750 cubic feet per second. Storage water may be released upon demand of both states concurrently or separately in amounts depending upon the amount of stored water available. Under concurrent demands Colorado is entitled to 60 percent of the water released, and Kansas 40 percent.

H. *Costilla Creek Compact*[24]

This Compact negotiated by Colorado and New Mexico apportions the waters of Costilla Creek, a tributary of the Rio Grande which traverses the state line three times before entering the Rio Grande in New Mexico. Allocations are also made of storage water from Costilla and Eastdale Reservoirs.

I. *Animas - La Plata Project Compact*[25]

This document establishes the priority of New Mexico users of water from the Animas - La Plata Project (if and when it is constructed) as equal to the priority of Colorado water users who will receive water from the project. The Compact was deemed necessary by Colorado and New Mexico to clarify the relationship between potential Colorado and New Mexico water users.

VI. EFFECTS OF INTERSTATE RIVER COMPACTS ON THE STATE

A. *Impacts on Water Supply*

In analyzing the effects of interstate river compacts upon the State of Colorado, the first question that presents itself is,

---

23. Arkansas River Compact, Pub. L. No. 81-82, 63 Stat. 145 (1949) (signed by the States 14 Dec. 1948).

24. Amended Costilla Creek Compact, Pub. L. No. 88-198, 77 Stat. 350 (1963) (original signed by the States 30 Sept. 1944).

25. Animas - La Plata Project Compact, Pub. L. No. 90-537, §501(c), 82 Stat. 885, 898 (1968).

"How has the ultimate water supply of the state been affected?" Table 1 illustrates the effects on the state in quantities of water committed to other states in relation to the total water supply available in Colorado from five major river systems.

Table 1 shows that Colorado is using an average of about 5.6 million acre-feet per year of a total of 15.6 million acre-feet of water produced. Colorado will be able to increase its use about 1 million acre-feet to a total of about 6.6 million acre-feet per year for the state as a whole, or about 42 percent of the produced water supply. Colorado is furnishing nearly 8.8 million acre-feet of water to sources outside the state to meet compact commitments.

TABLE 1

*Colorado — Surface Water Supply
and Use Within Colorado*[26]

River System	Surface Water Supply	Import	Use (1975)	Compact Commitments	Remainder Available **
Arkansas	.88	.16	.84	.05	.15
Colorado	10.74	0	2.15	7.75	.84
Platte	2.04	.34	1.66	.52	.20
Republican	.35	0	.23	.12	0
Rio Grande	1.58	0	1.26	.32	0
Total	15.59	.50*	6.14	8.76	1.19

*This item also counted as a depletion in Colorado River Basin. Actual use by State of Colarado = 6.14 − .50 = 5.64.

**State + Import — Use — Compact Commitments = Remainder Available.

Table 1 also shows that the drainage basins in Colorado, excluding the Colorado River Basin, produce a total of 4.85 million acre-feet of water per year of which Colorado uses 3.99 million. Compact commitments to the other states amount to 1.01 million acre-feet per year of which 860,000 acre-feet per year are being used. The remaining 350,000 acre-feet are still

---

26. Adapted from Table VI-11 of U.S. DEP'T OF THE INTERIOR, CRITICAL WATER PROBLEMS OF THE ELEVEN WESTERN STATES 261 (1975).

available at the state boundary. The compacts pertaining to these drainage areas, insofar as protection of Colorado's right to use water therefrom, have been a distinct advantage to the State of Colorado which is using 82 percent of the water originating in the state.

In the Colorado River Basin over 70 percent of the virgin flow of the river, as measured at Lee Ferry, originates within the State of Colorado.[27] According to Table 1 about 72 percent of this supply is allocated by compacts to be used in other states.

B. *Administrative Impacts*

Administration of compacts by Colorado officials to implement the expressed purposes of the compacts, including the delivery of waters allocated, have at times presented problems of varying complexity to the state. These problems are usually unique to a given river basin and compact. Therefore, a brief mention of a few problems facing the state will be made.

1. La Plata River Compact

On some occasions the flow of the La Plata River is so low that under the 50-50 compact split of the waters between Colorado and New Mexico neither state can receive a usable supply. In order to alleviate this situation the states agreed to adopt a system of rotation of the streamflow between the water users of the two states. In recent years a problem of maintaining an agreeable rotation system has developed. The ultimate impact of this problem on the state is unknown, and a solution is yet to be attained.

2. South Platte River Compact

Presently Colorado is planning to construct the Narrows Reservoir near Fort Morgan. Although Nebraska has not yet formally complained about this potential reservoir, officials of that state are reported to be investigating the possible effects upon Nebraska water users. Under present conditions during the non-irrigation season, a large quantity of water flows in the South Platte River from Colorado into Nebraska. Also a large

---

27. *Final Report, Engineering Advisory Comm. to Upper Colorado River Basin Compact Comm'n,* in 3 Official Record of Negotiations of Upper Colorado River Basin Compact (1948). Lee Ferry is the point of delivery of water to the Lower Basin under the Colorado River Compact.

number of irrigation pumping wells have been drilled in Colorado in the river basin since execution of the Compact in 1923. There is reason to speculate that the storage of water in the Narrows Reservoir may not only affect the amount of water delivered to Nebraska but may also affect pumping from wells and diversions of water made in Colorado after the date of the Compact. Officials of the State of Colorado will need to watch this situation carefully in order to assure compliance with the South Platte River Compact.

3. Rio Grande Compact

The Rio Grande Compact has been a bone of contention among Colorado, New Mexico, and Texas for about 20 years, principally because Colorado failed on many occasions to deliver sufficient quantities of water at the New Mexico state line. The deficits in deliveries finally became of sufficient magnitude that Texas entered a lawsuit in the U.S. Supreme Court against Colorado in an endeavor to force Colorado to meet its obligations under the Rio Grande Compact.[28] The Supreme Court in 1967 granted leave to Texas to file a complaint. New Mexico intervened in the case on the side of Texas.[29] In 1968 the Court issued a continuance order. As long as Colorado meets its annual Compact water delivery commitment at the state line each year, the case will remain in abeyance. Meanwhile, an administrative solution is being developed.

Colorado has had to enforce the curtailment of the use of water by irrigators in the San Luis Valley in recent years in order to meet the Compact commitment. The state has also sponsored the construction of the Closed Basin Project in the San Luis Valley as a federal reclamation project to make possible the continuance of irrigation in Colorado and at the same time deliver the required amounts of water to New Mexico and Texas.

The restrictions of the Rio Grande Compact have caused serious impacts on the development and economy of the local area and the state.

---

28. Texas v. Colorado, 389 U.S. 1000 (1967), *continuance granted,* 391 U.S. 901 (1968).

29. Kansas v. Colorado, 185 U.S. 125 (1902); Kansas v. Colorado, 206 U.S. 46 (1907); and Colorado v. Kansas, 320 U.S. 383 (1943).

4. Republican River Compact

Colorado law treats underground water in the same manner as surface water, *i.e.,* as being a part of the total supply of a river basin. If the pumping of water from this basin in Colorado increases to such an extent that deliveries of water to Kansas are affected, Kansas will undoubtedly object.

5. Arkansas River Compact

Prior to the Arkansas River Compact of 1948 the use of the waters of the Arkansas River was a subject of litigation between Colorado and Kansas in at least three different legal proceedings.[29] There have been continuing problems with the administration of the interstate Compact. Although Kansas was given the right to 40 percent of the water stored in John Martin Reservoir, there are times when Kansas' share of the water does not arrive at the state line. There is also a problem related to a large number of irrigation wells in Colorado that are depleting the groundwater and thus contributing to the overall problem of compact administration.

6. Costilla Creek Compact

Problems with administration of this compact have been minor.

7. Animas - La Plata Project Compact

The Animas - La Plata Project, which was authorized by the Congress in 1968,[30] has not been constructed. Therefore, this Compact has not been put into effect.

8. Colorado River Compact

The Colorado River Compact does not provide for a permanent administrative agency. There are two articles in the document that indicate that a certain amount of administration was anticipated. For instance, the Compact specifies that the chief official of each state charged with the administration of water rights, together with the Director of the U.S. Reclamation Service and the Director of the U.S. Geological Survey shall cooperate, *ex officio,* to determine and coordinate facts relating to water supply and consumption, publish a record of annual flows of the Colorado River at Lee Ferry, and perform

---

30. Colorado River Basin Project Act, Pub. L. No. 90-537, 82 Stat. 885 (1968).

such other duties as may be assigned by mutual consent of the seven basin states.[31]

The Compact also provides that if any claim or controversy arises between any of the signatory states, the governors of the states affected, upon the request of one of them, shall appoint commissioners with power to consider and adjust such claim or controversy, subject to ratification by the legislatures of the affected states.[32] This provision of the Compact has never been invoked. The 1964 decision of the U.S. Supreme Court in the fourth *Arizona v. California*[33] lawsuit requires the Secretary of the Interior to act as water master or administrator for operation of the lower main stem of the Colorado River for deliveries of water to Arizona, California, and Nevada.

9.   Upper Colorado River Basin Compact

Unlike any of the other river agreements to which the State of Colorado is a party, this Compact created an interstate agency known as the Upper Colorado River Commission to administer the Upper Colorado River Basin Compact.[34] The Commission is composed of one commissioner appointed by each state and one commissioner appointed by the President to represent the United States of America. The Commission is charged with certain well-defined powers and duties, among them that of making findings as to the necessity for and the extent of curtailment of use of water by each of its member states in the event such curtailment becomes necessary, in order to maintain the river flow to the lower basin in compliance with Article III of the Colorado River Compact.[35] Due to the fact that none of the member states of the Commission have used their full apportionments of water it has not been

---

31. Colorado River Compact, art. V. The present Commissioner of the U.S. Bureau of Reclamation is the successor to the Director of the U.S. Reclamation Service.

32. Colorado River Compact, art. VI.

33. Arizona v. California, 373 U.S. 546 (1963).

34. Upper Colorado River Basin Compact, art. VIII.

35. Upper Colorado River Basin Compact, arts. IV & VIII(8). Under art. III(c), (d) of the Colorado River Compact the Upper Division States, which are the same as the member states of the Upper Colorado River Commission, are required to: (a) deliver at Lee Ferry water to supply their obligation under the Mexican Treaty, whatever that may be determined to be by some future Supreme Court decision; and (b) to not cause the flow of the river at Lee Ferry to be depleted below an aggregate of 75 million acre-feet for any period of 10 consecutive years.

necessary to invoke this power of the Commission.

VII. Protection of Colorado's Rights to Use Waters of Interstate Streams

Although there have been administrative problems, compacts have been beneficial to Colorado in protecting the use of interstate waters against prior appropriation and use in other states. This beneficial impact far outweighs any administrative problems that have been encountered, some of which have been caused by Colorado water users themselves combined with poor administration of water rights within the state. The Rio Grande situation is an example of this point. The pending *Texas v. Colorado* lawsuit can be regarded as an outgrowth of the Rio Grande Compact. It certainly was not caused by the Compact itself, but by the failure of Colorado to meet its commitments thereunder.

Certainly, there are other related benefits from water-use compacts to the State of Colorado. Some of the compacts, notably the Upper Colorado River Basin Compact, made possible the construction of a number of water development projects that otherwise would have had to be foregone. This Compact also led to close interstate cooperation in promoting Congressional legislation to authorize the Colorado River Storage Project and participating projects of which Colorado is a major beneficiary.[36] The allocation of water resources by means of amicable mutual agreements has saved much time and energy through the avoidance of litigation. Compacts have defined the respective rights of all parties to the use of water, have resolved mutual interstate difficulties, and bound Colorado and her neighbors together with regional development ties.

The federal government with its vast resources on public lands and its deep interest in water resource development has been effectively kept within reasonable bounds in its pursuit of dominance by Colorado's interstate compacts. Most federal agencies seem to feel a moral obligation to stay within the limits of interstate river compacts to which the Congress has given its approval. In fact, federal-state cooperation has led to the development of a large portion of Colorado's compact-allocated water supplies.

---

36. Colorado River Storage Project Act, 43 U.S.C. § 620 (1970).

VIII.   SPECIAL PROBLEMS FOR COLORADO UNDER THE COLORADO
RIVER COMPACT

A. *Litigation*

The existence of interstate river compacts has not always been used to the benefit of Colorado, especially in the political arena. In spite of the fine language utilized by capable negotiators in the past in writing compacts, they are susceptible to different interpretations by different parties under different political situations at a later time. This is especially true if all of the facts are not at the disposal of the compact negotiators. An excellent example of a compact in this category is the Colorado River Compact.

In 1922 when the Compact was being negotiated, it appeared that the annual average virgin flow of the Colorado River at Lee Ferry was about 17 million acre-feet. Data collected during the last 54 years indicate that this average annual virgin flow may be less than 14 million acre-feet. Based upon the 1922 assumption as to water supply, the negotiators wrote into the Compact the provision that the upper states should not deplete the flow at Lee Ferry below 75 million acre-feet for each period of ten consecutive years.[37] Obviously with annual allocations totaling 17.5 million acre-feet (1.5 million to Mexico,[38] 8.5 million to the lower basin, and 7.5 million to the upper basin[39]) some allocations cannot be met.

In the 1950s California knew about this shortage. California bitterly opposed the Congressional authorization of water development projects in the Upper Colorado River Basin for the benefit of Colorado and her sister states on the grounds that there was insufficient water in the river, and that the upper basin should bear all of the shortage in water supply under the compact allocation.[40]

Arizona interprets the Compact in such a way that Colorado and the other upstream states would be charged with all

37. Colorado River Compact, art. III(d).

38. Mexican Water Treaty, 59 Stat. 1219, T.S. No. 994 (1944).

39. Colorado River Compact, art. III(a), (b).

40. *See Hearings on S. 1555,* 83d Cong., 2d Sess. (1954); *Hearings on H.R. 270, 2836, 3383, 3384, 4488, & S.500,* 84th Cong., 1st Sess. (1955) (Bills to authorize the Secretary of the Interior to construct, operate, and maintain the Colorado River Storage Project and participating projects).

of the shortage in water supply plus the delivery of one-half of the United States annual water obligation to Mexico (not one-half of any deficiency) plus losses in the river to deliver one-half of the Mexican water delivery.[41] The Secretary of the Interior, although he denies he is interpreting the compacts, in his calculations of available water supply assumes that Colorado and her sister upper division states should bear the shortage and deliver to the lower basin an amount equal to one-half the entire United States annual water delivery to Mexico in addition to 7.5 million acre-feet per year (1/10 of 75,000,000 under Article III (d) of the Compact). The effect of these interpretations, according to the Secretary of the Interior, is to leave 5.8 million acre-feet of water for annual consumption by Colorado, New Mexico, Utah, and Wyoming.[42] This arbitrary method of calculation reduces the water available to Colorado under the Compact from 3.8 to 2.98 million acre-feet per year—a reduction of 23 percent of the amount intended for Colorado when the Compact was executed in 1922.

Arizona also contends that the waters of the Gila River which flow through parts of New Mexico and Arizona are not included under the Colorado River Compact water apportionments, although those apportionments are made from the Colorado River system which is defined by the Compact to include the Colorado River and all of its tributaries within the United States.

The State of Colorado is strongly opposed to the above interpretations of the Compact and the actions of the Secretary of the Interior in his decisions affecting the river which result in an inequitable distribution of the benefits. These issues will

---

41. W. Steiner, Water for Energy as Related to Water Rights in the Colorado River Basin, May 1975 (presented at the Conference on Water Requirements for Lower Colorado River Basin Energy Needs, University of Arizona). *See also* Weatherford & Jacoby, *Impact of Energy Development on the Law of the Colorado River,* 15 NATURAL RESOURCES J. 171 (1975).

42. U.S. DEP'T OF THE INTERIOR, CRITICAL WATER PROBLEMS OF THE ELEVEN WESTERN STATES (1975). The Governor of Arizona apparently believes that the Secretary of the Interior does interpret the compacts in arriving at 5.8 million acre-feet per year for the Upper Basin. Thus, the Governor has written:

The 5.8 m.a.f. is supportable by interpretation of Compacts and was derived on the basis of an interpretation. It may not be the final or right interpretation, but it is an interpretation.

Letter from Governor of Arizona to Secretary of the Interior, 7 Aug. 1974.

have to be settled by the U.S. Supreme Court. At the present time there is no other alternative that can be reasonably anticipated. Because of the basic differences in philosophy among involved parties there is no chance of seeking a more equitable apportionment of water through renegotiation of the Colorado River Compact.

The issues involving inclusion of the Gila River under the compact, the determination of the upper and lower basins' shares of the Mexican Treaty burden, equitable distribution of the water storage, consumptive use, and energy generation benefits are all interrelated. They are also of great importance in the determination of the course of Colorado's future water development and related resources conservation program, especially as related to social and economic values.

B. *Water Quality*

The Environmental Protection Agency under the Federal Water Pollution Control Act Amendments of 1972[43] has declared that salinity in the Colorado River system is a form of pollution, and therefore falls under its jurisdiction.

On other river systems where the administration of the use of the waters is not under the terms of interstate river compacts, the attitude of the Environmental Protection Agency has been that a part of the water resource, including water from reservoirs constructed for other purposes could be released under edict of the federal government for dilution purposes to enhance water quality. When the EPA and its predecessor agencies first became active on the Colorado River this concept was also expressed. To anyone who has been closely associated with the salinity problem, it is apparent that the presence of the Colorado River Compact and the Upper Colorado River Basin Compact, combined with the close political unity of the seven basin states concerning this problem, caused the EPA to look at it in a more reasonable light. In fact, the EPA cooperated fully to the extent possible under the law with the seven basin states in seeking a completely different kind of solution to the salinity problem, a solution that was acceptable to both the states' and federal interests. The result was a cooperative

---

43. Federal Water Pollution Control Act Amendments, 33 U.S.C. §§1251 *et seq.* (Supp. III, 1973).

effort by the states to sponsor the passage of legislation[44] by the Congress that should cause the salt concentration in lower reaches of the river to become no worse that it was in 1972, *if the authorized salinity control measures are effective.* The states, also with the cooperation of the Environmental Protection Agency and the Department of the Interior, established salinity criteria at several points on the main stem of the river, as required under the Federal Water Pollution Control Act Amendments, and adopted a plan of implementation to meet those criteria.[45]

The two Colorado River compacts aided in reaching a solution to the salinity problem that will have far less adverse social and economic impacts on the State of Colorado than would a solution involving the use of large quantities of high quality water for dilution purposes to improve water quality in downstream states. Representatives of the EPA in the beginning complained that the compacts impaired their ability to accomplish the purposes of the water pollution laws to control and enhance water quality. The important point is that the compacts inhibited the EPA in any designs it may have entertained to revolutionize the entire scheme of river management.

IX. CONCLUSIONS

The State of Colorado has heavily influenced the history and development of the compact concept; compacts are a mutually agreeable means of settling existing water disputes and preventing future controversies over the waters of interstate streams. Colorado, a party to the first interstate water allocation compact in the United States and to a total of nine similar agreements, together with her sister states, has had a great impact on the process of interstate water allocation. Conversely, water compacts to which the state is a party have had and will continue to have their influences on the nature and

---

44. Colorado River Basin Salinity Control Act, Pub. L. No. 93-320, 88 Stat. 266 (1974) (codified in various portions of 43 U.S.C.). It is acknowledged that the negotiation of Minute No. 242 to the International Boundary and Water Commission, United States and Mexico, to settle an impending salinity problem between the two countries, stimulated action and gave impetus to the passage of the Salinity Control Act by the Congress. Title I of the Act also implements Minute No. 242 exclusively for the benefit of Mexico. *See also* 24 U.S.T. 1968, T.I.A.S. 7708 (1973).

45. 41 Fed. Reg. 13656 (1976) (water quality standards for salinity of the Colorado River System, promulgated by the Environmental Protection Agency).

direction of actions of state officials in the future development, conservation, and utilization of the water resources of Colorado. Compact terms have served as parameters for resource development processes.

Officials of the state have done an effective job in preserving the rights of Colorado citizens to use waters of interstate streams. It can be said with respect to river systems with headwaters in Colorado that, without compacts, other states probably would have obtained the permanent rights to use the bulk of interstate waters by prior appropriation due to their more rapid settlement and development. The benefits of this compact protection greatly outweigh the adverse effects of administrative problems that have been created, or the trials and tribulations that will be associated with seeking judicial corrections of inequities through Supreme Court interpretations of the Colorado River Compact. This is not to say that such judicial determinations should not be sought, because they certainly should be whenever inequities are believed to exist and the remedy will be beneficial to the state.

Changes in the overall economy have made possible the great expansion of groundwater pumping in several of Colorado's river basins in recent years. The interweaving of Colorado laws related to groundwater and surface water may lead to future disputes with neighboring states, if extraction of water from wells materially affects the streamflow across state lines. In that event, litigation under the compacts can be expected, and the legal position of Colorado will be tested under compact interpretation.

Although compacts have attained a great stature in the allocation of the use of water resources of interstate streams in the West, they should not be regarded as the means of permanent resolution of all water problems. Many years ago the writer attended a water conference in Colorado at which the century-old East Slope-West Slope controversy over the transmountain diversion of Western Slope Colorado River water to the Eastern Slope was being aired in no uncertain terms. One of the participants facetiously suggested that a permanent settlement of the fight could be attained by dividing Colorado at the Continental Divide, giving the western portion to Utah and the eastern portion to Kansas, and negotiate an interstate streams compact between Utah and Kansas!

In Colorado as well as in other parts of the West, exploitation is gradually being superseded by a sense of conservation. As the ultimate limit of the use of available water resources is approaching it is hoped that interstate water compacts may prove to be effective devices in aiding members of society to live together and make the most of what remains. As the goals and desires of Colorado society change, time may prove that too much rigidity in one or more of the interstate compacts could impair or preclude arriving at the best possible combination of social and economic benefits. Such changes ordinarily do not happen in one state alone. They usually occur on a regional basis. An atmosphere may be created in which trade-offs can be possible. At that point it is hoped that reasonable men will be able to sit around the table and reach interstate agreements that will be as successful as those of the past.

Interstate river compacts notwithstanding, one conclusion seems certain. To paraphrase a noted water authority of the State of Colorado, the final chapter in the continuing struggle over the waters of Colorado's rivers has not yet been written, and may never be.[46]

---

46. F. Sparks, Synopsis of Major Documents and Events Relating to the Colorado River, 20 July 1976 (presented at a symposium sponsored by the Colorado Water Congress and Western State University).

Appendix

INTERSTATE WATER ALLOCATION COMPACTS TO WHICH THE STATE
OF COLORADO IS A PARTY

Colorado River Compact, COLO. REV. STAT. ANN. §§37-61-101 *et seq.* (1973), approved by Congress, Pub. L. No. 70-642, §13, 45 Stat. 1057, 1059 (1928) (signed by the States 24 Nov. 1922). Text may be found at 70 Cong. Rec. 324 (1928).

La Plata River Compact, Pub. L. No. 68-346, 43 Stat. 796 (1925) (signed by the States 27 Nov. 1922).

South Platte River Compact, Pub. L. No. 69-37, 44 Stat. 195 (1926) (signed by the States 27 Apr. 1923).

Rio Grande Compact, Pub. L. No. 76-96, 53 Stat. 785 (1939) (signed by the States 18 Mar. 1938).

Republican River Compact, Pub. L. No. 78-60, 57 Stat. 86 (1943) (signed by the States 31 Dec. 1942).

Upper Colorado River Basin Compact, Pub. L. No. 81-37, 63 Stat. 31 (1949) (signed by the States 11 Oct. 1948).

Arkansas River Compact, Pub. L. No. 81-82, 63 Stat. 145 (1949) (signed by the States 14 Dec. 1948).

Amended Costilla Creek Compact, Pub. L. No. 88-198, 77 Stat. 350 (1963) (original signed by the States 30 Sept. 1944).

Animas-La Plata Project Compact, Pub. L. No. 90-537, §501(c), 82 Stat. 898 (1968).

SUBCOMPACTS

Little Snake River, in Upper Colorado River Basin Compact, Pub. L. No. 81-37, art. XI, 63 Stat. 31 (1949) (signed by the States 11 Oct. 1948).

Yampa River, in Upper Colorado River Basin Compact, Pub. L. No. 81-37, art. XIII, 63 Stat. 31 (1949) (signed by the States 11 Oct. 1948).

San Juan River, in Upper Colorado River Basin Compact, Pub. L. No. 81-37, art. XIV, 63 Stat. 31 (1949) (signed by the States 11 Oct. 1948).

15

Colorado, Water, and Planning for the Future

*Richard D. Lamm**

One of the things that intrigued me when I was at the University of Denver law school and now as Governor is the whole question of natural resources and the way in which we commit those resources. In 1968 my wife and I had the opportunity to view the remains of the ancient civilization of Angkor Vat in Cambodia, and we heard the story of its discovery by a French priest in the 1860s. Angkor Vat was built in incredible proportions; it extended over 50 square miles with various buildings and settlements. As one settlement after another dried up, due to misuse of water resources, they would simply build another city, much as the Mayan and other civilizations of the time did. One of the least understood questions in our civilization is the relationship of natural resources to our standard of living and to our well-being in every way. Let me illustrate.

There is a book, titled *Topsoil and Civilization,* written about twenty years ago, which says that "one man has given a brief outline of history by saying that civilized man has marched about the face of the earth and left a desert in his footprints." This may be an exaggeration, but it is not without foundation. Civilized man has spoiled most of the land upon which he has lived, and this is the main reason why civilizations have moved from place to place. Despoilation of land was the chief cause for the decline of civilizations in older settled regions and is a dominant factor in historical trends. Historians seldom note the importance of the wise use of resources; they seem not to recognize that land and resource use may determine the destinies of empires and civilizations. Most historians point out that many wars and colonial movements began because someone wanted more land, but they fail to note that conquerors often ruined their own land prior to seizing that of their neighbors. Current historians know that the strong and wealthy nations of today are those with abundant natural resources, but they often forget that many poor and weak nations

---

* Governor, State of Colorado; former Professor of Law, University of Denver College of Law.

were once similarly blessed. Some of the poor people on this earth are poor because their ancestors wasted the natural resources upon which present generations must live.

It is apparent that one of the major issues facing the United States, the West, and Colorado is the question of how we use our land, our water, and our natural resources and how we are inextricably tied to the natural resource base of the world. One of the pressures on the West comes from the energy crisis and the increasing number of resource cartels in many valuable minerals or materials upon which the United States depends. The cartel list is a long one. There are 12 OPEC nations. Seven countries have formed a bauxite cartel with great success and have increased the price of bauxite by a factor of seven. Six nations have formed a semi-successful phosphate cartel. Four countries have banded together on copper. Tin or other natural resource cartels may be formed. The same thing is happening with coffee and bananas, and we may be seeing a whole new chapter in world history, where, in the wink of an historical eye, the power to set prices and control availability of resources has been transferred from the consuming nations to the producing nations. I suspect that one of the current trends of history is movement from the politics of plenty to the politics of scarcity. This of course brings us to the topic of water.

An exorbitant amount of my time in the last two years has been spent on dealing with water problems—either too much water, or too little. Walter Orr Roberts, of the National Center for Atmospheric Research in Boulder, speaks articulately about the next drought, which in his opinion is likely to hit Colorado and the West in the near future. At the same time we have disasters such as the Big Thompson flood where we got much more water than we wanted in one place. In addition to the problems created by nature we face problems in planning for the use and distribution of normally available water. As you know, competition for water in this state is tremendous. I recently looked up the figures for the number of adjudications under the 1969 Water Rights Act. The number of adjudications has increased from 85,000 in 1969 to 121,000 by the end of 1974. Over 7,000 cases have been filed in Division One of the Water Court alone. We are being swamped with a backlog of adjudication claims, petitions for change of use or point of diversion, and other adversary actions arising out of water administration. Both Texas and New Mexico have recently sued Colorado over the water of the Rio Grande. A few years ago Kansas initiated action against Colorado over the water of the Arkansas River. Recent federal and state legislation concerning water pollution controls have imposed standards which a number of people in this state find intolerable.

Geographically, Colorado is unique. There is an old Chinese proverb that states: "He who rules the mountain rules the river." That may be true in China, but it certainly is not true in the West. Almost 50 percent of Colorado's mountain water is obligated to other states. As far back as 1900 the dependable flows of the Rio Grande, the Arkansas, and the Platte Rivers had already been appropriated. Since that time we have spent hundreds of millions of dollars in diverting water and capturing flood flows. At this point the Colorado River is also fully appropriated, but not yet fully utilized. The whole question of how we manage Colorado's remaining water is now of vital importance, perhaps of greater importance than the traditional question of how we can develop additional water. In short, the only water available in Colorado is the water we now have. Faced with this, with the rapid growth of energy development, and with growth in the Front Range and elsewhere, the challenge will be to manage the use of our remaining water without destroying the quality of life in the state.

One lesson from history is that when a commodity becomes scarce, the government comes to play at least a mediating role. One can like it, decry it, or bemoan it, but whether the scarce commodity is game animals, petroleum products, or natural gas, the government invariably intrudes into the system of allocation in some way to try to assure equity and fairness in the method of distribution. Thus it seems clear to me that we are in a transition period moving from the development and storage of water to a period which will be characterized by management and distribution. This new era will be characterized by increasing conflicts between the agricultural use of water and the transfer or attempted transfer of agricultural water to municipal, industrial, recreational, and other environmental uses. We will not be as preoccupied with the development of new water supplies as we have been in the past.

Any government intrusion in water matters has historically been only on the supply side of the demand and supply
equation. In the last hundred years we have never really looked
at different methods of allocation of water, other than the appropriation doctrine. In the future I suspect that we are going
to have to look at how government may have some control, or
at least some influence, on the demand side of that equation.
We must, therefore, focus our attention on the changes in use
of available water. The whole question of continued exploitation of water and land is before us, and I think that to preserve
Colorado as a livable, attractive place, we must reconcile ourselves to some increase in governmental control over natural
resources. Some controls will be at a federal level, some at a
state level, and perhaps some at an international level. Human
society, through government, must exercise controls to insure
that we do not destroy those resources upon which we depend.
Unlike water and air, land masses have a fixed location, and
are thus more susceptible to degradation. Land use and water
use are, however, inseparable. Unlike land, water is an easily
transportable commodity, and the method and place of using
water is nearly always dictated by the use of the land. It is
difficult if not impossible to control the use of water unless we
also control the use of land.

The present Colorado water laws were designed as the result of virtually unrestricted use of land. Water can be appropriated for almost any use incidental to the use of land. Such
appropriations can be modified to change the place and purpose of use with no restriction other than protection of other
appropriators. It, therefore, seems both proper and logical to
attach the same type of control over the use of water as we do
over the use of land. For example, if certain land is owned for
agricultural use, then perhaps water decreed for those lands
might not be changed to serve another use unless that change
would be in the best interest of the people of Colorado. The
current test, however, is not the overall public welfare, but only
whether the proposed change would injure other appropriators.
This problem poses one of the more difficult aspects of managing our water—how do we establish and measure our values?
Historically the yardstick has been the measure of economic
values. We all know that water runs uphill toward money.
Other values are largely ignored. A clear mountain stream is

nice; irrigation water might be helpful in the future to produce food; but there is a greater dollar value when we divert that same water for municipal or industrial use. I hope that we are beginning to realize that other values have at least some importance in water matters and that today's economic values might, in the long run, be counterproductive to the economy of tomorrow.

Some of you may have seen an equation dealing with social change. The first stage is "no talk, no do." There is no conversation about a subject, and there is nothing done about it. The second stage is "talk, no do." People are starting to talk about a problem, but still nothing is done. The third stage is "talk, do." People are both discussing the problem, and acting on it. The end result of the discussion results in some sort of plan. The final, fourth stage is "no talk, but do." The social change has become an accepted reality. I suspect that as to water in Colorado, we have arrived at the "talk, no do" stage. The past few years have brought an increasing crescendo about the way in which Colorado appropriates and allocates its water. A recent executive order on growth and development policy identifies water as an important component. In addition, we are working toward a more comprehensive and coordinated planning of our resources through a Policy Coordinating Council. More than 4.2 million dollars in federal funds are now being spent for local planning in regions along the Front Range and in other areas of rapid energy development. A water policy study is now underway in the Department of Natural Resources which will provide guidelines for me and the Executive Branch on water and water related decisions.

During the past 15 years we have seen a phenomenal growth of agencies dealing with development, use, and control of water resources at both the local and national level. The Congressional Select Committee on National Water Resources has produced voluminous reports on the state of the nation's water. Congress created the National Water Commission to follow up on the work of the Select Committee, and they have produced more reports. The Water Resources Council was created by Congress to coordinate the national water policy, and the Environmental Protection Agency has the responsibility for water quality standards. The question of implementation of §208 of the Water Pollution Control Act is one of the more intriguing and complex problems the state will face in the next year. We certainly do not lack for agencies to deal with problems relating to water. The agencies, however, will not produce automatic answers, because there will never be a simple or even a best answer. Water will continue to be a contentious area of endeavor.

If there is any future to water planning, however, some assumptions must be made. Let me share with you those now being made on a state level. First, population and industrial growth in Colorado will continue, but at a less accelerated rate. Secondly, continued agricultural production at present or greater levels is absolutely essential to the welfare of the state and the nation. We are genuinely concerned about agriculture in Colorado, its relationship to municipal water supply problems, and the fact that twenty dollar per acre-foot agricultural water cannot compete with energy water at two hundred dollars per acre-foot. Assumption number three is that the use of water for the production of energy will continue to grow. Number four is that the pressures for more water-oriented recreation and for protection of the natural environment will continue to increase also. Finally, we assume that the amount of water available for use within Colorado will remain relatively unchanged for the foreseeable future. It is an illusion to think we can develop as much water in the future as we have in the past.

With these assumptions in mind, the objectives of the state as they relate to water resource planning are as follows:

1. To examine closely the feasibility of encouraging industrial growth in Colorado on a selective basis, considering those industries which are heavy water consumers and which would have a significant adverse effect on the natural environment as less welcome than others.

2. To maintain Colorado's agricultural industry and the amount of land dedicated to agriculture at or near the present level and to strengthen the agricultural industry whenever possible.

3. To insure that the allocation of water for the energy industry is consistent with other state goals and will not undermine the agricultural goals of the state.

4. To prevent further depletion of our mountain streams at the higher elevations so we can preserve our mountain environment and our recreation opportunities to the greatest extent possible.

5. To explore the possibilities of amendments to our laws relating to changes in points of diversion, or changes in use of existing water rights, so that such changes can be made to conform with state and local land use laws and policies.

6. To dedicate the energies of state government to research in water use efficiency and water conservation.

I am aware that it will be difficult to reach many of these objectives, but difficult or not, these goals are essential to the maintenance of the quality of life in Colorado. I am of course not the only person in the state concerned with the proper management of water. Others are giving serious thought to waste and inefficiency and are proposing innovative solutions to some water problems. I know that the Pikes Peak area is considering the use of effluent from secondary sewage treatment to irrigate golf courses and parks, and Denver is looking at a project to pump its wastes out to a drying process for use as fertilizer. In the Grand Valley there are demonstration projects to reduce salinity in the Colorado River. Sterling has a water project under way, and the city of Northglenn is working out a relationship for use and return of nearby agricultural water. This last item is an innovative idea that has generated great interest. With greater efficiency and better management the available water resorces can be made to serve us better. Since we have no feasible way to manufacture water, we have no choice.

In summary then, it is difficult, if not impossible, to control the use of water unless the use of land is also controlled. In Colorado we are beyond the stage of only developing our water resources; they are already largely developed. We must instead look to better management and careful allocation of this important resource. This is truly an historical shift, but it must come. Thank you very much.

16
The Role of the State in Water Planning, Research, and Administration

Harris D. Sherman[*]

Other papers in this series have touched upon the role of the state in water planning and development. We at the Colorado Department of Natural Resources have a unique perspective on what that role should be. In the first place, we are confronted daily with the whole spectrum of opinion as to the degree to which state government should be involved in water projects. The opinions range from almost no government control or influence to heavy government involvement, regulation, and control. Secondly, we are now coming to recognize that historically the absence of controls over water was a function of the abundance of water and of the consequent limited number of conflicts over water. It goes without saying that over the years things have changed dramatically, and the following discussion highlights five or six areas where this change has taken place.

One area of great change is the degree to which Colorado's water has been consumed. You have heard many statistics, but a few more may be in order here. In the Arkansas Valley, my understanding is that about 86 percent of the water is now being consumed. The remainder is held by conditional decrees; the total of which most likely goes far beyond 100 percent. In the South Platte/Missouri River System, 91 percent of the water is being consumed. In the Rio Grande, there is little, if any, water left unconsumed. In the Colorado, approximately one-half the water is consumed (possibly a very conservative estimate) and the remaining 50 percent is undoubtedly committed under conditional decrees. In addition, there is little question that salinity problems will cut into Colorado's share of the water. In any event, "free water" is simply no longer there for the taking. As the Governor reiterated in his paper, we are facing times of water scarcity. Transfer of water rights, change in point of diversion, and change of use will be the name of the game in the future.

---

[*] Executive Director, Colorado Department of Natural Resources.

A second change is that an era of large-scale water resource development in this state is rapidly coming to an end. Since 1960 Colorado has witnessed a phenomenal boom in water projects, particularly federal projects. The federal government has spent approximately seven hundred million dollars on water projects in Colorado since 1960. We have eight authorized projects on the Western Slope, some of which are under construction and some of which are awaiting construction. On the Eastern Slope we have two Bureau projects that are either under construction or awaiting construction. The Corps of Engineers has several projects in Colorado. I have not even listed the numerous and significant private development and storage projects now planned or under construction. When the current series of public and private projects is completed, the water that was available for development will no longer be available; most of the prime sites will have been taken; and the most economical projects already built. When that day arrives, the thinking will have to change from how do we increase supply to how do we best use the water. Generally speaking, the state has not seriously considered this question in the past; it is time to begin such consideration.

The third area of change is that of state government growth policy. Each recent Colorado Governor, back through Governors Love and Vanderhoof, has articulated the kind of growth and development policy he would like to see for the State. Last month Governor Lamm released his own growth and development policy as an executive order. The interesting thing is that none of the growth policies—Love's and Vanderhoof's included—are synchronous with the actual use, allocation, and transfer of water. It is a rather remarkable thing that there is so little similarity between the policy and the actuality. Each Governor and Legislature knows generally where they want to go, but the way in which Colorado's water is used does not necessarily match the way they would have the State grow.

The fourth observation is that up to now the State has played a ministerial role as opposed to a managerial role in water. We have been the bookkeeper and the referee. The major function of both the State Engineer and the courts has been to keep the books and to be the referee of water use by private parties. The main emphasis of state involvement has been to facilitate the use and to provide enforcement for water users. I do not mean to detract from the efforts of various state agencies who work with the federal government on water development projects, but those are basically federal, not state, projects.

Fifth, I would like to note that as of now the State has little if any role in the allocation, transfer, or appropriation of water. The 1972 Holland and Hart Report to Governor Love said it succinctly:

> The existing water law in Colorado does not recognize that appropriators may seek to develop water rights which although of beneficial use under the existing law are nonetheless socially undesirable for the public at large.

If the use is "beneficial" in terms of the applicant's economic needs, that suffices. Colorado water law now assumes that all growth and all development give rise to beneficial use of water, and water is allocated to the first claimant. Thereafter the free market may cause a shift in uses, but the law is not concerned with the merit or demerit of the choice made by the market. Only a few so-called public interests are taken into account by our water law today. We have a minimum stream flow law which is one example of the public right being put forward. However, that particular law has been under constant constitutional attack in the courts, and it may well be unconstitutional because there is no actual diversion of water as the constitution seems to require. The minimum stream flow bill is a rare example of public interests and public rights being given some recognition in water matters.

In view of all five factors or observations above the question must be asked: What should the state role be with reference to future management of our water resources? This is, of course, an immensely controversial, difficult subject, and, as one can see from watching the legislature, no one agrees on the answer. However, let me offer a few thoughts for discussion.

The Governor and others have discussed what happens when there is a scarcity of natural resources. Usually the government gets involved. There are parallels between what is happening in water and what has happened elsewhere with other natural resources. I think we need to reevaluate the wisdom of the pure appropriation system. Our neighboring Western States do in fact have different ways of dealing with water appropriation, and when critical levels of scarcity are reached, maybe their system will work better than ours. For example, the Wyoming Constitution states that "[a]ppropriations for beneficial use shall not be denied, except in the public interest." The last five words, ". . . except in the public interest," which have a profound meaning, are not found in Colorado water law. In Utah the state engineer is allowed to reject an otherwise valid application for water if it will interfere with more beneficial potential uses, or if it will prove detrimental to the public welfare or the natural stream environment. I also believe that Utah sets a statutory time period in which an applicant must perfect a conditional decree. Perfection of conditional rights is, of course, a very controversial subject in Colorado, and I know that some applicants for conditional decrees have a difficult and costly time perfecting their decrees because the projects involved are large, expensive, and long term. New Mexico's constitution, another example, speaks to the public interest in terms indicating more than just consideration of public health and safety.

The State of Idaho has recently completed a basin-by-basin water study, and Colorado now has a similar project underway. There are a number of suggestions and ideas in the Idaho report which are quite interesting and worth noting here. One idea is that the state should encourage, in whatever way possible, the efficient use of water and the reduction of water waste. Idaho also suggests transferring water from areas of abundance to areas of need as a matter of state policy. The Idaho study is replete with other examples which might have application in Colorado. The point is that I think we can make some slight modifications of the appropriation system which will permit consideration of the public interest and be of benefit to us all. I think that administratively, legislatively, and judicially the state can play a much more important role in water matters. We should begin to think about changes in the definition of beneficial use and how an amended definition could be enforced.

Any discussion about increasing the role of state government in water matters leads inevitably to the question: Who should make the decisions? The legislature ought to make decisions about any change in the meaning of "beneficial use," and it is clear that we have never really attempted a definition. I think a legislative definition is certainly possible without changes in the state constitution. I also think that the legislature and the executive ought to develop guidelines for state water policies. Our efforts now underway in the Department of Natural Resources are just a beginning, but an important step, nevertheless. We should give the State Engineer and the Attorney General a more active role in judicial proceedings regarding changes in water rights. The state should take a more active role in helping to shape federal water programs. The state should develop water rights on its own land and purchase water when necessary for public benefit. I think the legislature ought to begin to set standards for waste of water and give the State Engineer or other state agencies tools to enforce the prevention of waste. These and many other ideas should be weighed carefully by the citizens of Colorado and by the various branches of government. If we realize that times of water scarcity will soon be upon us, and if we take the reappraisal of our water rights system seriously, then we may emerge with a state water plan which will have some relationship to growth policy. It makes no sense at all to have divergent policies that cancel out each other. In the end, I hope that the public interest will be served, for, after all, there is no reason why private interest cannot be compatible with public interest.

17

Colorado: The Problem of Underground Water

*C. J. Kuiper**

Probably one of the most difficult areas to resolve in water law is the right to appropriate and put to beneficial use underground water. Because of the short and seasonal supply of surface water in many parts of the world, including the state of Colorado, we have no alternative but to cope with the problem. If existing economies are to be enhanced, or even preserved, underground water is probably the last frontier for water resource conservation and development in the vast arid and semiarid areas of the world. The ever-increasing population growth, need for food, fiber, and essential exploitation of natural resources, and the preservation of the environment for a decent quality of life are dependent on adequate water supplies. The impetus for maximization of the beneficial use of available supplies demands treatment of underground water by imaginative and innovative legislation designed to provide the framework for sound development.

Promulgating and implementing laws on the use of underground water is a relatively new and extremely challenging field. Without a thorough knowledge of the physical characteristics and ramifications of effect, an ill-advised groundwater law can be a total disaster.

The first step in devising a groundwater law must be to categorize this water into one or more of the several types and deal with each category as a separate entity when and if applicable. Underground water can be considered under two broad general categories: tributary to a surface stream and non-tributary.

Even this broad categorization must be approached with caution. Judgment based on policy and on local situations must be made, because from a purist's viewpoint there is no such animal as non-tributary groundwater. The purist maintains, and rightly so, that there is no magic source of groundwater. It all derives from surface sources, whether it be precipitation, stream percolation, or recharge from surface application.

In Colorado, considerable work is still necessary on the

---

* Colorado State Engineer.

groundwater law. In the area of non-tributary groundwater, further dissection is necessary for proper definition and treatment, as follows: (1) transient water—groundwater with little or no hydraulic connection to surface streams and/or little or no utilization of surface water; (2) water in bedrock aquifers—not hydraulically connected to surface streams; (3) perched aquifers; (4) closed basins—isolated by geological formation from either surface or other groundwater; and (5) water trapped in solid rock zones. Generally speaking, these non-tributary waters are being or soon will be mined, causing the withdrawal of water in excess of the natural recharge rate. The policy of the State is to exploit these waters, realizing that at some future date we will reach a point of no return. The solution to this seemingly short-sighted policy would be a rather nebulous hope that technology might provide economically-justifiable recharge programs before the axe falls.

Transient water with little or no hydraulic connections to surface streams was given special consideration in the statute, under the title, "Designated Groundwater." Seven basins now exist which have been designated in eastern Colorado by the Colorado Groundwater Commission and are under the jurisdiction of the Commission rather than the courts. Although appellate recourse from any decision of the Commission is provided for in the district courts, I would call your attention to the policy of the Commission on mining groundwater. Each application for a well permit is analyzed on the basis of permitting 40 percent depletion of the saturated thickness of the aquifer within a circle three miles in radius and a time period of 25 years.

Groundwater, as defined in (2), (3), (4), and (5) above, might be recategorized as static rather than transient water, although each has its own peculiarities and its own unique problems. Some bedrock aquifers are considered as non-tributary because historic depletion has caused declines in the static water tables which would take centuries of natural recharge to restore to their past hydraulic connection with surface water. These bedrock aquifers were treated separately in the statutes, with the proviso that the State Engineer may grant a well permit to an applicant if the annual withdrawal of water did not exceed 1/100 of the recoverable water underlying his property: a 100 year aquifer. This was designed to answer the question of adequacy of the water supply for subdivision development dependent on these aquifers. Although this may not be in strict compliance with the constitutional doctrine of prior appropriation, expedience often dictates policy, and this may be a good example.

Numbers (3), (4), and (5) above would probably be best defined as static aquifers which are "a little bit" tributary, since natural recharge does occur, but at a rate less than the rate of withdrawal. I suppose if there is a condition being "a little bit pregnant," then we can have aquifers which are "a little bit tributary." But again, expediency dictates the terms. The hazards involved in applying the doctrine of prior appropriation and the right to divert unappropriated water to these conditions are obvious, especially for subdivision development. The ramifications of circulation of water in a closed system by well withdrawal and recharge with sewage effluent boggles the mind. Our legislature has not addressed this rather nauseous problem as yet.

The general category of tributary water superficially presents fewer problems than non-tributary groundwater if one were to adopt a simplistic approach under the priority system and order all tributary wells to cease and desist diverting, because of injury to senior vested rights. Unfortunately, the realization that diversions of tributary groundwater eventually diminish surface flows, to the injury of prior vested rights, was recognized only after the fact. In the interim, a substantial economy has developed around the use of this groundwater. The legislative body is thus faced with closing the barn door after the horses have been stolen.

In Colorado, this sin of omission was thought to have been atoned for by declaring a policy to integrate surface and tributary groundwater, *i.e.*, conjunctive use. The more knowledgeable legislators recognized the fallacy of this atonement because there simply was not enough water available without some innovative management plan. The policy statement further proclaimed that the doctrine of prior appropriation would be honored and the economy dependent on groundwater would be preserved. This was to be accomplished, despite the overappropriated water supply, through the provisions requiring plans of augmentation to be reviewed by the State Engineer for approval or help in devising a viable plan, and through another statute granting the State Engineer authority to adopt rules and regulations.

By consulting Mr. Webster's published works, I renewed my understanding of augmentation as meaning increasing, especially in size or amount. I knew I should have been more attentive in advanced mathematics because with an over-appropriated river I kept adding zero to not enough and coming up with not enough.

The best answer had to be better management of the resource. That included converting the root of the problem—tributary aquifers—from a culprit to an asset. Starting with the general concept that underground storage is far superior to surface storage, the solution seemed to be to divert water from this underground reservoir during times of deficient surface supplies and to recharge that reservoir during times of surplus surface supplies.

The next question was who would pay the bill for recharge projects and pumping back to the river? Quite obviously the beneficiaries of the project are the underground water appropriators who are junior to injured vested rights. Probably the most Herculean task of the entire exercise was to convince well owners, especially those most remote from the river, that (1) their pumping affected the surface flow, (2) they did not own the water underlying their property, (3) they were injuring senior vested surface rights, and (4) they had to finance remedial measures for that injury.

The difficulty of this public relations task was aggravated by procrastination of previous legislatures and polarization of diametrically opposed positions by well owners and surface appropriators, almost to the point of anarchy. We then organized a task force of experts in the fields of geology, hydrology, and administration to conduct a series of well-advertised informational meetings along the entire reach of the South Platte River Basin. Hostility was the name of the game at the earlier meetings. However, our bullet-proof vests received nary a dent after the well owners understood: (1) the interaction between surface and groundwater, (2) the constitutional doctrine of prior appropriation, (3) the new law, (4) our mutual problems, and (5) our willingness to help them devise ways to remedy injury at a reasonable cost. Their cooperation since that time has been remarkable. It certainly brought home to me the adage that a person's greatest fear is that of the unknown.

The culmination of our meetings in the South Platte River Basin was a general meeting to discuss ways and means of organizing some kind of legal entity to implement the plans for remedying the injury to prior rights. The result was a non-profit corporation under the name, "Groundwater Appropriatiors of the South Platte, Inc.," G.A.S.P. for short. Membership in the corporation is voluntary with a board of directors elected by members from the several districts. The board has done an outstanding job of furnishing replacement water to the river at a price to the members of about 25-35 cents per acre-foot of diversion. How can the corporation provide water at such a low rate, when the price of water in the South Platte in particular is inflated beyond all comprehension? A careful analysis of the law will answer that question. Groundwater appropriators are required by law to remedy any injury only during times that an injured senior right is demanding water and only in the amount of the injury occurring at that time. The first function in determining injury is consumptive use derived from, in the case of irrigated agriculture, irrigation efficiency. That water which is not consumed percolates back to the aquifer and does not constitute injury. The next function is timing of effect, which varies with the distance from the extreme channel, among other parameters. Given the physical characteristics of the aquifer, distance from the stream, and rate of pumping the lifetime and amount of effect can be determined by computer programming for any number of wells. This injury, at that given point in time, must be remedied when and if a downstream senior is demanding water. With the time frame of demand narrowed down to a small percentage of the year, the total injury is again reduced by that percentage factor. The end result is that an acre-foot of replacement water goes a long way toward remedying the net injury of considerable groundwater diversions.

Two projects have been completed that demonstrate the capability of utilizing groundwater storage for replacement water, one in the South Platte River and one in the Arkansas River, both of which have been very successful. The lower reaches of the South Platte ditch had been abandoned for some time because of excessive seepage losses, and a small holding pond was also abandoned for the same reason. That was the very thing we were looking for, the means to recharge the aquifer during times water not demanded by a senior was available in the river. In cooperation with other agencies the lower reach of the ditch was rehabilitated and water was diverted into the pitch and pond during periods when there was no call on the river. Instrumentation of the recharge area recorded the effect on the water table to ascertain the amount of recharge attributable to the project. The cost accounting indicated that this water in storage, and available for diversion during the following irrigation season, cost about $1.00 per acre-foot when the minor capital cost for culverts, and so forth, was disregarded.

In the lower Arkansas, wells were constructed along the Buffalo Canal to pump replacement water into the canal during times when the canal would have demanded curtailment of upstream junior rights, namely, wells. The first year of operation happened to be one of the driest on record. These wells provided water to the Buffalo Canal during the most critical part of the season, saving crops along the canal estimated to be worth about $225,000.00. This benefit was accrued in one year. With a construction cost of some $70,000.00, it more than paid for the project in the first year of operation. Further, the member wells of the Lower Arkansas Water Management Association, which was the sponsoring entity, were permitted to pump without restriction and grew crops also valued at many times the cost of the project. I had to contract as State Engineer with the Four Corners region in order to get this project built as a demonstration project, and the State of Colorado owns it for five years, at which time it will revert to the ownership of the association.

Other proven means of remedying injury include the purchase of reliable surface water rights and storage water, transmountain diversions for release to the streams, changes in points or alternate points of diversion with the replaced surface right released to the stream, and use of non-tributary developed water augmenting the stream.

In summary, good management planning solves many of the problems of the State of Colorado and other arid and semiarid areas of the world. Good management must include maximum utilization of groundwater in conjunction with surface water.

18

Conflicting Demands for Allocation of Water: A Roundtable

Municipal
JAMES L. OGILVIE*

As suggested by the conference chairman, Professor Ved Nanda, I prepared a suggested reading list for inclusion in the preconference materials. The list includes studies that are several volumes in length and obviously could not be read in advance of the meeting by conference participants, nor could they be included in total in the preconference materials. But, in line with this conference theme, I highly recommend them to you for your water libraries as research documents and background material. My brief remarks will center around a few quotations from each of the recommended reading materials.

Water Policies for the Future,[1] the study by the National Water Commission, deals with municipal and industrial water supply programs. The section on municipal water supply programs starts out saying:

> From the earliest days of the Nation, cities and industries have provided their own water supplies. In general, there is no reason why they should not continue to do so. For many years this was recognized by the Congress, and several laws contain statements to the effect that the Federal Government will confine itself to an ancillary role in this field. The Water Supply Act of 1958 made it possible to increase the capacity of major Federal reservoirs, constructed primarily for purposes other than the provision of water supply, in order to store water for municipal and industrial (M & I) purposes. This did not add to the Federal responsibility for M & I water as non-Federal interests were required to assume the full cost of the added capacity.[2]

I do not wish to denigrate the efforts of the federal government in financing flood control projects and wastewater control efforts throughout the United States, but it sometimes seems incongruous that the federal government and, for that matter,

---

* Manager, Denver Water Department, Denver, Colorado; former Director, Frying Pan-Arkansas Project, Bureau of Reclamation.
1. NATIONAL WATER COMMISSION, WATER POLICIES FOR THE FUTURE (1973) (final report to the President and to the Congress of the United States).
2. *Id.* at 161-62.

the state government have very little interest in financing potable water projects that are so vital to the health and welfare of our municipalities. In the case of municipal supplies, the federal and state governments seem to be saying:

> We will tell you how pure the water must be, we will tell you the standards you must adhere to, and we will tell you how to build the plants and meet the environmental safeguards you must guarantee, but you will finance both the cost of the projects and the ancillary expense caused by the regulations we establish.

This study also points out that 75 percent of the nation's population now lives in metropolitan communities comprising less than two percent of the country's area. The chapter concludes by stating in part:

> It seems certain that population growth, increasing per capita use, migration of people to urban areas, and expanding economic activity will strain many existing municipal and industrial water supply systems in the years to come. Effective planning followed by effective implementation measures will be required if serious shortages of water services for the nation's cities are to be avoided. In the more water-scarce and rapidly growing areas, competition for water supplies will mount and improved water husbandry will become increasingly necessary.[3]

Rivkin/Carson, Inc., a Washington consulting firm, did the study for the National Water Commission called *Population Growth in Communities in Relation to Water Resources Policy.*[4] On population in metropolitan areas, this consulting firm found that: "New communities and large developments have followed and are at present being planned to follow the general trend of growth in the outer areas of metropolitan concentrations."[5]

The study also reached the following basic conclusions:

> Fundamental economic and location factors determine whether a community will grow or decline, and the availability of water related facilities and services plays a minor role. Since population growth will continue to be predominantly metropolitan, relationship to a metropolitan area is the principle factor influencing growth of small communities.[6]

. . . .

---

3. *Id.* at 169.
4. RIVKIN/CARSON, INC., POPULATION GROWTH IN COMMUNITIES RELATIVE TO WATER RESOURCES (1971) (prepared for the National Water Commission).
5. *Id.* at 121.
6. *Id.* at i.

> When carefully applied to funding and regulatory matters within metropolitan areas, it [water resource policy] can have considerable influence in directing the form of metropolitan settlement. Water policy can help to achieve a more efficient, environmentally sound pattern of development than currently exists. Indeed, water policy can have more impact on directing the *form* of community growth than its *location*.[7]

This firm also asked whether investment in water resource development and water allied facilities stimulates population growth. The question was answered thusly:

> The hypothesis that water investment affects the growth of population was tested in four representative states across the country. Expenditures made by Federal agencies were arrayed against population trends in each of the counties in the four states and regression analyses performed. Neither the metropolitan population nor the least populous counties appear to be influenced in their rates of growth by water resource investment. Indeed, across the board for all counties there was no correlation. The test confirmed earlier more limited studies that water resource projects in and of themselves seem ineffective tools for promoting economic development.[8]

The so-called "West Side Study," *Critical Water Problems Facing the Eleven Western States*, conducted by the Bureau of Reclamation,[9] found that the population of the West will increase at a rate more than twice that of the rest of the nation. Every year between now and the year 2000 the West will add a population increase equal to the 1970 population of Idaho or Montana. Stated another way, this means the addition of the equivalent of a city of 65,000 people every month throughout the eleven states between now and the year 2000. Colorado and the Denver metropolitan area will receive more than an average share of this growth.

The West Side report found what we all know: that while the Colorado River is a facile source of water for these states, the river is not going to be able to supply enough water to support the new influx of population, particularly to the desert metropolitan areas and southern California.

---

7. *Id.* at ii.

8. *Id.* at viii.

9. BUREAU OF RECLAMATION, U.S. DEP'T OF THE INTERIOR, CRITICAL WATER PROBLEMS FACING THE ELEVEN WESTERN STATES (1975) (often referred to as the West Side Study Report).

Critical water problems facing the eleven Western states have been catalogued in the report. It recommends over 70 additional detailed investigations to be conducted by the federal government in cooperation with state governments. A total of 20 federal agencies were involved in the West Side Study, 10 from the Department of Interior. Future investigations are considered necessary to find solutions for water resource development to meet expected demands on the West's limited supplies through the year 2000.

It is interesting to note that projects requiring national planning, such as Columbia/Colorado Interbasin Transfers or the procurement of Canadian water, have not been considered in this particular study.

At the state level one of the most interesting recent reports was made to Governor John Love on Colorado water law problems in December of 1972.[10] Holland & Hart, a prominent Denver legal firm, reviewed the doctrine of prior appropriation and other existing water law in Colorado. While the authors of the report did not come to any firm conclusions or recommendations, they did offer a series of "observations," including the observation that our water law should be flexible enough to accommodate noneconomic values which the public may hold, such as social and environmental water values. In fact, the report notes, the failure of various western states to accommodate social and environmental values in water is one of the justifications offered by federal officials for the United States claims to reserved water rights.

The Colorado State Legislature studied metropolitan Denver water requirements and resources for a two-year period.[11] The study was under the direction of the Denver Regional Council of Governments and consists of three volumes: a text, a primary area appendix covering the urbanized areas around Denver, and a secondary area appendix covering the remainder of the nine-county study area. The report represents an update and an expansion of the earlier study, *Metropolitan Water Re-*

---

10. Carlson, *Report to Governor John Love on Certain Colorado Water Law Problems*, 50 DEN. L.J. 293 (1973).

11. DENVER WATER DEPARTMENT, METROPOLITAN WATER REQUIREMENTS AND RESOURCES, 1975-2010 (1975) (prepared for the Metropolitan Denver Water Study Committee of the Colorado State Legislature).

quirements and Resources, 1968-2010, commissioned by the Denver Regional Council of Governments and conducted by the Denver Water Department.[12] The 1975 report indicates that the metropolitan area will be short of both raw and potable water in the near future, that the importation of transmountain water appears to offer the best potential for the largest amount of additional supply, that development of water will continue to be controversial and more expensive than ever before, and that:

> a new horizon is coming into focus for those who make water supply decisions. By 1980, most present water projects will be completed, and after that time the projects appear to be ever-more controversial, costly, and complex. Because of these frustrating factors, an attempt is being made by most agencies to find some other agency to assume water supply responsibilities. While the desire for a metropolitan-wide water agency to solve the problems appears to be very clear to everyone, there is no consensus regarding details of the structure and responsibility of such an agency.[13]

The Denver Water Department does operate as a metropolitan water agency. It serves some 900,000 people in a relatively small geographical area. By City Charter[14] it must serve all the people in the City and County of Denver and by contract it serves another 400,000 people in a 200 square mile area surrounding the core city.

The Department's studies indicate a sufficient raw water supply to meet present needs. However, treatment capacity is strained to the limit, and we foresee a restricted use of water in the summer months ahead. These restrictions will continue until a new treatment plant, under planning for several years, is completed in Douglas County. The Foothills Treatment Plant, already delayed more than three years, is the subject of an environmental assessment study under review by the Bureau of Land Management.

The Board and the staff of the Water Department recognize the controversial aspect of many of its planned projects. It also recognizes the need for environmental concern,

---

12. DENVER WATER DEPARTMENT, METROPOLITAN WATER REQUIREMENTS AND RESOURCES, 1968-2010 (1969).

13. II DENVER WATER DEPARTMENT, *supra* note 11, at xxvii.

14. CHARTER OF THE CITY AND COUNTY OF DENVER, ch. c, § 4.14 (1904).

stream flows, minimum flows, fish life, and aesthetic and recreational aspects of water. But our critics should recognize that all municipalities in Colorado, including the metro Denver area, use less than three percent of the water diverted annually from our streams to meet the needs of millions of people.

The Water Department recognizes its primary responsibility to the people of the metropolitan area. That responsibility is to provide an adequate and safe supply of water for present customers, as well as those that all population projections tell us will be here in the years to come. These people also are entitled to a quality of living that a green environment assures, one that is possible only when there is sufficient water.

We shall continue to meet that responsibility until and unless some other agency created by the people and their elected representatives are willing and able to meet the needs of the people of this great and growing metropolitan Denver area.

Agriculture

John Stencel*

Since the early days of Colorado's history, agriculture has played a dominant role in its development. However, its population has grown and cities have expanded along the Front Range. The general consensus is that the importance of agriculture has declined. That is not true. In recent national ratings, development of new water supplies for irrigation was ranked well down on the list in terms of priority. This low priority may be due largely to the high productivity of American agriculture and our surpluses.

But recent world food shortages indicate a need for reconsideration of our priorities. Even today, agricultural production and related activity such as food, fiber, and livestock processing still constitutes a substantial share of our state's total economy. In 1970, for example, cash receipts from farm marketing totaled almost 1.2 billion dollars. And more recently until the

---

* President, Rocky Mountain Farmers Union.

recent farm price decline, it was approaching the 2 billion dollar level.

Much of the productivity of agriculture in Colorado stems from its supply of irrigation water. In fact, of the estimated water depletion of 5.3 million acre-feet per year in Colorado, about 4.2 million goes to irrigated agriculture. For the entire state the irrigation depletions represent 79 percent of the total, and are even higher—90 percent—if the Rio Grande basin is excluded. In comparison, only .25 million acre-feet, or 4.8 percent, is depleted by municipal and industrial use.

In the marketplace, irrigated agriculture is able to pay substantially less for water than can be paid by some of the other productive uses, such as municipal and industrial development. In the past, this situation has resulted in many irrigation water rights being converted or transferred to other uses. In the future, the ultimate result is likely to be a significant decline in overall irrigated acreage and in livestock production from irrigated hay and pastureland. This decline will occur more rapidly if cities have prescriptive rights to the water they need for expanding population.

A definite need exists to determine, adopt, and implement a water-use policy that will direct Colorado's future development on the basis of criteria other than just the ability to pay. A state water plan is needed.

Some water is used for problems that relate to specific areas that deserve special mention. For instance, in some cities along the South Platte River the municipal and industrial water supply is becoming critical, and, in the absence of other alternatives, agricultural water rights have been purchased. There is a danger here that the basic agricultural economy will be destroyed. In the Arkansas basin shortages and rationing of municipal and industrial (M & I) water supply have already occurred, even though irrigation water rights have been converted to M & I use. In the Colorado River basin, potential mineral development, especially in connection with oil shale development, offers substantial threats to agricultural water use. Through programs to rehabilitate existing private irrigation systems there is much opportunity to increase the efficiency of use of limited water supplies.

However, the careful redesigning of systems that is necessary is often beyond the financial capability of private individuals or companies. Similarly, farm irrigation efficiency can also be greatly improved, but the essential equipment and structural changes can be costly, and widespread adoption of new practices cannot be accomplished on short notice. Existing programs need to be funded and new ones developed.

In the southeastern portion of the state there are numerous localized groundwater aquifers which have been mined in the past, and yet may offer opportunities to recharge. This is not a program that an individual can undertake for private benefit, but one which requires public investment in order to be practicable. The same principle holds true for managing the snow melt and heavy summer rainfall which runs off the land without full utilization. Storage reservoirs could control the majority of this water and provide opportunity for the release of downstream appropriations to increase the useable supply of Colorado water.

However, the realization of these opportunities nearly always requires public investment rather than private. In 1969, lands totalling nearly 36.7 million acres were included in Colorado farms and were used for agricultural purposes. These lands constitute approximately 55 percent of the total land area and are widely distributed over the state. In western Colorado, more than one-half of the agricultural land is used for grazing. The plains area, which includes the major part of both the Arkansas and Missouri River basins in Colorado, has most of the cropland. The intensively cultivated lands are those that have been developed for irrigation. The irrigated lands constitute 27 percent of the cropland and account for a large percentage of crop production.

This state needs to retain a diversified economy. The loss of water for irrigation purposes would be detrimental to our entire agricultural economy—the agricultural segment of Colorado and Wyoming economies would be greatly hindered—and it would drop from its present ranking and become minimal in its contribution to the overall condition of the economics of our state. Conservation of our water resources by farmers and ranchers is necessary, and we need to utilize our resources to a greater degree.

There are no trade-offs when it comes to maintaining irrigated agriculture in our region, but two important questions need to be answered: (1) Should there be additional federal and state aid for developing water for irrigation? And, (2) are we going to maintain or expand our present acreage of irrigated agriculture in this region through the protection of prime agricultural land, together with incentives to promote agriculture and open space utilization? Other questions that need to be answered are: What really is beneficial use? What is considered domestic use of our water? What do we do about condemnation rights as they concern irrigation water? What do we do about the outright purchase of water by municipalities? What do we do about mineral development and energy production: the coming of coal plants, coal gasification, and nuclear development? These questions all affect our water.

In closing, we in agriculture would like to remain an important part of the economy of this state. Irrigation does play a significant role in the economy of our entire region. However, if we do not consider the alternatives to water-use justly, we will return to a dry-land type of agriculture in this state.

Energy

T. W. Ten Eyck*

One of the most important facts of life this Nation must face is that it takes water to produce energy under the technology available to us now and for the rest of this century.

The United States, with 6 percent of the world's population, consumes about 30 percent of all of the energy used in the world. That same 6 percent of the world's population produces 31 percent of the gross national product of the world. There is a direct correlation between energy consumption and the GNP.

The only way we can hope to guarantee our high level of productivity in America is to produce as much energy as we can from sources within our own borders. I think we should be realistic. We are going to continue to need and want energy, and we know that dependence on foreign oil for 40 percent of our national needs is dangerous. Another embargo would be far

* Vice President for Governmental, Community, and Public Affairs, Rio Blanco Oil Shale Project.

more serious than the one three years ago. Further, whether we like it or not, oil and gas, oil shale, coal, and nuclear power are the sources we will have to use in the next several years. Increased conservation and use of renewable forms of energy such as solar power should be part of a national energy policy, if we ever get one. But, they will not contribute significant amounts of energy for many years to come.

The production of the kind of energy which is available to us now and will be in the next 20 to 25 years requires the use of water. Necessary water quality ranges from very low for such duties as water flooding of oil fields and moisturizing processed oil shale, to a very high quality water required for such jobs as high pressure boiler feed and production of hydrogen by reforming hydrocarbons with steam.

To give you some perspective on the use of water in the energy-producing industries, a few comparisons are in order. Here are some typical water requirements for various materials on a "per ton of material produced" basis: gasoline from the refining of petroleum requires 350 gallons of water per ton; shale oil by surface retorting, 1,000 gallons per ton; water flooding for secondary recovery of petroleum reserves, 7,000 gallons per ton; synthetic liquid fuel from coal may require from 1,000 to 7,000 gallons per ton; production of a ton of corn requires 10,000 gallons per ton; and wheat, 35,000 gallons of water per ton.

When push comes to shove, I believe it likely that powerful economic forces will exert a tremendous influence on the decision of who gets how much water for energy development and agriculture. The first test will likely take place here in the semi-arid West before it does in the rest of the country.

A recent study by the U.S. Department of Agriculture and the Environmental Policy Institute shows that the dollar value of produced wheat is only about 4 percent of the dollar value of synthetic fuel produced from coal. This is based on each using the same amount of water. That is, if it takes 100 gallons of water to produce about one-half million B.t.u.'s of synthetic coal liquid worth one dollar, the same amount of water would produce about one-hundredth of a bushel of wheat worth four cents. These numbers could indicate that irrigated crops in the

West may be unable to compete economically with synthetic fuels for the use of water. There might be political constraints which would overcome some of the economic considerations in favor of increased agricultural use of water. Nevertheless, economic pressures are very likely to have an effect on future water-use decisions.

Now, I would like to be more specific about the use of water. The United States petroleum industry has pioneered the use of a zero discharge concept for use in petroleum refineries. In this concept, the total amount of water taken into the refinery, whether it be in the form of raw water required for cooling purposes or rainwater falling on the plant premises, is recycled and evaporated until it is totally consumed. There is no discharge of waste waters into surrounding streams with the concomitant problems of water quality and treatment required before discharge.

In the case of shale oil production, we find that the zero discharge concept fits in very nicely with the requirements of moisturizing the processed shale prior to discharge. The moisturizing serves the triple purpose of reducing the dust from the processed shale, providing a proper consistency for compaction, and avoiding the need for final evaporation. As I noted above, about 1,000 gallons of water are required per ton of shale oil produced. This is a total consumption of water. About one-half is used for moisturizing the processed shale and the other half is evaporated to the atmosphere, largely to take care of cooling certain process streams. There is not much potential for reduction of water consumed unless a way can be found to dispose of the processed shale without moisturizing. If water becomes too costly to be economical, the water cooling requirements could be partially reduced by substituting air cooling. However, there is only a limited potential because air cooling cannot completely replace water cooling.

The Rio Blanco Oil Shale Project proposes to kill two water birds with one stone. The saline groundwater, which must be pumped out in order to de-water the mine, is estimated to be capable of supplying all the water required for more than 50,000 barrels per day of production. Production at this level for us is probably more than 10 years into the future.

This means there will be no discharge of pumped saline water into the White River. As a matter of fact, our studies project a reduced natural flow of saline water into the White River as a result of our pumping. Another advantage is that we will not need to import more expensive water to our tract until our production increases. If and when our production does expand above 50,000 barrels per day to a potential ultimate of 300,000 barrels per day, we would import water from the White River through use of an existing industrial water right on which we have an option.

Our plans for use of water are more completely spelled out in our detailed development plan submitted to the U.S. Department of the Interior in March 1976. We stand ready to modify these plans if new information becomes available which would indicate a better solution.

In summary, the kinds of energy available to this country require the use of water. While there will probably be some competition for this valuable resource, it is probable that energy development will take much of it simply because we will not have that much of a choice in the next several years. In the case of the Rio Blanco Oil Shale Project, we can get by with underground water for production of some 50,000 barrels per day.

Industry

LYLE E. BUSH*

We as members of the water resource department of a large Eastern Slope industry in Colorado feel like a rare breed. It is unusual for manufacturers here to be self-sufficient to the extent that they provide their own water resource and water treatment systems. We appreciate the opportunity to present several ideas from that point of view.

Coors is the largest single brewing complex in the world. Our water diversions last year were a little over 40,000 acre-feet. Most of that water is used for cooling mechanical equip-

---

* Manager, Water Resources, Adolph Coors Co., Golden, Colorado.

ment and is returned directly to the stream, so our depletions—the true measure of our impact on the state's water supply—totaled less than 2,000 acre-feet. That makes us a relatively minor user of water in the South Platte basin. In fact, municipal and industrial users together consume only about 10 percent of the total flow of the South Platte. Therein lies one of the major problems facing us today. We, like many of the outlying municipalities in the metropolitan Denver area, are simply not a large enough water user to justify sophisticated water resource projects similar to those developed by the Denver Water Board. This forces us to rely almost entirely on Eastern Slope water, and, because almost all of that water was originally used for agricultural purposes, results in the potential for conflict with the farming community in addition to spirited competition with the municipalities in the area.

We hope that those conflicts can be minimized. We have a good many friends in the agricultural industry, and we have to live every day with members of the communities near us with whom we share the area's water resources, so it is important to us that the situation not get out of hand. In order to reduce the potential for this conflict we feel that there are two conditions which should be encouraged.

The first of these factors is the continued use of the marketplace as the means of allocating water to the various users. As a large industry, we would be hesitant to spend millions of dollars to construct manufacturing facilities if the availability of the water supply required to operate those facilities was in the hands of an administrator whose goals and objectives could change each time the state's winds of political fortune change direction. But even beyond that, the marketplace recognizes the value of the water right which is owned by the individual irrigator. We at Coors directly support about 7,000 families with our 2,000 acre-feet of depletions, but a farmer with whom we negotiate for water is able to determine whether the economic value offered by us exceeds the value of the water to him on his farm.

The marketplace system has another advantage in that it easily allows acquisition on an equitable basis of water required or desired for scenic or recreational uses. The people, acting through their government, need merely determine that a flow for aesthetic purposes is worth more than the next highest and best use and then go to the marketplace to acquire that flow through a system that protects the rights of the former owner.

The second condition which we feel will help to reduce conflicts between Eastern Slope users is the cooperation of those users in as many ways as possible in both the joint use or successive use of water, and in the development of additional usable supplies of the water resource. As an example, municipalities and industries are forced to plan their water resource programs around the possibility of an extremely dry year. Much of the water they acquire might be available for other purposes, perhaps the irrigation of agricultural lands, for seven or eight years out of a 10-year period. Perhaps the agricultural lands from which that water is removed could produce foodstuffs for those seven or eight years to be stockpiled for use during the two or three years when the water is needed for domestic or industrial consumption.

A second area of potential cooperation involves the "first use" of an agricultural right by a municipality or industry, with the return flow resulting from that use then being delivered to the irrigation ditch for successive use by the farmers who presently own the right.

In the area of resource development, significant improvement is possible by having several moderately-sized water users band together to build reservoirs to capture some of the 200,000 to 300,000 acre-feet of water which leaves the South Platte basin in an average year. The statutes, as they presently exist, may not encourage an industrial user to participate in this type of activity, but it is certainly a direction toward which we must work if we are to make the fullest and best use of water supplies available to us.

A second possibility in resource development is a joint venture to import out-of-basin flows from water-rich areas—a concept which is normally far beyond the scope of small cities or industries acting individually.

In summary, because nearly all Eastern Slope water was originally diverted for agricultural purposes, some conflict is inevitable as a portion of that finite supply is converted to support municipal and industrial activities. We feel that conflict can be minimized if significant efforts are made to cooperatively develop additional supplies of usable water and to encourage the joint and successive use of the supplies available as efficiently as possible. We also feel that reallocations of water are equitable only under a marketplace situation which recognizes that a fair price will be set when a willing buyer and a willing seller agree to a transaction, and that water is automatically directed toward its highest and best use when such a situation exists.

Part 3
Technological

19

Alternative Strategies for Closing the Supply/ Demand Gap[*]

J. Gordon Milliken[**]

I. INTRODUCTION

This paper presents a conceptual framework for policy analysis to assist decisionmakers in future water supply planning for semiarid metropolitan areas where water resources are limited. These policy analysis principles can be applied by urban decisionmakers in areas of the United States where projected water demands seem likely to outstrip assured supplies.

Until fairly recently it has been possible to develop new water supplies to keep pace with the requirements of continuous urban growth. In many areas in the United States today, however, the continued concentration of population in urban industrial clusters is outstripping municipal efforts to develop additional water supplies. Water supply agencies face diminishing returns of water and increasing development costs. The problem of providing urban water resources grows increasingly complex, especially because it is interrelated with the issues of economic growth and environmental quality. Just when traditional sources of water are becoming exhausted resistance is growing to damming scenic rivers, to transferring water supplies from agricultural to municipal use in an era of world food shortage, and to constructing ever more remote water collection and transmission facilities as cities grow and compete for water.

The purpose of this paper is: (1) to present and discuss briefly several alternative water strategies, including some that are nontraditional such as wastewater reuse, which can be used by urban policymakers working to resolve the technological, economic, environmental, and social issues of municipal water

* This paper derives from a forthcoming Denver Research Institute report, *Policy Analysis for Metropolitan Water Supply Planning* by Milliken, Taylor, Cristiano, Schooler, Creighton & Martz, prepared for the U.S. Environmental Protection Agency.

** B.S., B.E., Yale University; M.S., D.B.A., University of Colorado; Senior Research Economist at the Denver Research Institute, University of Denver.

supply; (2) to present a framework for analysis of these alternative strategies; and (3) to indicate a method for arriving at a rational least-cost decision based on this analysis.

The methodology proposed here is intended to lead to a thorough systems analysis (involving economic, social, and environmental considerations) of known alternative means to increase water supplies or to reduce water demands and to help select a least-cost mix of actions that will achieve a supply/demand balance throughout the chosen planning period. Techniques of cost-effectiveness analysis are recommended to help determine the least-cost actions that will achieve the desired goal of matching water supply and demand.

It should be emphasized that this methodology must be considered within the framework of overall community goals, *i.e.*, the desires of the citizens, as expressed through the ballot or other forms of political action, concerning the future of their community, which will differ from one community to another. It should also be recognized that a least-cost supply of water implies a weighing not only of economic costs but also of social costs which will differ from one area to another. Thus, a best solution for one metropolitan area will not necessarily be best for another.

II. Alternative Strategies for Closing the Supply/Demand Gap

The next section of the paper briefly discusses 10 alternative strategies for closing the water supply/demand gap in a metropolitan area. Two are strategies for reducing or alleviating demand: (1) conservation measures (voluntary or involuntary) and (2) changes in water pricing. The remainder are alternative ways of adding to the supply of water, increasing its effective yield, or reallocating it among users. Some of the supply alternatives may be effective in certain geographic areas but infeasible or inappropriate in others. They are described briefly in the following paragraphs.

Alternative 1—Water Conservation Measures

Conservation of water encompasses many activities: from encouraging people to fix leaky faucets through low key public relations campaigns, to requiring the installation of water saving devices in new households, imposing mandatory lawn watering restrictions, and limiting the service area of a water supply agency. Each measure is relatively inexpensive in economic terms, but as a measure shifts from "conservation" to "restriction" to "prohibition," in terms of the user, the political and social costs increase, as does the potential for a decline in the perceived quality of life. The impact of these costs falls directly upon an administrator's constituents whereas traditional means of increasing supply have their primary negative impacts on persons outside the service area. Therefore, conservation measures, other than encouraging wise use of water, are considered politically undesirable by most urban administrators, and their exact potential for effecting a reduction in demand is largely unknown.

Alternative 2—Water Pricing to Reduce Demand

If a water supply agency is seeking to motivate more efficient use of existing and future supplies of water, nothing is as simple, comprehensive, and effective as the pricing mechanism. The demand for domestic water exhibits some price elasticity; therefore, a change in pricing structure can be an effective option for reducing the supply/demand gap. In many respects it is an especially attractive option in that the market forces will encourage residents to reduce demand for unnecessary water voluntarily. The effects of implementing a new water rate structure are almost immediate, the environmental impact is relatively minimal, and the benefits to be derived in terms of optimal use of existing water resources and reduced demand for future resources could be quite substantial.

There are other potential advantages as well. Pricing structures can be used to distribute more equally the costs of providing water to those persons receiving the greatest benefits and can promote a greater degree of efficiency in the allocation of productive resources by relating water prices to the costs of developing new water supplies.

In general, other than increased administration, pricing techniques have few monetary costs attached to them. There are, however, substantial social and political impacts, as well as some legal impediments, which should be considered prior to implementing any new pricing structure.

Alternative 3—Water System Management

Some water-short metropolitan areas must store water provided in periods of peak supply to satisfy the water demands during the rest of the year. They may also face periods of shortage and the need for short term water allocation procedures during these periods. For these water-short areas it is very important to provide an adequate amount of available storage and to establish techniques to best manage that storage so that evaporation and distribution (conveyance) losses are minimized and so surface runoff is captured and stored for later use, rather than flowing by unused. Techniques of water system management that may increase yield include proper design and operation of storage facilities and reduction of conveyance losses. A third technique, reduction of evaporation losses, has not yet been proved effective.

Alternative 4—Diverting Additional Water Supplies Into the Study Area

Many U.S. cities obtain their municipal water supplies from rivers which run through the city, from lakes which border them, or from wells which tap groundwater. When these sources are inadequate, cities will "divert," or take water from rivers at some distance from the city and bring it through aqueducts to reservoirs serving the city. Even if an ample quantity of water is nearby the municipality, if the local water quality is poor because of pollution or mineral content, diversion of distant river sources may be used to obtain a cleaner, purer supply of water.

A municipality which contemplates a river diversion must first obtain rights to the water through appropriation or purchase. This can be a complex process involving negotiations with numerous landowners over the value of water and the damage caused by its diversion.

Once a water right is purchased or appropriated, the city must construct a physical system to collect the water through dams or diversion works; must transport it through canals, aqueducts, or natural river channels; and must construct storage reservoirs to accumulate and store the water for later use. Depending on circumstances, the water may be brought directly from the reservoir by aqueduct for treatment, stored in the reservoir until needed, or exchanged (*e.g.*, traded to another water user for an equivalent amount of water located more conveniently for the using city).

In the case of transbasin diversion the water must be transported from points of collection or storage in one basin through or over the basin divide to the other basin. This may require pumping to a higher elevation, tunneling under the divide, construction of siphons or pipelines to carry the water, or construction of additional storage reservoirs. Such facilities are costly, and so may be the acquisition of land to hold them.

Direct costs attributable to the diversion project, besides construction costs, are the continuing operating and maintenance costs of the water system. The secondary costs of diverting water include environmental effects and social costs. There may also be political costs in the source area, *i.e.,* the area of export.

Alternative 5—Reallocation of Agricultural Water Supplies

In many water-short regions the agricultural land adjacent to the metropolitan area is irrigated. It is possible, therefore, to reallocate or divert water from agricultural to municipal uses, and this change in water use sometimes accompanies a change in land use from agricultural to urban. The cost of reallocating agricultural water has usually been established through the market system. The direct monetary costs of reallocation are competitive with those of other techniques for increasing water supply, as there is a very high percentage of water currently used for irrigated agricultural purposes, and its value in use is lower than the current value of water used for municipal purposes. However, indirect costs which include the effect on agriculture and agriculture-related businesses of the diversion of irrigation water to domestic use are apt to be very high and to fall on a relatively small part of the population. Because of its high indirect costs, agricultural water reallocation should be carefully evaluated before being considered as an alternative.

Alternative 6—Using Groundwater

Nearly one-fifth of the water withdrawn for use in the United States come from groundwater. The water is found in two types of aquifers: shallow or unconfined, which are closely related to the surface flow of rivers, and confined or deep aquifers, which are recharged only through faults or fissures in the overlying layers of impervious rock. The principal advantages of using groundwater, as opposed to surface water, are that: the total volume in storage is enormous, the storage is available at "no cost" with no environmental damage, and groundwater does not suffer the high evaporative losses associated with surface transmission and storage. Other advantages of groundwater include the generally low temperature (*e.g.*, for industrial cooling) and comparative immunity from pollution and natural disasters such as earthquakes.

On the other hand, the disadvantages of using groundwater include the slow response and relative uncontrollability of the source, low water quality in some locations (due, for example, to dissolved solids), and the difficulty of treating or eliminating pollution once it has occurred. In some areas aquifer yields may not be great enough to provide sufficient water feasibly, or the cost may be exorbitant due to the depth of the wells which would be required.

Groundwater withdrawals which are balanced by recharge often constitute an attractive source of supply. Such withdrawals may exceed recharge during dry periods with the deficit being made up during wet periods. However, if long term natural recharge of the aquifers is insufficient to balance withdrawals, groundwater mining occurs. When this occurs, a natural resource is being used up, and the supply cannot be relied upon forever.

Alternative 7—Using Watershed Land Management Techniques

Wildlands (forests and associated brush and rangeland) are particularly important sources of water. Much of the U.S. streamflow originates from forested land as forests almost always occupy the higher elevations which receive the greatest amount of precipitation and yield substantially greater than average runoff. In the comparatively water-short Western United States it has been estimated that 90 percent of the usable water yield originates on the largely forested mountain watersheds.

In view of the significance of wildlands as water sources consideration should be given to managing these watersheds to enhance the water yield in areas which are short of water. In the United States it has been estimated that over 71 percent of the precipitation which falls on the watersheds is consumed locally and that only 29 percent reaches the streams; hence, it would appear that there could be significant potential for increasing streamflows. Such techniques are administratively feasible, as a major portion of the wildlands is publicly owned.

There are three groups of land management techniques which can be used to increase the runoff from watersheds. These are:

1. Localized snowpack enhancement by means of snowfences;
2. Modification of the vegetation within the watersheds;
3. Elimination of riparian vegetation.

The first technique is aimed at increasing the stream runoff from alpine areas and from brush and grassland. The second is effective in forest and brush areas. The third technique is oriented more towards conserving water in streams and rivers during its transmission to beneficial usage but is also applicable within forest and brush areas.

Alternative 8—Precipitation Augmentation

Man has been modifying the weather for centuries. For example, the presence of a city changes the average temperature, cloud cover, and wind speeds with respect to those which would pertain if the city were not there. It is only relatively recently that man has considered deliberate modification of the weather with the emphasis on changing the patterns of precipitation of rain or snow in a given location—a subject area more precisely termed "precipitation inducement" or "precipitation augmentation."

The first step in the process of estimating the potential increase in watershed yields resulting from a precipitation augmentation program involves identification of the cloud characteristics pertaining to the watersheds from which the municipal surface water supplies are or can be obtained. If these watersheds are extensive, they will probably need to be divided for planning purposes into a number of separate tracts with relatively homogeneous characteristics. However, it must be appreciated that in a practical program the dividing lines between tracts will be somewhat variable, as the effects of seeding one tract may spill over onto adjacent tracts. Expert opinion should be sought on the potential for increasing precipitation, the direct cost of such an operation, and the increased runoff which can be expected. These data should include information about the seasonality of the increased supply and predictions of the magnitude of the increases for dry and wet years as well as years with average rainfall. Allowance should be made for suspending seeding during inappropriate or potentially dangerous periods. For example, in the Colorado Rocky Mountains seeding has been suspended during holidays and the big game hunting season.

Alternative 9—Desalinization of Brackish or Salt Water

Desalting seawater is costly and to date has been justified only where there are virtually no feasible conventional alternatives. In the Florida Keys, for example, several small plants have been installed. However, desalting saline groundwater or surface water could be an almost indispensable part of plans for locations where all sources are of low quality. To raise slightly saline water to an acceptable quality with regard to dissolved solids need not involve desalting the entire flow. A portion of the water could be desalted and used to dilute the remainder.

There are four types of processes currently available for desalting:

1. Distillation;
2. Crystallization (freezing);
3. Membrane processes (reverse osmosis and electrodialysis); and
4. Ion exchange.

Use of ion exchange is normally restricted to removing limited quantities of salts to enhance water quality, *e.g.*, to reduce hardness.

In planning for desalting as a basic water supply source data should be obtained on the quantities of water available and the total dissolved solids content of the various possible sources; the data should include detailed chemical analyses to aid process selection. For inland areas land costs for evaporation ponds, feasibility of deep-well injection, and likely well depth should be determined. Availability and costs of alternative energy sources should also be investigated.

Alternative 10—Reuse of Municipal Wastewater

The case for directly recycling wastewater from municipal and industrial sewage is increasingly gaining support in the United States today. Although some people may view the prospect of having treated wastewater come through their household water taps with aversion, technology has made it possible to return wastewater to a quality level which, with few (though nevertheless important) exceptions, equals that of pure natural sources. While the cost of treatment is still relatively high, there is every expectation that it will decrease over the years as the technical processes are further refined. However, the most significant sources of support for the use of recycled water owe less to a technical ability to purify wastewater than to a number of other considerations having to do with problems of developing new "fresh" water supplies and of disposing of municipal and industrial wastewater.

The task of dealing with domestic and industrial wastewater becomes more onerous as population continues to concentrate in urban areas. The volume of such waste is increasing; it includes ever greater levels of pollutants; and it is difficult to dispose of. This waste is not only an aesthetic problem; it has led to the pollution of conventional sources of drinking water: both surface water and, in some cases, groundwater. Moreover, providing both for new water supplies and for safe effluent disposal has been made more difficult by recent changes in the public's attitude toward the environment. These changes, largely reflected in Environmental Protection Agency rules and regulations, have imposed restrictions on the development of new water supplies and on the unregulated disposal of untreated municipal and industrial wastes. It is not surprising, then, that recycling which takes wastewater and processes it into usable water supplies is being proposed as a solution to the problem of both fresh water supplies and used water disposal.

III. FRAMEWORK FOR ANALYSIS OF ALTERNATIVES

A conceptual framework for the rational analysis of alternatives is essential to the decisionmaking process. There are three prerequisites to establishing the analytical framework. One is to determine the water supply/demand gap for the metropolitan area over a multiyear period which extends as far as the chosen planning horizon. Another is to array all possible alternative techniques for closing the gap and to separate these techniques into their natural subdivisions (*i.e.*, their stages, or progressive degrees of application). The third prerequisite is to determine for each subdivision of each technique the direct and indirect effects of its adoption. This task involves identification of the parties-at-interest, that is, the organizations or identifiable groups of persons who share a common interest and who are significantly affected, for better or worse, by the application of a specific technique. The third task also involves an identification and assessment of the economic, social, and environmental impacts which result from application of a particular technique. Each of these prerequisite tasks is briefly outlined in the following sections of this paper.

A. *Determining the Supply/Demand Gap for Municipal Water*

The determination of the supply/demand gap for water in a municipality requires judgment, historical data, and a knowledge of the principles of risk analysis. In simplest terms, the relationship of water quantity to time is projected for both supply and demand over a chosen period of years.

Because water demand fluctuates as a function of annual climate, it is necessary to establish a series of confidence limits, showing the extent to which demand can be expected to differ (plus or minus) from the mean no more often than one year in 10 (*i.e.*, 90 percent confidence level), no more often than one year in 20 (*i.e.*, 95 percent confidence level), and no more often than one year in 100 (*i.e.*, 99 percent confidence level). The confidence levels can be established by statistical analysis of past years' per capita water demand. Since the supply/demand gap is most significant when demand is greater than average, it is necessary to show only the confidence levels above the mean.

Water supply also varies as a function of annual climate. Furthermore, water supply will increase over the baseline supply as assured future developments of new supplies are completed. (For planning purposes those potential developments that are not absolutely certain should not be shown.) The average year water supply (*i.e.*, the amount of water which the supply system will generate in a year of average climate) is determined first. Superimposed on the average (mean) supply are a series of confidence levels, showing the extent to which supply can be expected to differ (plus or minus) from the mean no more often than one year in 10 (*i.e.*, 90 percent confidence level), no more often than one year in 20 (*i.e.*, 95 percent confidence level), and no more often than one year in 100 (*i.e.*, 99 percent confidence level). These confidence levels can be established, at least for the baseline supply, by statistical analysis of hydrologic (*i.e.*, water flow) records of the supply system. Confidence levels for future developments increasing the supply system can usually be estimated by hydrologic records of flow in the new additions or by engineering judgment. Since the supply/demand gap is most significant when supply is below average, it is necessary to show only the confidence levels below the mean.

When the water supply and demand curves are superimposed, as in Figure 1, it is possible to detect gaps during certain time periods. In Figure 1, for example, it appears that a supply/demand gap appears during years of average demand and average supply soon after year 2005. That is, the curve D-D lies above curve S-S after that year. The height of the gap (*i.e.*, the cross-hatched area of the figure) represents the severity of the water supply gap.

Even though no gap may occur between the average supply and demand curves, there still can be a strong likelihood of a shortage during certain years. If climate variation causes a relatively hot, dry year every 10 years and during this year water supply is at a 10-year low while demand is at a 10-year high,[1] the water supply gap will be significantly increased. Figure 2 illustrates this.

Some gaps may occur only in extreme cases, *e.g.*, when the 95 percent confidence level in demand overlaps with the 95 percent confidence level in supply or when the 99 percent confidence levels overlap. The overlapping of the 95 percent curves can, by definition, occur no more often than one year in 20, and the likelihood is still lower that the low supply and high demand curves will occur simultaneously. However, this possibility may still occur frequently enough that the policymaker will wish to plan for it. For extremely unlikely cases, *i.e.*, the overlapping of the 99 percent curves, it is probable that the policymaker would accept the risk rather than spend money to avert

---

1. The probability of the 10-year low supply coinciding with the 10-year high demand is less than 1.0 percent, due to variability of climate. Yet it is not an unlikely case since the same hot, dry conditions which produce one tend to produce the other. It may be appropriate to plan for this worst case and to use the possibility that the years do not coincide as a form of safety factor.

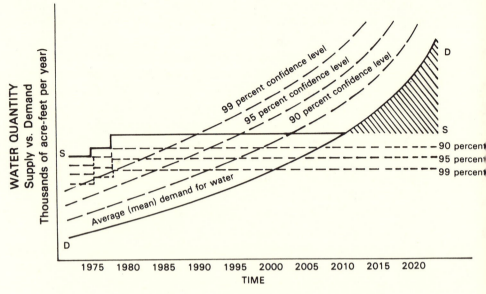

Figure 1. Water Quantity vs. Time, with Demand and Supply
Curves Superimposed

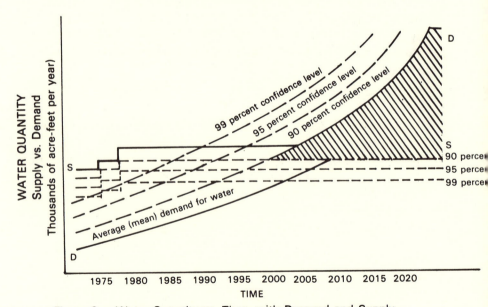

Figure 2. Water Quantity vs. Time, with Demand and Supply
Curves Superimposed, Illustrating the Supply/Demand Gap Which
Could Occur During One Year in Ten (Assuming Coincident Low
Supply and High Demand)

this unlikely shortage. Certain undesirable alternatives (*e.g.*, severe water use restrictions that limit use to drinking and cooking) could be reserved for such unlikely contingencies.

Perhaps the single most important decision made by the water resources policymaker is that of deciding how much risk to avert in developing alternative ways to reduce the potential supply/demand gap. In this decision the policymaker must be guided by a knowledge or probability and particularly by a familiarity with risk analysis. Risk analysis permits a manager to understand the range of possible gains and losses from a proposed action and to avoid actions which may lead to disastrous outcomes, even where the predicted (probable) outcome is favorable.

B. *Arraying Alternative Techniques for Closing the Gap*

A suggested method of approach is first to eliminate techniques which are completely impractical in the study area of interest (*e.g.*, desalting sea water in Denver, orographic weather modification in California's Imperial Valley). Second, each technique should be analyzed to subdivide it into its various subtechniques or its various degrees of application. For example, watershed land management can be divided into subtechniques of snowfencing, forest cutting, modifying watershed vegetation, and controlling phreatophytes. Each subtechnique has different effectiveness in augmenting water supply and has different direct costs and impacts. Thus, each should be analyzed separately.

Similarly, some techniques have natural stages or degrees of application which should be analyzed separately. For example, conservation should probably begin with a first stage of voluntary public information conservation programs, which have a low cost in relation to the quantity of water which can be saved and few, if any, undesirable secondary effects. The next stage might be the voluntary installation of cost-effective water saving devices, followed by a stage of mandatory installation in newly-constructed houses and buildings. Water use restrictions represent more advanced degrees of application of the conservation technique and should be subdivided into stages according to the severity of the restrictions: (1) limited restriction of lawn watering hours; (2) a severe restriction on watering to the minimum quantity necessary for lawn and tree health; and (3) prohibition of all but inside house uses.

C. *Determining Effects of Each Technique on Parties-at-Interest*

For each technological or policy action which may be taken there are several identifiable groups of persons whose common interests are affected. These have been termed parties-at-interest and have been categorized roughly as follows:

1. Parties internal to the affected industry (or activity);
2. Suppliers and customers of an affected industry (or activity);
3. Government, at different levels and in certain roles, *e.g.*, taxer, regulator, or keeper of social welfare;
4. Affected bystander, *e.g.*, those concerned with resources, wildlife, recreation potential, or aesthetic effects.

The basic question used to identify parties-at-interest is:

What are the goals of identifiable social or cultural or locational groups which lead them to perceive problems differently, to set different priorities for solving problems, or to respond differently to a particular policy/program?

For municipal water supply planning involving 10 alternative techniques to close the supply/demand gap, the authors of the University of Denver Research Institute (DRI) report have analyzed and identified 20 distinct parties-at-interest. These include an affected industry (water supply agencies), customers of the affected industry (residential, industrial, and commercial water users), government (metropolitan area political officials, Forest Service, and public health officials), and affected bystanders (environmentalists and several others). The vertical axis of Figure 3 lists the 20 parties-at-interest, subdivided into five parties-at-interest in most policy decisions, and 15 parties-at-interest in some decisions. The horizontal axis of Figure 3 lists the various alternative techniques and distinct subtechniques to close the supply/demand gap. The first column distinguishes between effects of increases in water supply and effects of specific techniques.

The DRI report next analyzed the impacts[2] which application of each of the various techniques would have on the various parties-at-interest. By consensus judgment these impacts have

---

2. In earlier DRI research on environmental policy analysis, impact was defined as a change from the present state of things or from the way things are clearly evolving. Any impact may be either positive or negative depending on the interests, values, or goals of different parties-at-interest. It may fall on individuals, economic entities, social or political institutions, or cultural characteristics.

Figure 3. Matrix of Impacts on Parties-at-Interest

ALTERNATIVE TECHNIQUES TO CLOSE SUPPLY/DEMAND GAP vs. **PARTIES-AT-INTEREST**

Legend:
- `++` Very favorable impact
- `+` Favorable impact
- `+|` Mixed good and bad impacts
- `|` Unfavorable impact
- `:` Very unfavorable impact
- (blank) No significant impact

Parties-at-Interest in Most Decisions: Water Supply Agencies; Residential Water Users; Industrial and Commercial Water Users; Metropolitan Area Political Officials; Environmentalists.

Parties-at-Interest in Some Decisions: Wastewater Treatment Agencies; Power Supply Agency; Forest Service; Public Health Officials; Downstream Water Users; Present Groundwater Users; Surface Water Rights Holders; Farmers and Stockmen; Agri-Dependent Sectors of the Economy; Transbasin Development and Water Conservation Interests; Still Water Recreationists; Moving Water Recreationists; Hunters; Metropolitan Area Developers; Water Project Construction Sector.

Technique	WSA	RWU	ICWU	MAPO	ENV	WTA	PSA	FS	PHO	DWU	PGU	SWRH	F&S	ADS	TDWC	SWR	MWR	HUN	MAD	WPCS
Reuse (Dual system)	++		+	+	++	+	+		|	:		|						|	|	++
Reuse (Potable)	+	:		:	+	+			:	:		|						|	:	++
Brackish Water Desalting	+				|		+													++
Desalting Seawater	+		+		|		++							+|						++
Precipitation Augmentation	+				|		+	+			+				++		+	|		
Riparian Vegetation Elimination	+				|				+		+						+	|		+
Vegetation Modification	+				|		+	++	+		+	+			+	+	+	+		+
Forest Cutting	+				|		+	++	+		+				+			+		+
Snowfences	+				|			|	+		+				+					+
Groundwater Mining	+|			|	|		+		+		|	+	:						+	++
Groundwater Withdrawal (at recharge rate)	+				++		+		+	:	+	|							+	++
Condemnation of Water Rights	|			|	:						+	:	|	:						
Purchase of Water Rights	+			+	|								++	|	:					
Construction of Transbasin Delivery Facilities	+			+	:		+								:		+	|	|	++
Construction of Water Collection and Storage Facilities	++			+	:		+	+			++					++	:	|		++
Chemical Substances on Reservoir Surface	|	|			:				|		:					:				
Reservoir Lining	+				:				|	|						:				+
Canal Lining	+				:							|					:			+
Optimum Management Strategy	++			+					+						|					
Surcharges	+	|		+|	+				:											
Peak Responsibility Pricing · Meters	+	|		+|	+	+														
Progressive Rate Structure · Assuming	+	+|	:	+|	+	+			+											
Marginal Cost Pricing	|	:	:	|	+	+			+									|		
Retroactive Installation of Residence Meters	+|	:	+	:	++	+													+	++
Limit Service Area			+|	+	+	|				:		|	|	+	+			+	:	|
Water Use Restrictions (high)	:	:	:	:	:				|	+	|							:		
Water Use Restrictions (moderate)	:	:	:	:	|				+	|								|		
Water Use Restrictions (low)	|	|	|	|	+				+	|								|		
Installation of Water Saving Devices	+	|	|	|	+	+			|										|	+
Voluntary Public Information Conservation Program	+		|	+	++	+														
Any Technique to Increase Water Supply	++	+	++	+				+											+	

been identified and weighted in gross terms according to significance.

IV. EVALUATING AND DECIDING AMONG ALTERNATIVES

The first step in the evaluation/decision process is to determine the effectiveness of each technique in terms of quantity of water produced (in added supply or reduced demand) annually. Where effectiveness is uncertain, a technique such as expected value or sensitivity analysis should be used to convert all effectiveness measures to an equal degree of certainty.

Next, all techniques should be arrayed on the effectiveness scale in terms of number of acre-feet of water which the technique could produce annually in the study area.

For each technique all associated costs and effects should be recorded:

1. Direct cost in dollars per acre-foot annually;
2. Indirect economic effects in dollars per acre-foot annually where possible to estimate;
3. Social effects, *i.e.,* quality-of-life effects;
4. Environmental effects;
5. Energy effects;
6. Political aspects;
7. Legal uncertainties;
8. Technical uncertainties.

A. *A First Trial Solution*

The next step in the process is to propose a tentative solution to the supply/demand gap by adopting a combination of techniques whose combined effectiveness in acre-feet of water provided annually equals the magnitude of the supply/demand gap in a given year. Theoretically, since any proposed solution will be compared with all other possible solutions before one is selected, it should not matter what combination is used to begin. However, to simplify comparisons and perhaps also to begin closer to the ultimate solution, it is suggested that the first tentative solution be made on the basis of least-direct cost.

Once the least-direct cost combination of selected techniques with their associated costs and effects is arrayed, the policymaker can identify certain costs which seem excessive. For example, the trial solution may include groundwater withdrawal involving a moderately high use of energy, a risk of land subsidence, and a possible loss of amenities caused by well drilling throughout the metropolitan area.

B. *Improving the Trial Solution*

The next step in the process is to look for an alternate technique to substitute for one in the trial solution. For example, if groundwater mining were rated at 60,000 acre-feet a year on the effectiveness scale, the policymaker might substitute a brackish water desalting plant also rated at 60,000 acre-feet a year.[3]

Should this substitution be made? First, the changes in costs and effects due to the substitution must be analyzed. Using hypothetical figures, the direct cost for groundwater mining may be $70 per acre-foot while brackish water desalting costs $170 per acre-foot. The indirect economic effects involving short term and long term construction and operating employment vary for the two techniques. The effects on quality of life, the environment, energy use, and political aspects also differ. Table I displays these differences as a policymaker might view them.

Table I shows that the substitution of brackish water desalinization would cost $100 times 60,000, or $6 million annually in direct cost. This would be partially offset during the first 18-month construction period by stimulated construction employment of $10 million which would produce, directly and through a multiplier effect on the local economy, jobs and tax revenues. The operation of the desalting plant would also provide more, permanent jobs. However, the heavy capital and operating costs of the desalting plant make it clearly inferior to groundwater mining on the basis of quantifiable direct and indirect economic effects.

In cities concerned about "urban sprawl," groundwater mining, which encourages further horizontal urban development, is particularly undesirable. In other cities, where residents desire the amenities of lawns and gardens and decentralized, low-density housing, use of groundwater is more acceptable, particularly as it reduces the cost of water collection and distribution systems.

---

3. It is not, of course, necessary that an alternative have exactly equal effectiveness to be substituted. An alternative with limited effectiveness could be substituted for a *portion* of the trial solution. For a desalting plant rated at 30,000 acre-feet a year might be substituted for half of the planned 60,000 acre-foot groundwater mining program.

TABLE I.

TYPICAL COMPARISON OF ALTERNATIVES

(Note: All quantitive data are hypothetical; they will differ from one metropolitan area to another)

	Groundwater Mining	Desalinizing Brackish Water
1990 Effectiveness:	60,000 acre-feet/year	60,000 acre-feet/year
1990 Cost/acre-foot	$70	$170
Indirect Economic Effects:	Stimulated basic employment in well-drilling: $3,500,000 income over 3 years	Stimulated basic employment in constructing plant: $12,000,000 income over 18 months Capital cost = $35,000,000
	Continued employment in maintenance of pumping plants, $100,000/year	Continued employment in operation of desalting plant: $300,000
Quality of Life effect	Encourages horizontal urban development	Small, if any
Environmental effect	Risk of land subsidence Depletion of nonrenewable resource	Depletion of brackish water resource Problem of brine disposal through deep well injection
Energy effect	Moderately energy intensive in operation 1,500 kwh/acre-foot Energy used in well drilling	Energy intensive in operation 3,500 kwh/acre-foot Energy used in plant construction
Political aspects	Considerable concern by present groundwater users over lowering of water table	Some concern over cost risk
Legal uncertainties	Risk of not obtaining state approval of approriation of groundwater Risk that groundwater may be ruled to be directly connected to surface source.	Question over right to appropriate brackish water. Risk of disapproval of method used to dispose of residual brine (e.g., deep well disposal)
Technical uncertainties	Yield of formations varies widely, hence cost is uncertain Quantity stored is most uncertain and hence duration of supply is not known As drawdown continues, pumping cost increases.	Little is known as to plant cost and reliability due to limited experience with plants. Substantial future cost reductions are anticipated

	Groundwater Mining	Desalinizing Brackish Water
Effect on Parties-at-interest:		
Water supply agencies	±	+
Metro political officials	+	0
Environmentalists	-	-
Power supply agency	+	+
Public health officials	-	0
Downstream water users	+	0
Present groundwater users	--	0
Metro area developers	+	0
Water project construction sector	+	++

Each alternative method has environmental drawbacks: desalinization depletes a visible but little-valued resource of brackish water; groundwater mining depletes an invisible but valuable resource. The problems of brine disposal and possible land subsidence, additional environmental problems, are somewhat difficult to compare in severity.

The effects on parties-at-interest vary, and it requires a subjective analysis to determine which is superior for society as a whole.

Faced with the differences shown in Table I, the policymaker would weigh the possible effects according to criteria chosen for applicability to the specific metropolitan area. By identifying and isolating the effects of the proposed substitution, the policymaker can judge it according to any of several values: reduced risk of horizontal urban development, greater direct cost of $6 million per year, increased energy expenditure of 120 million kilowatt-hours (KWH) per year, etc. Correctly, it would be judged according to all of the factors listed in Table I interpreted through the subjective criteria of the policymaker. The policymaker should consider all the various possible substitutions until it is clear that, according to the criteria selected, the optimum solution has been found.

The analysis technique described herein has an important advantage: it permits the policymaker to measure the direct dollar cost of any proposed substitution of one technique for another. By doing so, the policymaker can place an approximate minimum dollar value on a normally nonquantifiable effect, such as preservation of an environmental feature, if these are the key factors in the substitution decision. It is this aspect of the analysis process which is critical; only by weighing all costs can an optimal decision be made.

20

Augmentation and Conservation of Water Resources

Lewis O. Grant* and Kelvin S. Danielson**

I. INTRODUCTION

⌈The management and use of existing and potential water supplies is a topic of critical importance. As the demands for the available supplies increase, the problems of water allocation and distribution will increase, and hard decisions on optimal societal utilization will be needed. An increasingly high premium must be placed on the management of the *total* water resource: surface water, underground water, and atmospheric water. If additions are to be made to the total volume of water supplies to land areas over the globe, the additional water must, as does natural precipitation, come from the atmosphere. Diversion and transfers can redistribute surface water but do not increase the initial supply. The atmosphere, in addition to being the initial source for surface water, also constitutes the primary "sink" to which this water is lost.

How Much Water is There in the Atmosphere?

Huge quantities of water vapor pass over the watersheds of the semiarid Western United States. However, not more than about one percent of the water vapor present in the air that passes over Colorado annually, for example, is condensed into clouds that can form precipitation. Most of the atmospheric water remains in vapor form and is not potentially available for precipitation. There are extensive periods, however, when the local atmosphere is saturated and some of the water vapor condenses into liquid drops or ice particles forming clouds. Some of this water is in a suitable state for precipitation and is the water from which all natural precipitation comes. Only a portion of this condensed cloud water actually reaches the ground as precipitation.

The type of cloud in which condensed water is contained is important in considering how much of the cloud water reaches the ground as precipitation. Orographic clouds are

---

* Professor, Department of Atmospheric Science, Colorado State University.

** Ph.D. candidate, Atmospheric Sciences, Colorado State University; Research Associate/Scientist, Department of Atmospheric Science, Colorado State University.

formed when air is forced over a mountain. Orographic clouds are relatively simple and therefore their physical descriptions are relatively complete and accurate. Cumulus clouds are usually associated with summertime weather phenomena. Cumulus clouds can be small, white, puffy clouds typical of many warm summer days, or they can be large storms, sometimes resulting in lightning, hail, and heavy rains. A small fraction of the summertime cumulus clouds in Colorado are highly efficient in converting condensed cloud water into drops or ice particles large enough to fall out and reach the ground. Many others, however, are not. Most summertime thunderstorms of the High Plains region of the United States probably precipitate 5 to 20 percent of the cloud water, while the remaining portion reevaporates as the clouds move out of their source area and into a drier region. A few summertime cumulus clouds are highly efficient precipitators and convert 70 to 80 percent of the cloud water into precipitation. Still other cumulus clouds have zero efficiency, and none of the cloud water is precipitated.

Some orographic clouds are also highly efficient in converting cloud water to rain or snow while others are highly inefficient. Overall, the natural precipitation efficiency of orographic clouds in wintertime may be higher than for summertime cumulus clouds. It is the water that condenses to form clouds but does not reach the ground as precipitation that constitutes the potential for weather modification to augment precipitation. Under some conditions, this potential is large since in these cases conditions are suitable for the formation of additional precipitation by enhancing cloud efficiency through cloud seeding. Under many other conditions, the natural inefficiencies are inherent in the system and cloud seeding cannot be an aid.

The amount of atmospheric water vapor and the existing weather conditions are also important in the rate of depletion of existing surface and underground water supplies. Some 90 to 95 percent of the average annual precipitation over Colorado is returned to the atmosphere by evaporation and evapotranspiration while the other 5 to 10 percent is transported out of the state in the form of runoff. A major portion of the water transfered back to the atmosphere is in the form of useful transpiration or unavoidable evaporation losses. An important portion of it, however, might be conserved or utilized more effectively by employing good management practices.

This paper briefly considers the potential of weather modification as a technology for increasing usable water resources. It considers both the augmentation of water supplies by enhancing the efficiency of cloud water conversion to precipitation and the conservation of water by modifying evaporation and evapotranspiration losses.

II. Cloud and Precipitation Modification

Clouds and weather can clearly be modified under some circumstances. However, given differing weather conditions, one could either cause more efficient use of cloud water and produce more precipitation, produce no change in cloud efficiency or precipitation, or even decrease the natural precipitation efficiency of the cloud and thereby possibly reduce the precipitation on the ground. Clearly one must be able to define and recognize just which effect will occur before practical operational weather modification efforts can be undertaken. The important point is that there are many situations when the natural precipitating efficiency is low and can be increased by treatment. Since summertime cumulus cloud systems are very complex and the technology for their modification is very primitive, we will only briefly summarize their potential for modification. Precipitation augmentation prospects for the simpler and better defined wintertime orographic clouds will be discussed in greater detail.

A. *Summertime Cumulus Cloud Systems*

While changes in both the clouds and precipitation have been shown from seeding certain individual convective summertime clouds, the augmentation of precipitation over an area has not been demonstrated with a satisfactory degree of certainty for most geographical regions. The results from at least four carefully conducted experiments suggest (but not at a statistically significant level) a decrease in precipitation following seeding. At least two or more recent experiments using more advanced concepts provide results indicating precipitation increases, but still without a substantially high degree of certainty.

These cloud types are complex, very short-lived, and difficult to study. A probable reason for present conflicting evidence is that differing effects resulting in both precipitation increase and decrease are incorporated in existing experimental samples. Clearly, cloud conditions and seeding methods leading to precipitation increases or precipitation decreases must be defined before extensive operational field programs are feasible. The Bureau of Reclamation in its large High Plains precipitation augmentation research experiment, and other groups, such as the South Park Area Cumulus Experiment (SPACE) at Colorado State University, are addressing these problems with the parallel and complimentary efforts of laboratory simulations, field cloud studies, and field seeding experiments. The benefits can be large, particularly in the semi-arid, Western United States.

B. *Wintertime Snowpack Augmentation*

The basis for considering augmentation of snowfall from wintertime orographic clouds is considerably more advanced than summertime cumulus precipitation augmentation, and the basic technology for augmenting precipitation in many geographical areas on a determinate basis now exists. Careful research over a 15-year period has provided the basis for defining which clouds are efficient and which ones require treatment to improve their efficiency. These concepts have been confirmed in carefully designed, long term field experiments.

During two randomized seeding experiments carried out by Colorado State University, an average of less than half of the cloud water was converted to precipitation reaching the ground on unseeded days defined as having naturally inefficient cloud water utilization. On similarly defined days that were seeded, actual precipitation averaged nearly twice as much as on the unseeded days. These results, of course, apply only to certain weather situations, and in the Northern Colorado Rockies these days constitute only about 15 to 30 percent of the cloudy days. On the other 70 to 85 percent of the days, the natural precipitation process was efficient so that no seeding effects should have been expected, and none were observed. The large increases on certain days, however, can be shown to have the potential for augmenting overall snowfall in most Colorado mountain areas by 10 to 20 percent over a winter season. Results of another six-year field test by Colorado State

University in the Wolf Creek Pass area of southern Colorado indicated even larger percentage increases since there was a higher frequency of warmer, more seedable weather episodes. A subsequent randomized experiment in this same area by the Bureau of Reclamation provided confirmation and refinement of the physical concepts but demonstrated the difficulties involved in trying to predict the seedability of the respective cloud systems for 24 to 30 hours in advance. In fully operational programs with automated data observation systems, seeding operations can and should be based primarily on current observations rather than forecasts.

Streamflow from snowpack increases should be at least comparable to corresponding natural increases in snowfall in various watersheds. The Colorado State University Wolf Creek Pass experiment provided strong, statistically significant evidence of a streamflow increase of about 23 percent during the continuously seeded winter seasons.[1] This amounted to a total of 276,000 acre-feet of water, of which half was produced in the head waters of the San Juan River Basin and the other half in the Rio Grande. Based on the changes in precipitation determined to be feasible and the results of this Wolf Creek Pass streamflow analysis, the potential for water augmentation from Colorado watersheds should be of the order of 1.5 to 2.0 million acre-feet per year.

C. *Societal and Environmental Impacts of Augmented Precipitation*

Augmenting water resources in the Western United States can make a substantial contribution to the solution of current regional and national water resources problems. The direct cost of the augmentation would be low in relation to present water values and particularly those to be expected in the future. Weather modification affects entire communities or regions, not just individuals or individual groups. Thus, the entire spectrum of societal and environmental impacts must be considered.

First, studies to date have not identified any short term

---

1. Mielke, Williams & Wu, Covariance Analysis Technique Based on Bivariate Log-Normal Distribution with Weather Modification Applications (1977) (to be published in 16 J. Applied Meteorology).

environmental impacts that are of a magnitude that would preclude the use of weather modification for augmenting mountain snowpack.[2] Most of the undesirable effects that might occur can be managed. For example, treatment can be terminated during particularly bad storms or heavy snow years. It also appears that most adverse environmental impacts that might arise are reversible by subsequently terminating the augmentation treatment.

Second, as in naturally occurring heavier snow years, augmented precipitation will cause added expenses at the locale where precipitation is being augmented. It seems likely that expenses incurred could be borne as part of the cost of the added water without seriously affecting the cost-effectiveness of the technology. A method for distribution of the direct costs, benefits, and reimbursements does present a difficult problem that will have to be addressed.

Third, water ownership and cost sharing for its production will have to be established.

Fourth, special societal problems are introduced by increasing water in western watersheds[3] since the relatively small community affected by the additional snowfall has little or no use for the additional water while the relatively large user community, frequently hundreds of miles downstream, is the beneficiary. At least some, and likely many, of the affected communities may object to this arrangement even though they, by choice, live in the water source area of many downstream agricultural, urban, and industrial water users. Land use issues are raised. Perhaps the greatest present and potential land use value for these mountain watersheds is for the production and storage of usable water supplies. This may or may not be compatible with present recreation, mining, and agricultural uses. Expanded working relationships will have to be developed to facilitate multipurpose land use planning and implementation.

---

2. STANFORD RESEARCH INSTITUTE, THE IMPACTS OF SNOW ENHANCEMENT: A TECHNOLOGY ASSESSMENT OF WINTER OROGRAPHIC SNOWPACK AUGMENTATION IN THE UPPER COLORADO RIVER BASIN (1974).

3. B. Farhar, Weather Modification in the United States: A Socio-Political Analysis, 1975 (Ph.D. Thesis, University of Colorado).

III.   MANAGEMENT TO REDUCE UNPRODUCTIVE EVAPOTRANSPIRATION

The reduction of water returned to the atmosphere through evaporation, sublimation, and transpiration at the surface-atmosphere interface has a high potential for enhancing water supplies in the Western United States.

A.   *Low Precipitation Agricultural Areas*

In agriculture on semiarid lands, water conservation techniques are aimed at maintaining limited subsoil moisture supplies by reducing evapotranspiration. One conservation technique involves keeping soil free of vegetation for a growing season to reduce evapotranspiration and to allow the precipitation which occurs that year to replenish subsoil moisture. This moisture is then used to enhance the water supply for the crops which are planted the following season. A second widely-used agricultural technique, mulching, involves only partially removing crop stubble after the crop has been harvested. The plant stems are left standing to intercept blowing snow during the winter. If the snow had not been trapped it probably would have sublimed and returned to the atmosphere. Thus, in the first example, evapotranspiration is reduced, and, in the second, sublimation losses from blowing snow are reduced. A number of additional techniques are routinely used in agriculture aimed primarily at reducing evapotranspiration losses.

B.   *Low Precipitation Range Area*

Ranchers in semiarid areas conserve moisture for productive vegatative growth by reducing nonproductive evapotranspiration losses.[4] This is accomplished by controlling vegetation types on rangeland. One example of this type of control is reduction of big sagebrush. The moisture which would normally be used by the sagebrush can then be used by plants which are better food producers for grazing animals. In addition, Sturges has estimated that reducing big sagebrush foliage[5] on rangeland can result in up to a 15 percent increase in water yield under the most favorable conditions.

---

4. D. Sturges, Hydraulic Relations on Undisturbed and Converted Big Sagebrush Lands: The Status of our Knowledge, Mar. 1975 (U.S.D.A. Forest Service Research Paper RM-140).

5. *Id.*

C. *Alpine Areas*

In addition to water savings resulting from management of agricultural and rangelands, the management of watersheds in the West has a high potential for enhancing streamflow. Mountain watersheds often have a region above timberline which is typically referred to as the alpine region. Estimates of the alpine area coverage in Colorado range from 1.9 to 4.5 million acres, which corresponds to approximately 3.5 percent of the surface area of the state. The runoff resulting from this relatively small area produces about 20 percent of Colorado's total water yield. The amount of water returned to the atmosphere from this region by evaporative losses as a whole has not been well-defined. A major portion of these losses are probably due to sublimation of windblown snow. Santeford defined water losses due to sublimation on a mountain ridge line at 62 percent of the total wintertime precipitation for the area.[6] Twenty percent of this amount was due to direct sublimation from the snow surface, and 60 percent was due to losses related to blowing snow. This study and a subsequent study[7] investigated snow entrapment by inducing avalanches on the lee slopes of the ridge. The Santeford study indicated that approximately half of the windblown snow losses in his study plot could be saved using this technique. Such savings would produce an increased water yield of 270 acre-feet of water per mile of treatable ridge line. Other studies in the alpine region have investigated the possibility of enhancing runoff and changing the timing of runoff through the interception of blowing snow by snowfences.[8] Terrain modification is another technique which is aimed at reducing sublimation losses resulting from blowing snow. Estimates of water savings from these techniques are not well-defined. It should be recognized that treatment of the relatively small alpine area may result in significant streamflow increases.

D. *Subalpine Areas*

In the high elevation, forested regions (often referred to as

---

6. H. Santeford, Management of Windblown Alpine Snows, 1972 (unpublished Ph.D. Thesis, Colorado State University).

7. M. Pope, Snow Surface Modification in the Alpine to Augment Water Yield, 1977 (unpublished M.S. Thesis, Colorado State University).

8. M. Martinelli, Water Yield Improvement from Alpine Areas: The Status of our Knowledge, Mar. 1975 (U.S.D.A. Forest Service Research Paper RM-138).

subalpine) watershed management techniques can enhance streamflow significantly. The Colorado River Basin has a total alpine and subalpine areal coverage above about 9000 ft.msl (2900 m) which is 17 percent of the basin area, yet this portion of the basin is responsible for 80 percent of the streamflow. Thirty years of study have shown that the subalpine region is capable of producing 25 percent more streamflow if 40 percent of the watershed area is occupied by small, protected openings. This study by the National Forest Service in the Fraser National Experimental Forest indicates that the openings should be 5 to 8 tree-heights in diameter and 5 to 8 tree-heights apart.[9] The pattern results in a redistribution of snow with more snow in the openings and less snow in the trees. The net effect is that the snow melts earlier in the spring and, due to reduced evapotranspiration, streamflow is increased. The increased streamflow remains stable at approximately a 25 percent increase for 30 years with lesser increases evident for up to 60 years. The increased runoff is a by-product of timber harvest. It should be emphasized, however, that only when the harvest is appropriately planned and managed will increases in streamflow result. This technique is silviculturally sound, does not degrade water quality, and, if planned to fit the terrain, is not aesthetically displeasing. Watersheds with commercial forests to which this type of treatment might be applied comprise about ten million acres in Colorado alone.[10] Leaf and Alexander have numerically simulated a forest management technique which considered optimal forest growth and watershed runoff enhancement for the South Tongue River of the Bighorn National Forest in Wyoming.[11] The simulation was run for a 120-year time period with a stepwise harvesting and rejuvenation of the watershed. The simulated treatment resulted in increased streamflow ranging from 10 to 20 percent for the entire period. This method pro-

9. C. Leaf, Watershed Management in the Central and Southern Rocky Mountains: A Summary of the Status of our Knowledge by Vegetation Types, Mar. 1975 (U.S.D.A. Forest Service Research Paper RM-142).

10. R. Alexander, Silviculture of Central and Southern Rocky Mountain Forests: A Summary of the Status of our Knowledge by Timber Types, Apr. 1974 (U.S.D.A. Forest Service Research Paper RM-120).

11. C. Leaf & R. Alexander, Simulating Timber Yields and Hydraulic Impacts Resulting from Timber Harvest on Subalpine Watersheds, Feb. 1975 (U.S.D.A. Forest Service Research Paper RM-133).

vides a very lucrative potential for enhancing streamflows in the West.

E. *Streambeds and Standing Water Areas*

Rivers of the West are bounded by phreatophytes (Greek word meaning "well plants"). These plants use the water that flows in the streams and, through evapotranspiration, release the water to the air. It is estimated that phreatophytes occupy 16 million acres along streams in the 17 Western States.[12] Horton and Campbell have estimated that one to two acre-feet of water per acre of phreatophyte can be saved each year by removing the phreaophytes.[13] If only 25 percent of the phreatophyte area were treated, this translates into 4 to 8 million acre-feet of additional streamflow per year in the 17 Western States.

F. *Environmental and Social Impacts of Water Conservation Treatment*

Establishment of optimum multiple-use management techniques for mountain watersheds and phreatophyte areas often requires a compromise between the environmental factors and the needs of society. Seldom are areas best managed by devoting the land to a single use. Most of the environmental difficulties associated with these techniques are or can be defined. Intelligent decisions cannot be made on the use of watershed management techniques unless the environmental ramifications are carefully considered.

Social and legal difficulties associated with water ownership, treatment cost, and compensation for those receiving disbenefits must also be resolved for optimal technique utilization to occur.

IV. SUMMARY AND CONCLUSIONS

The atmosphere under some meteorological conditions is a source for additional surface and subsurface waters. The atmosphere is also a sink for evaporative losses under other conditions. By utilizing well-defined techniques for augmenting wintertime orographic precipitation, it is possible to increase

---

12. SELECT COMMITTEE ON NATIONAL WATER RESOURCES, 86TH CONG., 2D SESS., WATER RESOURCES ACTIVITIES IN THE UNITED STATES: EVAPO-TRANSPIRATION REDUCTION (Comm. Print 1960).

13. J. Horton & C. Campbell, Management of Phreatophyte and Riparian Vegatation for Maximum Multiple Use Values, Apr. 1974 (U.S.D.A. Forest Service Research Paper RM-117).

the atmospheric source. Management of watersheds provides a means for reducing evaporation and evapotranspiration losses, thus reducing the atmospheric sink for moisture. Combined, these treatments constitute potential major water supplies to assist in meeting the water needs of the future for Colorado, the United States, and the world.

Specifically, weather modification for augmenting orographic precipitation over many western watersheds, using existing or near-ready techniques has the potential of adding 10 to 20 percent to natural supplies. In Colorado, this can involve the addition of up to 1.5 to 2.0 million acre-feet of water annually. The increase in available water supplies from management practices to reduce unproductive evaporative losses are comparable and likely greater. In addition, a synergistic relationship has been suggested for these two techniques.[14]

Each of these resource utilization techniques involves societal and environmental impacts that must be addressed. The total water resources, including the atmospheric component and the impacts of its utilization, must be included in water planning for the future.

---

14. A. Rango, Possible Effects of Precipitation Modification on Selected Watershed Parameters, 1969 (unpublished Ph.D. Thesis, Colorado State University).

21

Legal System Requirements to Control and Facilitate Water Augmentation in the Western United States

Kelvin S. Danielson, *George William Sherk, Jr.,*** *and Lewis O. Grant****

I. INTRODUCTION

Water is a basic necessity for both plant and animal life. The availability of water has had a pronounced effect on the physical and social organizations which develop in any particular region. This inherent value has been recognized for centuries. Historically, water has been used for human consumption, irrigation, industry, transportation, recreation, and power generation.

In many regions of the world, water supply is not adequate to meet societal water requirements. The Western United States, in general, and Colorado, in particular, have only limited surface and underground water supplies. Water diversion projects have been instituted to remedy this situation. However, expanding population, increasing industrial and agricultural demands, and inefficient water use have displaced the interim solution of water diversion.

One possible solution to the problem is to limit population, industrial, and agricultural growth in the semiarid western region of the United States. An alternative solution could be to increase the total surface and subsurface water supply through the use of watershed management techniques and wintertime orographic weather modification.[1] When used in combination,

---

* Ph.D. candidate, Atmospheric Sciences, Colorado State University; Research Associate/Scientist, Department of Atmospheric Science, Colorado State University.
** J.D. candidate, University of Denver College of Law; Graduate Research Assistant, University of Denver Research Institute.
*** Professor, Department of Atmospheric Science, Colorado State University.

1. Orographic clouds are formed when air is forced over a mountain. Unlike cumulus clouds, they are relatively simple and their physical descriptions are relatively complete and accurate. The potential for water augmentation from orographic clouds relates to the amount of water that condenses to form the clouds but does not reach the ground as precipitation. Seeding operations can improve the efficiency of such clouds resulting in increased precipitation. It must be noted, however, that this is not a long-term solution. Both watershed conservation and wintertime orographic weather

these techniques are estimated to be capable of increasing streamflow in the Western United States by 15 million acre-feet annually.[2] Even though this water might enter the water use priority system at the lowest end of the value structure (irrigated agriculture), the value of this additional water would be approximately three hundred million dollars per year.[3] When reuse and higher valued uses are considered, the direct gains in production in 1976 prices could amount to several billion dollars per year.[4] The direct costs of weather modification and appropriate watershed management techniques are not high. In fact, a considerable margin in the cost/benefit structure would exist.[5]

The ability to enhance streamflow in the Western United States through wintertime orographic weather modification is a technique which has been studied extensively for well over a decade. The physical principles are understood, and the capability of the technique to enhance streamflow is well documented in the literature.[6] Similarly, the physical principles

---

modification will serve to meet the water needs of the Western United States only until such time as augmented water supplies are utilized by ever-expanding water demands.

2. This would result from 10 million acre-feet being produced by wintertime orographic weather modification and an estimated 5 million acre-feet resulting from watershed management. The region-wide potential of watershed management to increase water supplies has not yet been fully evaluated. Experimental results to date indicate that the potential of watershed management to augment water supplies may be equal to or greater than that of weather modification. For the purposes of this analysis a conservative projection of 5 million acre-feet was utilized. NATIONAL ACADEMY OF SCIENCES, COMM'N ON NATURAL RESOURCES, NATIONAL RESEARCH COUNCIL, COMMITTEE ON CLIMATE AND WEATHER FLUCTUATIONS AND AGRICULTURE AND RENEWAL RESOURCES, CLIMATE AND FOOD 131-62 (1976) [hereinafter cited as CLIMATE AND FOOD]; R. ELLIOT, J. HANNAFORD & R. SHAFFER, TWELVE BASIN INVESTIGATION: ANALYSIS OF POTENTIAL INCREASES IN PRECIPITATION AND STREAM FLOW FROM MODIFICATION OF COLD OROGRAPHIC CLOUDS IN SELECTED RIVER BASINS OF THE WESTERN UNITED STATES 1-200 (1973); C. LEAF, WATERSHED MANAGEMENT IN THE ROCKY MOUNTAIN SUBALPINE ZONE: THE STATUS OF OUR KNOWLEDGE 1-28 (1975) (U.S.D.A. Forest Service Research Paper RM-137)[hereinafter cited as LEAF].

3. This projection is based on an assumed cost of $20.00 per acre-foot for agricultural water.

4. The costs of water for industrial and domestic water users has been estimated to range up to ten times the cost of water for irrigated agriculture. The specific values vary substantially with location.

5. CLIMATE AND FOOD, *supra* note 2.

6. *See generally* L. GRANT, C. CHAPPELL, L. CROW, J., FRITSCH, & P. MIELKE, WEATHER MODIFICATION—A PILOT PROJECT (1974) (Final Report, Bureau of Reclamation Contract No. 14-06-D-6467). *See also* note 2 *supra* and note 8 *infra*.

and application techniques utilized in watershed management are defined, tested, and documented.[7]

The major problems encountered in applying these techniques to increase water supplies do not lie with scientific understanding or technological limitations. The fundamental problems are environmental, social, and legal.

The direct environmental problems introduced by employing these techniques (not including increased population growth) have been addressed on a limited basis.[8] Numerous studies have defined many of the environmental problems. The problems thus far identified, while important, do not present any major obstacles to the development of operational water augmentation programs. As such, they are not considered in this analysis.

Problems relating to sociological considerations are quite complex. For watershed management, these are relatively minor. For weather modification, they present significant difficulties.[9] The primary issue is that those people who benefit from water augmentation activities (senior water right holders) are generally not the same individuals who incur disbenefits from the activities (increased snowfall plus associated inconveniences and costs). It is unlikely that those individuals receiving disbenefits will voluntarily accept a degradation in their quality of life for the benefit of others. It may be that monetary compensation will not remedy this situation.

The responses of local, state, and federal governments to legal problems related to water augmentation have been varied. The bulk of legal system actions have been at the state level, though a number of proposals have recently been considered by the federal government.

The problems of water augmentation are twofold. First, the complexity of the weather modification portion of water augmentation must be considered. Weather modification can

---

7. LEAF, *supra* note 2.

8. *See generally* STANFORD RESEARCH INSTITUTE, THE IMPACTS OF SNOW ENHANCEMENT: A TECHNOLOGY ASSESSMENT OF WINTER OROGRAPHIC SNOWPACK AUGMENTATION IN THE UPPER COLORADO RIVER BASIN (1974); *see also* note 2 *supra*.

9. B. Farhar, Weather Modification in The United States: A Socio-Political Analysis, 150-367, April, 1975 (unpublished Ph.D. dissertation in Dep't of Sociology, University of Colorado).

be used on wintertime orographic clouds to enhance precipitation and on summertime cumulus clouds to reduce or enhance precipitation or to decrease hail; additionally, to dissipate cold and warm fogs, to control cirrus clouds in order to control surface temperatures, and for many other purposes.[10] Some of these treatments are well defined. Others, however, are not. The legal system response to the problems of water augmentation should facilitate the application of those techniques which are well defined while controlling, and in certain cases limiting, the application of other weather modification techniques. Only wintertime orographic cloud seeding, for which modification techniques are well defined, will be considered as weather modification in the following discussion.

Water augmentation via watershed management, which has both well defined and developing techniques, must also be analyzed. Many watershed management techniques will require legal system responses to protect both water rights holders and the general populace.

The second aspect of legal uncertainties concerning water augmentation involves the issue of water rights. Questions of subsidizing and controlling augmentation activities, taxing for compensation, liability, record-keeping, and the administration of streamflow enhancement programs all depend on the ownership of "new" water. The following analysis examines different approaches to the ownership of water. Because of the application of the *Shelton Farms* decision of the Supreme Court of Colorado[11] to the question of the ownership of water produced by water augmentation activities, specific attention will be focused on it.

II. General State Claims to Water

State claims to the ownership of water which may have a critical impact on the ownership of water produced by water augmentation must be evaluated. All eight appropriation doctrine states of the Western United States, without exception, claim the waters within the state. Their claims are based on the presumption that state waters are the "property of the public,"

---

10. W. Hess, Weather and Climate Modification 227-765 (1974).

11. Southeastern Colo. Water Conservancy Dist. v. Shelton Farms, Inc., 187 Colo. 181, 529 P.2d 1321 (1975) [hereinafter cited as Shelton Farms].

"belong to the public," or are the "property of the state."[12] Traditionally, the appropriation states have acted as a public trustee, administering the waters of the state in the public interest. The appropriation system, the usufructory nature of a water right, and the requirement of beneficial use as the basis, measure, and limit of a right, exist in all eight states.

The questions of those waters subject to state jurisdiction and appropriation for beneficial use come into critical focus when the ownership of waters developed by water augmentation activities is considered. It is possible that a theory of ownership might be developed based on a definition of the waters produced by water augmentation as "unnatural" waters. This may free such waters from state ownership claims. Four of the eight western states consider the "natural" characteristics of the water to which they assert a claim.[13] Three of the appropriation doctrine states do not make mention of the "natural" characteristics of the waters within their jurisdiction.[14]

The claims of the State of Colorado appear to be a combination of the "natural" claims of Wyoming, Arizona, Idaho, and New Mexico and the more inclusive claims of Utah, Montana, and Nevada. The Constitution of the State of Colorado includes a provision asserting claim to "the water of every

---

12. Colorado (COLO. CONST., art. 16, §5; COLO. REV. STAT. ANN. §37-82-101 (1973), Utah (UTAH CODE ANN. §73-1-1 (1953)), Nevada (NEV. REV. STAT. §533.025 (1975)), and New Mexico (N.M. STAT. ANN. §75-1-1 (1953)) all declare the waters of the state to be either the "property of the public" or to "belong to the public." Wyoming (WYO. CONST., art. 8, §1; WYO. STAT. §41-2 (1957)), Idaho (IDAHO CODE §42-101 (1947)), and Montana (MONT. REV. CODES ANN. §89-866(1) (Supp. 1975)) all assert title to waters as the "property of the state."

13. Wyoming states a claim to "the water of all *natural* streams, springs, lakes or other collections of still waters" (WYO. CONST., art. 8, §1). Idaho claims "all the waters of the state, when flowing in their natural channels" (IDAHO CODE §42-101 (1947)). Arizona asserts title to the "waters of all sources flowing in streams, canyons, ravines or other *natural* channels" (ARIZ. REV. STAT. §45-101(A) (1956), §45-180 (Supp. 1976)). New Mexico claims "all *natural* waters flowing in streams and watercourses" (N.M. STAT. ANN. §75-1-1 (1953)) and "the unappropriated water of every *natural* stream" (N.M. CONST., art. XVI, §2) (emphases added).

14. Utah asserts title to "all waters in [the] state, whether above or under the ground" (UTAH CODE ANN. §73-1-1 (1953)). Nevada claims "the water of all sources of water supply . . . whether above or beneath the surface of the ground"(NEV. REV. STAT. §533.025 (1975)). Montana appears to make the most expansive state water claims by asserting title to "all surface, underground, flood and atmospheric waters" (MONT. CONST., art. IX, §3(3)) and to "all water of the state, surface and subsurface, regardless of its character or manner of occurrence" (MONT. REV. CODES ANN. §89-867(1) (Supp. 1976)).

natural stream."[15] This claim, however, has been expanded by statute to include "all water originating in or flowing into this state."[16]

III. Water for Weather Modification

Four of the eight appropriation doctrine states make specific claims to the waters produced by weather modification activities. New Mexico claims "the right to all moisture in the atmosphere which would fall so as to become a part of the natural or percolated water" of the state.[17] Wyoming asserts a "sovereign right to . . . the moisture contained in the clouds and atmosphere."[18] The statutory provisions of Colorado regarding the ownership of water produced by weather modification, asserting claim to all water "suspended in the atmosphere"[19] or "artificially induced to fall,"[20] reflect the approaches taken by both Wyoming and New Mexico. Utah, which bases its water claims on very expansive definitions of cloud seeding, has provided that "all statutory provisions that apply to water from natural precipitation shall also apply to water derived from cloud seeding."[21]

Arizona seems to have taken a quite different approach. Its weather modification statute does not contain a statement of the ownership of the water produced. It does provide, however, that nothing in the statute is to be construed to prohibit the owner of land used for agricultural purposes from doing weather modification on the individual's property for exclusive benefit.[22] This statute seems to have been intended to deal with some forms of summertime cumulus cloud seeding. The application of a statute so designed for both wintertime orographic cloud seeding and watershed management would be doubtful as the benefits of these two activities frequently occur in areas other than the area where the activity was conducted.

Both Montana and Nevada assert claims to those waters which may have been produced by weather modification.

---

15. Colo. Const., art. 16, §5 (emphasis added).
16. Colo. Rev. Stat. Ann. §37-82-101 (1973).
17. N.M. Stat. Ann. §75-37-3 (1953).
18. Wyo. Stat. §9-266 (1957).
19. Colo. Rev. Stat. Ann. §36-20-103 (1973).
20. *Id.*
21. Utah Code Ann. §73-15-4 (Supp. 1975).
22. Ariz. Rev. Stat. §45-2406 (1956).

These claims, however, are not contained in the weather modification statutes of either state. Montana, in its state constitution, asserts a claim to "atmospheric" waters.[23] Nevada appears to be asserting a claim to atmospheric water when, by statute, the state claims water "above . . . the surface of the ground."[24] Finally it should be noted that only Idaho does not, in some way, address the problem of the ownership of atmospheric waters. Statutory claims to waters produced by water augmentation activities must be understood if the issue of ownership is to be resolved. It would appear, in some states, that private claims to such waters are impossible. In other states, private claims to water so developed would appear to be possible. Such ownership questions must be resolved by legislation if private water augmentation activities are to be encouraged.

IV. WATER FROM WATER AUGMENTATION

As with weather modification, the question of the ownership of water produced by water augmentation activities is critically important to those individuals and organizations contemplating water augmentation activities. It can be argued that the waters produced by these activities fall under the "water from all sources" types of water ownership policies previously considered. Such general policies, however, are not conducive to water augmentation activities in that they do not guarantee a water right to those individuals and organizations augmenting water supplies.

Colorado appears to be the only state in the region to have developed specific statutory provisions concerning water augmentation.[25] Under the statute, augmentation is defined, in part, as an increase in the supply of water "by the development of a new or alternate means or point of diversion, by a pooling of water resources, by water exchange projects, by providing substitute supplies of water, by the development of new sources of water, or by any other appropriate means."[26] The statute

---

23. MONT. CONST., art. IX, §3(3).

24. NEV. REV. STAT. §533.025 (1975).

25. This statute, however, is not aimed at the ownership question regarding new sources of water supply. It is primarily intended to encourage the development of alternate sources of supply to protect the rights of senior appropriators.

26. COLO. REV. STAT. ANN. §37-92-103(9) (Supp. 1976). While not specifically mentioned in the Statute, it would be difficult to argue that water produced by weather modification and watershed mangement falls outside the scope and intent of the legislation.

specifically excludes from the definition of water augmentation programs phreatophyte eradication and the use of water runoff collected from land surfaces which have been made impermeable.[27]

Under the Colorado procedure, an application and a plan for water augmentation are filed with both the water clerk of the specific division and the State Engineer. The State Engineer can then approve, on a temporary basis, the augmentation plan. The water judge of the specific division is then to hold a hearing on the augmentation plan to consider either a final approval or denial. At this hearing, the conclusion of the State Engineer is *prima facie* evidence unless challenged by "competent countervailing evidence."[28] It is apparent, under the Colorado water augmentation statutes, that one augmenting water supplies pursuant to an approved plan has first claim to the waters produced in accordance with the plan.

V. ARTIFICIAL WATER: DEVELOPED WATER

New Mexico has defined artificial water as water "whose appearance or accumulation is due to escape, seepage, loss, waste, drainage, or percolation from constructed works."[29] In both New Mexico and Arizona, artificial waters are not subject to appropriation.[30] In New Mexico, however, the exemption for such waters from appropriation exists only as long as the water is on the property of the individual who created the artificial waters.

The aforementioned definition of "artificial waters" is very similar to the definition of "salvaged waters" developed by the Supreme Court of Colorado.[31] Under both Colorado and Utah law, however, persons salvaging water do *not* have first claim to the water. Such waters remain a part of the stream system and are subject to a call on the river.

The Supreme Court of Colorado has, however, drawn a distinction between "salvaged waters" and "developed wa-

---

27. *Id.*

28. COLO. REV. STAT. ANN. §37-92-307(5), (6) (Supp. 1976).

29. N.M. STAT. ANN. §75-5-25 (1953).

30. Hagerman Irrigation Co. v. East Grand Plains Drainage Dist., 25 N.M. 649, 187 P. 555 (1920); Fourzon v. Curtis, 43 Ariz. 140, 29 P.2d 722 (1934).

31. Shelton Farms, *supra* note 11, at 1325.

ters."[32] Developed waters are those waters which are transported from another source, flood waters which are captured
and stored, or waters "which would never have reached the
river or its tributaries."[33] In essence, the definition of developed
waters "implies new water not previously part of the river system."[34] Under the *Shelton Farms* rule, developed waters "are
free from the river call, and are not junior to prior decrees."[35]
In the final analysis, it would appear that an individual developing waters under this rule, and in accordance with the aforementioned plans for water augmentation, would have first
claim to the water. Such issues must be resolved before private
water augmentation plans can be developed. This is particularly true when the cost of proving the quantity of water developed is considered.

VI. POSSIBLE SYSTEM RESPONSES: PRIVATE DEVELOPMENT

If the assumption is made that an increase in the total
water supply of the Western United States is in the public
interest, then legal institutions should seek to facilitate rather
than discourage the development of potential "new" water supplies. Review of the legal institutions of the eight western states
indicates that private claims to water developed through
weather modification and watershed management techniques
are open to question and subject to the claims of existing
appropriators. A study by F. B. Jones, C. F. Leaf, and W. H.
Fischer[36] points out that the private concern asserting a claim
based on water augmented through weather modification has
no assurance that such a claim would not be contested by
existing appropriators. Water augmented through watershed
management techniques may also result in contested rights
under the existing systems. Assurances of ownership are
critical if private water augmentation activities are to be conducted.

In fact, it is highly unlikely that development of augmented water supplies by private concerns will occur until

---

32. *Id.*
33. *Id.* at 1324.
34. *Id.*
35. *Id.* at 1325.
36. *See generally* F. JONES, C. LEAF & W. FISCHER, GENERALIZED CRITERIA FOR
PROOF OF WATER DEVELOPED THROUGH WEATHER MODIFICATION (1975) [hereinafter cited
as GENERALIZED CRITERIA].

legal and institutional assurances of ownership are developed. This is clearly apparent in light of the initial procedures and, in some instances, expenses which would be necessary for a private concern to prove the magnitude of the augmented water claim.[37] These assurances must guarantee that the actions of private concerns to augment and to prove augmentation will result in a legal right to the augmented portion of the water when adequate proof of augmentation is provided.

There are numerous legal system responses which would facilitate *private* concern development of "new" water. One option is legislation at the state level. This could be easily implemented if "new" waters resulting from watershed management and weather modification were defined as "developed" waters in the manner in which the Supreme Court of the State of Colorado has defined them.[38] In Colorado, it is established that "one who adds to an existing water supply is entitled to a decree affirming the use of such water."[39] Colorado recognizes that developed water includes "water within the system which would never have normally reached its tributaries."[40] Water created by watershed management and by weather modification would seem to fit these criteria. A definition of this water as "developed" water is advantageous since it is consistent with the distinction drawn between "developed" and "salvaged" water in the *Shelton Farms* decision. This would allow the augmentor first claim to "developed" waters.

Once state legislation has resolved the question of water rights in a manner that would allow development of this resource by private concerns, a number of additional issues must be addressed. Initially, proof of the amount and availability of augmented water supplies, which would meet "preponderance of evidence" requirements in judicial proceedings, must be developed. Methods for development of this proof of water based on weather modification have been proposed.[41] It should be noted, that specific proof may have to be offered following

---

37. *Id.*
38. Shelton Farms, *supra* note 11, at 1325.
39. *Id.* at 1324.
40. *Id.*; *see* notes 30-34 *supra.*
41. GENERALIZED CRITERIA, *supra* note 36.

each water augmentation activity from which benefit is claimed. If judicial notice of specific methods of proof had been taken, however, such repetitive proofs would be economically feasible. No example of a technique capable of proving the magnitude of augmented water from watershed management is available in the literature. Development of such a technique, however, would probably be less complex than for weather modification.

The statistical and numerical techniques proposed to prove the amount and availability of augmented water supplies may not conform to current evidentiary requirements. In essence, probability and fact may not be seen as synonymous. Since statistical and numerical techniques assert proof in terms of probabilities, their admissibility as proof of the characteristics of water augmentation activities may be questioned. Even though readily accepted by the scientific community, judicial acceptance of such procedures is as yet untested.[42]

A broad range of issues relating to the liability of individuals attempting to augment water supplies must be addressed. Initially, the question of procedures for compensation of individuals who experience a reduction in quality of life by virtue of their living in a treatment area is a serious one. An example of such a reduction would be increased snowfall in a region from wintertime orographic weather modification efforts. The question can be raised as to whether increased snowfall, and the resultant loss in the enjoyment of property (assuming it is not a ski slope), would constitute a "taking."[43] If the assumption is made that this does constitute a "taking," a possible solution would be to tax the concern performing the treatment while simultaneously providing a tax benefit to those individuals adversely affected. Another possible solution would be to make a one-time monetary compensation to those currently owning property in the region since those that move into the

42. Fischer, *Weather Modification and the Right of Capture*, 8 NAT. RES. LAW. 639 (1976). If judicial notice of the statistical method is taken, then by a preponderance of the evidence it would be necessary to show that the specific statistical method is appropriate and that it demonstrates the magnitude of the claim.

43. The question of whether the interference with private property would constitute a taking must be resolved. It would seem that minor interferences would not be a taking. By way of analogy, zoning requirements which limit the use of private property have not usually been seen as constituting a taking of property.

area "post hoc" have full knowledge of the quality of life that exists. Since the value of the water produced by water augmentation is substantially in excess of the costs of implementing the techniques, a considerable margin exists in the cost/benefit relationship. These revenues, which would initially accrue to the private developer, could be tapped by the state via taxation to compensate those adversely affected.

Liability for catastrophic occurrences resulting from water augmentation activities must also be considered. An example of such an occurrence, which might be construed to have resulted from these activities, would be an avalanche following heavy snowfall during which winter orographic weather modification activities were conducted. A second example would be a situation in which a percentage of trees in a watershed had been removed in order to enhance streamflow where, following the removal, heavy rainfall resulted in flooding within the watershed. In both of these examples, the legal issue which must be resolved is whether the water augmentation activities were, in fact, the proximate cause of the resulting damages.

If liability in such instances can be established, the legal system must develop means to insure that compensation is available to those injured. Two possible responses could be developed. The water augmentor applying for a permit would be required either to prove adequate insurance coverage or to post a bond sufficient to cover possible damages. In the event of an incident, either the bond or the proceeds of the insurance policy could be administered by the state (possibly through the office of the State Engineer) to compensate those damaged by water augmentation activities.

A problem with water augmentation with which many states have already dealt involves the qualification for the issuance of licenses and permits to do water augmentation. Licensing requirements are necessary to assure the state that competent individuals and firms are providing the treatment. Permits are needed to assure the state that water augmentation activities are coordinated on a statewide basis to reduce conflicting programs. Records of these activities, already required by some states, would be useful in providing a means of monitoring and evaluating program success. An additional use of records might be in the determination of liability for unforeseen occurrences.

VII. POSSIBLE SYSTEM RESPONSES: STATE DEVELOPMENT

Another approach to the question of water rights resulting from water augmentation programs would be for the state either to carry out the program itself or to contract with firms which would be responsible for carrying out the treatment for the state but which would have no right to the water produced. The additional water supplies would then go to current (and possible future) appropriators. It is assumed that the state would conduct such activities for the benefit of its citizens.

State funding of water augmentation activities could evoke a variety of public and private responses. The political feasibility of using public revenues to meet private water requirements is open to question. On the one hand, those who would argue against the state subsidies of private enterprise might question whether or not the use of state funds to meet the needs of a select few (existing and potential water rights holders) is a proper use of such funds. Under normal climatological conditions, this argument may have substantial merit.[44]

On the other hand, unusual climatological conditions resulting in reduced streamflow threaten the general welfare of the state. At such times, the general economy of the region suffers due to reduced water availability. This results in increased unemployment and reduced state revenue which, in turn, endanger social programs. The result is that both liberal and conservative policymakers and the general populace support efforts to enhance streamflows. In such situations, state-supported water augmentation programs have substantial merit and a high probability of being instituted.

The liability question could be more easily resolved since the state can exercise both taxing and eminent domain authorities. As with a private concern engaged in water augmentation activities, the state must provide compensation to those suffering injury in a treatment area. Regardless of the nature of the injury, be it an ongoing diminution in the quality of life resulting from water augmentation interference with the use and enjoyment of property, or a short-term cataclysm resulting from a catastrophic event, the liability of the state cannot be

---

44. It is interesting to note, however, that Utah allows only the state division of water resources to conduct cloud seeding activities. UTAH CODE ANN. §73-15-3 (1953).

denied. Toward this end, records, licensing, and permits would remain valuable and should be maintained.

VIII.   Possible System Responses: Multistate and Federal

Since many of the augmentation techniques could involve a number of states, simultaneously, it is conceivable that interstate agreements would be necessary. Such agreements might take the form of new multistate compacts or amendments to existing compacts. Federal legislation controlling private water augmentation programs, which would supersede state legislation, is also a possibility. The main advantage of such legislation would be its ability to control private concerns to prevent conflicting programs without regard for state boundaries. One issue, which would suggest substantial further research, is the relationship of water augmentation programs to interstate water compacts. It would appear that waters developed by private concerns would be free from "the call of the compact" whereas such waters, if developed by the state, would not be free from compact obligations.[45]

A federal program for water resource development through weather modification and watershed management would be yet another possible legal system response. The Bureau of Reclamation, which has been a lead agency in the development of weather modification programs, and/or the U.S. Forest Service, which has been responsible for major advances in watershed management, are likely candidates for administration of national programs. Under this approach, the federal government would assert a claim to all waters developed on federal lands or pursuant to a federal program. This situation might well develop regardless of federal action because the multistate nature of weather modification might well raise a "diversity of citizenship" issue. It is possible, however, that the federal government, under the "implied reservation doctrine," already has a valid claim to the waters produced by water augmentation activities on federal land.

IX.   Conclusions

The greatest land use value of the alpine and subalpine

---

45. Fischer, *supra* note 42, at 651-56. This article contains an excellent overview of the problems that may emerge if the states themselves conduct water augmentation activities. Specifically, the potential effects of existing interstate compacts are discussed.

portions of watersheds is as an area for the collection and storage of water. While recognizing the legal, social, and technological problems implicit in water augmentation activities, it is apparent that substantial public benefit could be derived from such activities.

Land use regulations which protect the watershed function of alpine and subalpine areas would not prohibit their use for other purposes (*i.e.,* mining, residential development, etc.). These other land uses, however, should not be allowed to interfere with water augmentation activities. In the final analysis, the optimal use of a watershed is to produce water.[46] Legal and political obstacles which impede this use must be overcome. The possible legal system responses presented herein may provide some insight into surmounting these obstacles.

---

46. This point is the subject of ongoing research. Initial conclusions indicate that the value of the water produced exceeds the value of the use of alpine and subalpine portions of a watershed for any other purpose.

22
Water and Inappropriate Technology: Deep Wells in the Sahel[*]

Michael H. Glantz[**]

> Science and technology represent a means of development and emancipation for Africa, but they also harbor—technology in particular—dangers inasmuch as they may, because of their foreign origin, become the vectors of ways of life and thought dangerous for the African personality . . . .[1]

This statement from a report of the United Nations Educational, Scientific and Cultural Organization (UNESCO) points to an apparent growing awareness of the social implications, both positive and negative, of the transfer and the application of new technologies across cultural boundaries.

This paper discusses the societal impact of the construction of deep wells in the arid and semiarid regions of West Africa. In order to understand that impact clearly it is important to be aware of the environmental as well as the social setting in which the wells have been constructed. Therefore, the following sections will examine the physical and social setting of the area, and present a case study of deep wells in the Sahel.

I. THE SETTING

The Sahelian zone in West Africa has recently been affected by a succession of below-average rainfall years. These years served to highlight many socio-political and economic problems that continually confront the inhabitants and the governments of the region.

* The research for the Study of the Social Implications of a Credible and Reliable Long-Range Climate Forecast, of which this paper is a part, has been funded and supported by the Rockefeller Foundation, the International Federation of Institutes for Advanced Study, the National Center for Atmospheric Research, and the Aspen Institute for Humanistic Studies.

** Visiting Scientist, Advanced Study Program, National Center for Atmospheric Research.

1. UNESCO, SCIENCE AND TECHNOLOGY IN AFRICAN DEVELOPMENT (Science Policy Studies & Docs. No. 35, 1974).

Debate on the major causes of the drought has crystallized into two major points of view, one attributing the drought to climatic change[2] and the other attributing the drought to normal climatic fluctuations.[3] While the two factions disagree on conclusions, they do agree on at least two basic points. First, climatic fluctuations are normal to the region, and in any event the region will continue to be faced with occasional periods of prolonged drought. The other point is the realization that human agricultural and livestock practices have had a negative impact on the ecologically fragile Sudan-Sahelian zone. Whatever the underlying cause or causes of the drought in the Sahel, it has been widely acknowledged that, at the least, the impact of harmful climatic fluctuations has been greatly exacerbated by human misuse of the land in this region.

Some of the factors cited as having aggravated the impact of the drought are herd size, herd composition, lack of water, excess of tube wells, human population growth, lack of managerial skills, political rivalries (within the bureaucracy as well as between the government and the pastoral populations, and between the pastoralists and the cultivators), veterinary medicine, and human health care, among others. Given the interrelationship between the various parts of the fragile Sahelian ecosystem, each of these factors has in some way played a role in the ecological deterioration of the Sahelian rangelands. Commenting on such interrelationships, a recent report noted that:

> It is . . . easy to see how reduction or destruction of vegetation in one part of a nomad's yearly travels could have disastrous consequences on other parts of the range, on the animals and on the existence of nomadism itself.[4]

It is highly probable that another major factor tending to make a bad drought situation worse was the uncoordinated construction and unregulated use of deep wells.

2. *See* R. Bryson, Climate Modification by Air Pollution; II. The Sahelian Effect (Univ. of Wis. Inst. for Environmental Stud. Rep. No. 9, 1973); Winstanley, *Climate Changes and the Future of the Sahel,* in Politics of Natural Disaster: The Case of the Sahel 189 (M. Glantz ed. 1976).

3. *See* H. Landsberg, Drought, A Recurrent Element in Climate 45-90 (WMO Special Environmental Rep. No. 5, 1975).

4. FAO, *FAO and Sahara Reclamation,* 23 UNASYLVA 12 (1969).

A. *The Sahel*

The Sahelian zone in West Africa encompasses parts of six states: Senegal, Mauritania, Mali, Niger, Upper Volta, and Chad. The populations of these states total approximately 24 million inhabitants, about 6 million of whom were directly affected by the drought. It has been estimated that at least 100,000 people and up to 40 percent of the 25 million cattle perished. A large part of those affected were herders who practiced some form of nomadism. According to Douglas Johnson,

> Nomadism can best be viewed as a continuum between purely sedentary society on the one hand and a hypothetically "pure" nomadism that has no contact whatsoever with agriculture on the other.[5]

The Sahel has been defined by various authors using variables such as precipitation,[6] vegetation,[7] and geography.[8] In this paper it is assumed to be a climatically defined zone in the sub-Saharan part of West Africa which receives 200 to 600 mm. of average annual rainfall. It is bordered to the north by subdesert (100 to 200 mm.) and to the south by the Sudanian Zone (600 to 900 mm.). The 400 to 500 mm. isohyets (lines of equal precipitation) have generally been accepted as a boundary north of which only irrigated crops should be grown. This guideline, however, has often been disregarded, especially during periods of good rainfall.[9]

During much of the year, precipitation is nonexistent. Yet, a four to five month period of summer rainfall does occur between as early as June and as late as October. The social value to the inhabitants of the rain that does fall is affected by other factors existing at the time, such as the potential evapotranspiration, wind speed, soil porosity, runoff, and the like. In such arid and semiarid regions precipitation variability is relatively high, and thus droughts, as well as dry spells, by most definitions are expected to be part of the climate regime.[10]

---

5. D. Johnson, The Nature of Nomadism 12 (Univ. of Chicago Dep't of Geography Research Paper No. 118, 1969).

6. UNESCO, Regional Meeting on Integrated Research and Training Needs in the Sahelian Region (Man and the Biosphere Program Rep. No. 18, 1974).

7. Stebbing, *The Threat of the Sahara*, 36 J. Royal African Soc'y 3-35 (1937).

8. Tanaka, Weare, Navato & Newell, *Recent African Rainfall Patterns*, 255 Nature 201 (1975).

9. See Figure 1. From Environment and Land Use in Africa (M. Thomas & G. Whittington eds. 1969).

10. H. Riehl, Tropical Meteorology (1954).

308

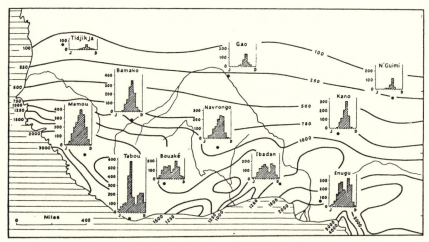

Mean annual and mean monthly rainfall in West Africa. Rainfall is in millimetres.

Figure 1.

Another factor affecting the social value of the rainfall is the geographic distribution of the rainfall that occurs in the region. The rainfall is delivered through "rows of self-propagating convective clouds giving showers and thunderstorms."[11] The local, small-scale nature of the thunderstorm activities produces widespread differences in amounts of seasonal precipitation within relatively small areas.[12]

B. *Pastoral Nomadism*

The availability, distribution, and timing of rainfall coupled with other sources of surface and groundwater have had an important effect on the type of social systems that developed in the Sahel. Pastoral nomadism developed in arid and semiarid regions where rainfall variability is extremely high. In Africa, pastoral nomadism takes on many forms determined by migratory patterns, degree of dependence on livestock, geographic location, and water availability, among other factors.[13] Several indigenous social systems in the Sahelo-Sudan region

11. Cocheme, *FAO/UNESCO/WMO Agroclimatology Survey of a Semi-Arid Area in West South Africa South of the Sahara,* in UNESCO, Agroclimatological Methods (1968).

12. Horowitz, *Ethnic Boundary Maintenance among Pastoralists and Farmers in the Western Sudan (Niger),* 7 J. Asian & African Stud. 105-14 (1972).

13. Widstrand, *The Rationale of the Nomad Economy,* 4 Ambio 146-53 (1975); Graham, *Man-Water Relations in the East-Central Sudan,* in Environment and Land Use in Africa, *supra* note 9, at 409-45.

have put a major emphasis on livestock for their livelihood as well as for their survival.

While some pastoral groups keep livestock by tradition and not necessarily for subsistence, others are dependent on their herds for fuel, food, fertilizer, trade, and transportation.[14] It is important to keep in mind that there are cultural as well as economic reasons for the pastoralists to try to maintain as large a herd as possible. On one hand, wealth and power are often measured in terms of cattle numbers. On the other hand, Leslie Brown has estimated that, in terms of survival, about five cattle are required to sustain one pastoralist, an estimate apparently considered low by pastoralists themselves.[15] To Brown, the current problems in the Sahel are the result of human, not just livestock, population growth.[16] He noted that "where rising human population becomes too great to permit each family to maintain this necessary minimum herd, damage to the environment through overstocking becomes inevitable."[17]

Given that there is a minimum number of cattle needed to support one herder and that the cattle fulfill at least three important economic objectives—milk production as cash income, large herds as insurance against the vagaries of weather, and maximum individual gains from communal land—it appears quite difficult to reduce herd sizes below a minimum number at which the group can survive as pastoralists. The importance of the insurance value of cattle numbers, overshadowed by other factors, is often underrated by observers outside the pastoral system. It is often difficult, for example, for the outside observer to understand the following response made by a Fulani herder to a question on how he had been affected by the recent Sahelian drought:

> I had 100 cattle, but, because of the drought, I lost 50. Next time I will have 200.

Yet, the land's carrying capacity, defined as the number of

---

14. D. JOHNSON, *supra* note 5.

15. Laya, *Interviews with Farmers and Livestock Owners in the Sahel*, 1 AFRICAN ENVIRONMENT 49 (1975).

16. Brown, *Biology of Pastoral Man as a Factor in Conservation*, 3 BIOLOGICAL CONSERVATION 93 (1971).

17. *Id.*

livestock the pasture can support without deterioration of either the pasture or the stock,[18] will be no greater next time; given the same circumstances again, the herder will still have 50 cattle remaining, but his losses will have been much greater. Thus, one of the main reasons that nomadic populations are reluctant to de-stock their herds, especially for cash, is that the cash payment cannot fulfill the many functions that the cattle fulfill in their societies.

While most governments in the Sahel have sought to sedentarize their nomadic populations for reasons relating to political control, economic development, or taxation, many observers agree that there is an important function that nomadism can perform. For one example, a substantial part of government foreign exchange comes from the sale of the relatively small number of cattle the herders do part with.[19] For another example, it is generally acknowledged that the cattle use the rangeland resources, resources that would otherwise be "under-utilized or not utilized at all."[20]

C. *The Process of Deterioration*

In times perceived to be "normal," that is, during periods of above-average rainfall,[21] the cultivators established themselves farther north into the relatively marginal agricultural areas. Nomadic populations were pushed even further north and became sandwiched on extremely marginal rangelands on the southern edge of the Sahara. Even during periods of what was considered acceptable rainfall, some of the marginal land that had been cleared for cultivation was later abandoned because of either low crop yields or unreliable rainfall. These areas were then left open to deflation (wind erosion) and to desertification. In other cases where the cultivators remained on the land, they tended to block the access of the nomads and their herds to some of the water sources.[22]

---

18. Boudet, as cited in A. RAPP, A REVIEW OF DESERTIFICATION IN AFRICA 1 (1974).

19. E. Berg, The Recent Economic Evolution of the Sahel, 1975 (unpublished thesis in Univ. of Michigan Center for Research on Economic Development).

20. J. Pino, Livestock Production in Tropical Africa (Rockefeller Foundation 1970).

21. Katz & Glantz, *Rainfall Statistics, Droughts and Desertification in the Sahel,* in DESERTIFICATION (M. Glantz ed. 1977).

22. Dresch, *Reflections on the Future of the Semi-Arid Regions,* in AFRICAN ENVIRONMENT 1-8 (P. Richards ed. 1975).

During periods of extremely favorable weather, such as the 15 years preceding the onset of the drought in 1968, the pastoralists inhabited, with relatively large herds, those areas that were classified as unreliable with respect to pasture productivity on a long-term basis. With consecutive shortfalls in precipitation in these ordinarily marginal areas the carrying capacity of the ranges was overtaxed, resulting in the destruction of the vegetative cover and the death of many animals. One of the end results was that the nomads, as well as the sedentary farmers in these marginal areas, believed themselves to be victims of a natural disaster, when in fact there was a return to the kind of "normal" rainfall conditions that are part of long-term average statistics. Reports have since supported the contention that the periodic regional droughts have only tended to aggravate a situation in which ecological deterioration was already well in progress. Summarizing the process of deterioration, a recent report noted that the present situation in the Sahel has been

> due to the buildup over the years before the drought, of high human (and animal) populations relative to the carrying capacity of the land. This trend has been magnified by even greater population increases outside the range areas, leading to an expansion of cultivation and hence, a reduction of available grazing area.[23]

II. Deep Wells

At least throughout this century it has generally been assumed that the most crucial problem facing inhabitants of the Sahel has been the availability of water. As a direct result of that assumption, various governments, independent as well as colonial, have sought to make more water available to the region's inhabitants. One of the popular methods has been to tap deep groundwater sources by constructing deep wells and boreholes. Given the existence of these wells, during favorable rainy seasons in the Sahel (200-400 mm.) the general process of water use by nomadic populations was reported to be as follows:

> 1. In the rainy season, grazing is in depressions and close to temporary ponds of water;
> 2. In the beginning of the dry season, grazing is in the vicinity of groundwater holes of shallow depth, where water is only 4-10 meters below the ground surface;

---

23. FAO, The Ecological Management of Arid and Semi-Arid Rangelands in Africa and the Near East: An Interdisciplinary Programme, AGPC/Misc/26, 27-31 (1974).

3. During the main part of the dry season, grazing is near rivers or near deep water holes, with water 80-100 meters below the surface.[24]

With repeated shortfalls in precipitation, along with large increases in human and livestock populations, grazing pressures sharply increased in the areas surrounding the sources of relatively permanent water, such as deep wells, as other sources of water became less reliable, or nonexistent.

Another problem associated with the wells is that they were often constructed with little consideration being given to the availability of adequate pastures. Rene Dumont wrote that

> the areas near the wells have been overgrazed and vegetation much reduced. The points of water supply were set up before a map of the pasturelands was drawn up, which would have established them on a more intelligent basis.[25]

J.A. Pino noted that there were also similar problems during wet periods as well:

> Water utilization [was] for the most part haphazard, and stock either had to travel too far for water or animals [were] concentrated near water to an extent that available forage [was] seriously reduced.[26]

It was, however, during the succession of low rainfall years that the lack of organization and planning with respect to well construction and herd size became apparent. As Jean Dresch recently observed:

> When a series of dry years succeeded each other, after 1968, the pressure of pastoralism became clear, particularly around wells, more and more of which had been dug, often with the best intentions but without the organization or any discipline in their use.[27]

A. *Deep Wells and Desertification*

Traditionally, nomadism resulted in the use of available water resources on a relatively rational basis.[28] This was done by keeping water resources in balance with the condition of the pastures. The existence of semipermanent water sources—shal-

---

24. Boudet, *supra* note 18, at 45-58.
25. R. Dumont, False Start in Africa 187 (2d ed. 1969).
26. J. Pino, *supra* note 20.
27. Dresch, *supra* note 22, at 6.
28. D. Johnson, *supra* note 5; Widstrand, *supra* note 13.

low water or wells that could be dug without the use of sophisticated mechanical equipment—encouraged herders to continually move their cattle from one location to another as the
sources of water dried up. The availability of these semipermanent (seasonal) watering points during the dry season determined the size of the herds that the watering points could
support.[29] This led to de facto rotational grazing and to a better
distribution of grazing pressures on the vegetation. In such a
situation,

> [l]ow yielding or temporary water sources are much less harmful
> [to the environment] . . .; when there is no pasture, there is no
> water either and hence pasture depletion is rarely acute in this
> case.[30]

The pastoralists understood their system as one of survival.
With the construction of sources of permanent water, however,
it was no longer possible to maintain this balance. The London
Drought Symposium report cited evidence that

> the availability of a more advanced technology than that of the
> subsistence farmer and pastoralist can lead to abuse of the envi
> ronment and to the disturbance of a previously unrecognized
> ecological balance.[31]

Permanent water sources, such as deep wells, disrupted
the unrecognized balance by converting seasonal pastures into
year-round ones "with far more cattle per area, resulting in
serious deterioration of the pasture."[32]

Soils and vegetation surrounding the wells were adversely
affected by the excessively high concentration of livestock. The
soils were affected, for example, by trampling, causing a reduction in soil porosity, and by removal of most palatable vegetation, leading to deflation and to desertification. The vegetation
was overgrazed; vegetation disappeared up to 20-30 kilometers
from the well sites, and less palatable species invaded these
areas,[33] surrounding the wells and forcing the livestock to travel
longer distances for forage.

---

29. J. DORST, BEFORE NATURE DIES (1970).

30. Le Houerou, *Ecological Management of Arid Grazing Lands Ecosystems*, in
POLITICS OF NATURAL DISASTER: THE CASE OF THE SAHEL, *supra* note 2, at 270.

31. DROUGHT IN AFRICA 13 (D. Dalby & R. Harrison eds. 1973).

32. *Id.* at 16.

33. Heady, *Influence of Grazing on the Composition of Themeda Trianda Grasslands, East Africa*, 54 J. ECOLOGY 705-26 (1966).

The livestock, for the most part in weakened condition, unable to survive the trek in search of water and forage, perished. Although the actual impact of the drought on livestock is somewhat difficult to ascertain and has, thus, remained a controversial issue, estimates as of April 1973 of the existing Sahelian livestock intimated that up to half of the approximate 25,000,000 cattle in the region at that time had possibly perished.[34] Some of those cattle may have been removed from the area through migration and through forced sales.

This situation which followed the uncoordinated and unassessed construction of wells and boreholes has been graphically portrayed in Figure 2.[35] It is interesting to note that a report of the FAO/SIDA Study Mission in 1974 suggested that "the cause of heavy mortality of stock in 1973 was lack of forage much more than lack of [drinking] water."[36]

The large number of livestock deaths resulted not so much because the wells were constructed, but because they were viewed apart from the ecosystem of which they were a part. Deep wells could have been put into the fragile ecosystem with minimal consequences to the system if, for example, their use had been regulated. Such controls could have been used to open and close wells in accordance with the availability of pasture, or used to distribute the grazing pressures more evenly among the pastures. Such controls suggest the need for at least a minimal level of planning, which in turn suggests the desirability of a systems approach to planning, given the fragile nature of the Sahelian and West African ecosystems.[37] Similar conclusions were also drawn for water problems caused by "an anarchic multiplication of wells and bore holes" in the Algerian

34. Temple & Thomas, *The Sahelian Drought: A Disaster for Livestock Populations*, 8 WORLD ANIMAL REV. 1-7 (1973).

35. Swift, *Disaster and Sahelian Nomad Economy*, in DROUGHT IN AFRICA, *supra* note 31.

36. FAO/Swedish International Development Agency, Report on the Sahelian Zone: A Survey of the Problem of the Sahelian Zone with a View to Drawing Up a Long-Term Strategy and a Programme for Protection, Restoration and Development, FAO/SWE/TF 117 (1974).

37. Secretariat of the U.N. Conference on Desertification, Report of the First Meeting of the Panel on Management of Livestock and Rangelands to Combat Desertification in the Sudano-Sahelian Regions (SOLAR), April 18, 1976 (UNEP unpublished manuscript).

Figure 2.
Relation between spacing of wells and overgrazing

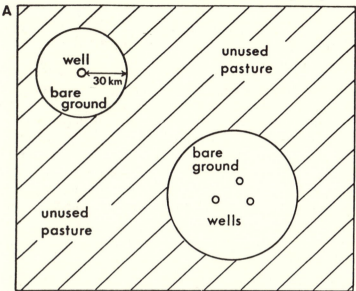

A. Original situation. End of dry season 1. Herd size limited by dry season pasture. Small population can live on pastoral economy

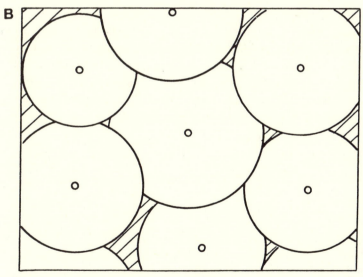

B. After well-digging project, but no change in traditional herding. End of dry season 2. Large-scale erosion. Larger total subsistence herd, and more people can live there until a situation when grazing is finished in a drought year. Then the system collapses.

Northeast Sahara[38] and in the Sudan.[39]

Swift[40] and Widstrand[41] drew attention to the importance of planning noting that while technology had been applied to some parts of the system, such as tapping sources of deep groundwater, it was not applied to other parts.

> Permanent increases in production are impossible since soil and vegetation receive no technological boost, and thus remain limiting factors. Nomad economies and societies are tightly integrated and functional wholes, with numerous checks and balances. Proposed changes must act ecologically on the whole system, not just isolated parts of it.[42]

A final but perhaps the most important plea for a systems approach to Sahelian range management was made by Baker in his article entitled *The Administrative Trap*.[43] Bureaucratic subunits within the Sahelian governments, such as veterinary, water, agriculture, marketing, security, and health departments, often fail to perceive the total range management problem given their limited jurisdictional mandates. Baker called for a redefining and a regrouping of such subunits based on the range management problem. Such regroupment would be a major step in reducing bureaucratic rivalries, jealousies, and piecemeal approaches to the important problems of range management.

As suggested by these examples, the lack of planning for this particular water resource and the unassessed use of it as a technological "fix" ultimately results in the death of livestock, but only after the vegetation cover has been totally destroyed and the denuded surface made vulnerable to deflation and desertification.

B. *"Technology is the Answer" Fallacy*

Technology is viewed by this author as being value-neutral. Thus, technological developments within, as well as technology transfer among nations, can have favorable as well

---

38. Achmi, *Salinization and Water Problems in the Algerian Northeast Sahara,* in CARELESS TECHNOLOGY 276 (M. Farvar & R. Milton eds. 1972).

39. Graham, *supra* note 13.

40. Swift, *supra* note 35.

41. Widstrand, *supra* note 13.

42. Swift, *supra* note 35.

43. R. Baker, Administrative Trap, 1-12, April 1975 (unpublished manuscript in the School of Development Studies, Univ. of East Anglia, Norwich, UK).

as unfavorable impacts on society.[44] Medical technology, for example, can be used to keep more people and livestock alive longer and in better condition; but an increase in population may in turn create greater pressure on scarce resources such as the rangelands in the Sahel.

The examples provided by deep well construction clearly suggest that vegetation more often became a more limiting factor in the Sahel than water. One can conclude that while technology may be value-neutral, its implications—social, economic, political, and ecological—are not. Therefore, the implications of technology development and/or transfer must be assessed as much as possible before the development is undertaken, so that unexpected side effects might be anticipated and mitigated. Failure to undertake such assessments often leads to situations in which temporary gains might eventually be outweighed by long-term losses of a more permanent nature.

> The man who drills wells [is not taught to] ask what will happen to all the animals which survive as a result of his activities . . . .[45]

Often technological fixes do not resolve basic problems but only tend to bypass them temporarily. For example, with respect to the misuse of wells it was suggested by one observer that it might be better, albeit more expensive, to consider taking water to the animals and thereby avoiding overconcentration at the well sites. Technological bypasses often tend to make "situations which are inherently bad more efficiently bad."[46]

Kenneth Boulding, commenting on the potential danger of technology, observed:

> There is a famous theorem in economics, one which I call the dismal theorem, which states that if the only thing which can check the growth of population is starvation and misery, then the population will grow until it is sufficiently miserable and starving to check its growth. There is a second, even worse theorem which I call the utterly dismal theorem. This says that if the only thing which can check the growth of population is starvation and misery, then the ultimate result of any technological improvement

---

44. CARELESS TECHNOLOGY, *supra* note 38.
45. R. Baker, *supra* note 43, at 178.
46. E. JANTSCH, TECHNOLOGICAL PLANNING AND SOCIAL FUTURES 12 (1972).

is to enable a larger number of people to live in misery than before and hence to increase the total sum of human misery.[47]

Awareness of the problems associated with the development, transfer, and application of technology (including technical information) may not be sufficient. Often such an awareness is acknowledged but only at an abstract level. Thus, while on the one hand the UNESCO conference representatives can acknowledge technology assessment needs, on the other hand the impact of any particular application of technology tends to be overlooked by decision makers, donors, and recipients. Often short-term expediencies overshadow relatively long-term implications. Thus, there can be no assurance that awareness of such problems will automatically lead to attempts at resolving them. Finally, while social assessment in itself is not sufficient to resolve the problems associated with the development, transfer, and application of technology, it is a necessary precondition for the achievement of rational solutions.

---

47. K. BOULDING, THE MEANING OF THE TWENTIETH CENTURY: THE GREAT TRANSITION 127-28 (1965).

23

Denver's Successive Use Program

*Kenneth J. Miller**

The Denver Water Department presently treats and delivers to the metropolitan area about 72 billion gallons of water each year. After serving a variety of purposes, about 40 percent of this water returns to the Platte River system through several sewage treatment plants. Under Colorado's appropriation doctrine, part of this return flow must remain in the river. A substantial part, however, of this now-wasted resource is available to the Department for successive uses.

Recognizing the potential of successive uses, the Denver Water Department began several years ago to investigate profitable possibilities. The Department conducted research into advanced wastewater treatment, investigated the economic and legal feasibility of water reuse, and studied marketing and public acceptance aspects of successive uses. This paper contains a summary of these studies and a description of the program developed as a result.

I. The Denver Water System

In order to understand the direction of Denver's successive use program, it is necessary to look at the Department's current water supply situation.

The safe annual yield of the Department's water supply system is approximately 300,000 acre-feet per year. Approximately 40 percent of this is obtained from Eastern Slope tributaries of the South Platte River. The remaining 60 percent of potential supply is derived from tributaries of the Colorado River by transmountain diversion. Recent Colorado Supreme Court decisions hold that return flow derived from the Eastern Slope must be returned to the river, but that the transmountain-diverted portion of Denver's supply is available to the City for successive uses. This situation is shown, in simplified form, in Figure 1. In actuality, the system consists of five major storage reservoirs totaling nearly one-half million acre-feet, four major trans-Continental Divide tunnels, and numerous canals, conduits, and intake facilities. Operation of

* Director of Planning and Water Resources Division, Denver Water Department, Denver, Colorado.

the system not only supplies water for the Denver metropolitan area, but also incorporates water for fish flows, recreation, and joint uses with other public and private agencies.

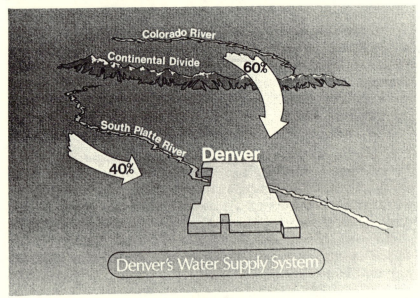

Figure 1.

Denver began operation of transmountain diversion projects in the 1930s in order to augment the Eastern Slope supply system. The most recent transmountain diversion consists of Dillon Reservoir and the 23-mile long Roberts Tunnel along with other facilities planned for development. As part of the court action granting Denver rights to build this project, the "Blue River Decree" effectively required that Denver investigate the possibilities of successive uses of Western Slope water.[1]

Figure 2 shows Denver's supply and demand situation. Supplies are presently adequate. The currently available 300,000 acre-feet will not meet demands beyond about 1980, however. Additional supplies will be needed, eventually doubling the Department's present capabilities. This water is available to the metropolitan area, but the costs of supplying

1. *In re* the Adjudication of Priorities of Water Rights in Water Dist. 36 for the Purposes of Irrigation, Civ. No. 5016 (D. Colo., Oct. 12, 1955); *In re* the Adjudication of Priorities of Water Rights in Water Dist. 36 for Purposes Other than Irrigation, Civ. No. 5016 (D. Colo., Oct. 12, 1955).

it will increase dramatically because of market factors, increasing distances from the City, lower elevations requiring pumping, and, most recently, various governmental constraints on development.

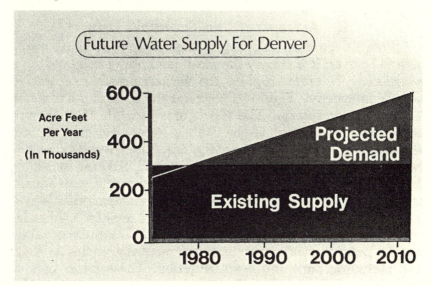

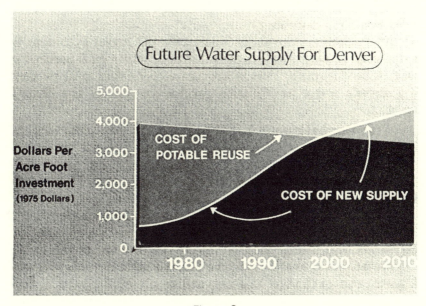

Figure 2

At some point in the future, the cost of treating sewage effluent, even to potable quality, will be competitive with the cost of developing new supplies. The exact date is uncertain, because potable reuse has never been tried in this country, but appears to be some time in the 1990s.

II. Alternatives for Successive Uses

Potable reuse is not the only form of successive use available to Denver; it is simply the most demanding and expensive alternative. In order to place the various possible successive uses in perspective, Figure 3 illustrates the present use of water in the Denver system. The top figures indicate that Denver uses about 1.3 percent of the State's water. Agriculture uses about 94.7 percent. Unfortunately, the Blue River Decree has been interpreted as preventing Denver from utilizing its return flow for agricultural uses.[2] The middle portion of Figure 3 illustrates water use within the Denver Water Department's system. The majority of water (52.1 percent) goes to residential customers. Industry takes 5.5 percent of the system's water, and 7.6 percent goes to various governmental agencies for their use, including park and lawn irrigation. These latter uses of relatively small amounts of water are spread throughout the metropolitan area, making a second distribution system to serve less-than-potable-quality water economically infeasible. Within the home, only about 7.3 percent of Denver's residential water goes toward human consumption, while 39.8 percent is used in landscaping. This latter figure correlates to 21 percent of Denver's water or 27/100ths of one percent of the State's water.

With this background, it is possible to make some choices regarding the direction of Denver's successive use program. The various alternatives are shown in Figure 4. Exchange, the simplest successive use, involving no treatment and relatively low cost, is the most attractive. Denver intends to implement exchange, or the trading of used water at the sewage treatment plant outfall for less polluted water at the existing intakes, in the immediate future. Unfortunately the amount of relatively unpolluted water available in the South Platte River is severely limited, and exchange will not utilize all of the return flow

---

2. Note 1 *supra.*

FIGURE 3
TYPICAL WATER USE

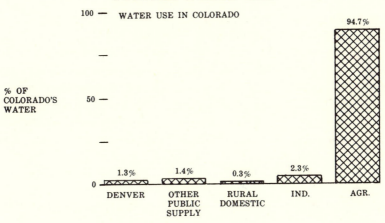

WATER USE IN COLORADO

% OF COLORADO'S WATER

100 —
50 —
0

				94.7%
1.3%	1.4%	0.3%	2.3%	
DENVER	OTHER PUBLIC SUPPLY	RURAL DOMESTIC	IND.	AGR.

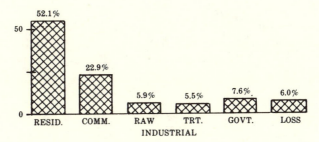

WATER USE IN DENVER

% OF DENVER SUPPLY

100 —
50 —
0

52.1%	22.9%	5.9%	5.5%	7.6%	6.0%
RESID.	COMM.	RAW	TRT.	GOVT.	LOSS
		INDUSTRIAL			

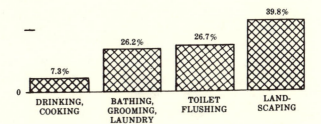

RESIDENTIAL WATER USE

% OF RESIDENTIAL USE

100 —
50 —
0

7.3%	26.2%	26.7%	39.8%
DRINKING, COOKING	BATHING, GROOMING, LAUNDRY	TOILET FLUSHING	LAND-SCAPING

resource available. Agricultural reuse may require some minimal treatment beyond that now applied depending upon the crop to be irrigated. Unfortunately this practice appears to be prohibited by the Blue River Decree. Industrial reuse and lawn and golf course watering with return flows require additional treatment and are uneconomical with the low, scattered demands found in the Denver area. Only the location of large, water-using industries in Denver would change this situation. Potable reuse is capable of utilizing the amounts of sewage effluent available and, as mentioned before, may be economically competitive with more conventional supplies some time in the future.

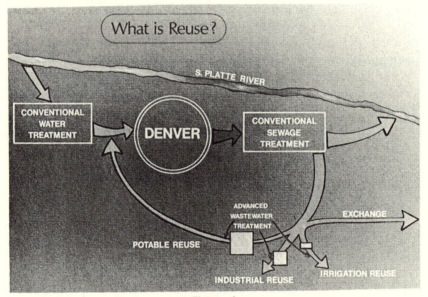

Figure 4.

Planned, conscientious potable reuse has never been practiced in this country. There exist many questions regarding the safety, acceptability, and legal and economic feasibility. Recognizing this, the Denver Water Department began investigating various aspects of potable reuse in the late 1960s. An advanced wastewater treatment pilot plant was constructed by a grant from the Federal Water Quality Administration (now EPA) through cooperative agreements with the University of Colorado. Since that time, the plant's processes have been upgraded, and it has served continuously as a laboratory for graduate student research operated jointly by the civil engineering department at C.U. and the Denver Water Department.

Recognizing the importance of an informed and approving public, the Denver Water Department has conducted an extensive public information program. In order to determine the success of this program, several surveys have been undertaken. The results of one survey, performed by contract in 1974, are shown in Figure 5. As with other surveys, the results indicate that Denver residents would accept potable reuse if the quality of the water were identical with that which they now receive.

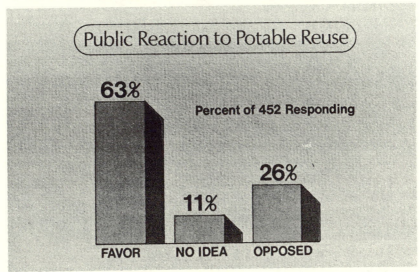

Figure 5.

III. DENVER'S DEMONSTRATION PLANS

Recognizing the importance of water quality in the public's mind, and noting a lack of national quality standards for water reuse, the Department has adopted a quality goal of equivalency with existing potable water. Advanced wastewater treatment will have to remove the "use increment," or the amount of each pollutant added between water supply intake and wastewater discharge, in order to meet this goal, as shown in Figure 6. Since no precedent exists for direct potable reuse and since many questions remain unanswered, a 5- to -10-year demonstration of appropriate treatment processes is planned. Interim recreational use and extensive health and quality testing will accompany this demonstration.

POTABLE REUSE DEMONSTRATION PLANT
QUALITY GOALS

VIRUS, PATHOGENIC BACTERIA, HARMFUL ORGANICS	NONE PRESENT
TRACE METALS, INORGANICS, ORGANICS, NUTRIENTS, BACTERIA	AT OR BELOW EXISTING POTABLE WATER QUALITY

EXAMPLE

TDS	157
Hardness	88
Suspended Solids	0.0
COD	<5.0
Turbidity	0.6 units

Figure 6.

In December 1975, the Department hosted a one-day design seminar at which national experts of advanced wastewater treatment and reuse health effects advised Denver and its engineering consultants on a proper process train for the demonstration project. This information was turned over to the design firm of CH_2M-Hill Engineers who prepared a conceptual design of the plant in August of 1975. As shown in Figure 7, the treatment train will link several processes in series to accomplish the quality goal. Lime will be added to raise the pH, precipitate phosphorus and heavy metals, and reduce suspended solids. Following two-stage recarbonation to remove the flocculated material and lower the pH, the water will enter a holding pond followed by conventional multimedia filtration to finish suspended-solids removals. Selective ion exchange and breakpoint chlorination will be utilized to reduce ammonia-nitrogen concentrations and disinfect the water. The flow will then enter carbon adsorption columns for organic removal. Lime, the ion exchange regenerant, and activated carbon will all be regenerated and reused in the processes. For economic reasons, only part of the flow stream will proceed to the remainder of the treatment processes. Reverse osmosis, a desalting process, will be used to reduce dissolved solids; ozonation will be utilized to disinfect the water and polish organic removals; and chlorination will serve to provide a residual disinfectant. Extensive quality and health tests will then be performed with the effluent flowing to a recreational lake and eventual industrial use.

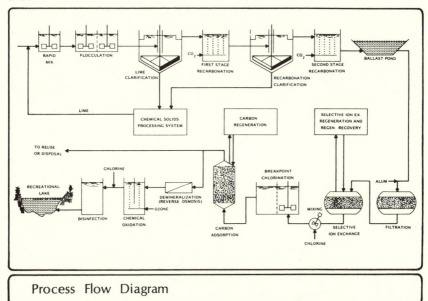

Process Flow Diagram

Figure 7.

IV. PROGRAM

As shown in Figure 8, the Department's current plans call for designing the demonstration plant in 1977 with construction to be complete by 1980. Operation of the plant will progress for perhaps 10 years, accompanied by extensive quality and health testing. If all goes well, a full-scale plant could be on line in the early 1990s.

The consultants estimate that the plant will cost 8.39 million dollars. This capital expenditure, coupled with other parts of the successive use program will cost in excess of 100 million dollars over the next 20 years. As shown in Figure 9, in addition to the demonstration plant capital cost, 6.48 million dollars will be spent on its operation and 1.1 million dollars on parts of the program common to both reuse and exchange, such as legal work, a quantity accounting system, and public relations. A reservoir to facilitate exchange operations will cost about 8.7 million dollars. Depending upon the results of the demonstration, a full-scale plant of approximately 100 MGD capacity will cost somewhere between 95 and 150 million dollars.

DENVER REUSE PROGRAM

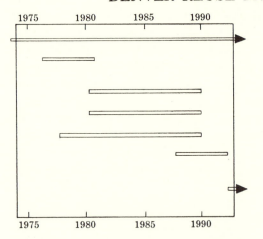

1. PUBLIC RELATIONS
2. DEMONSTRATION PLANT DESIGN, CONSTRUCTION
3. DEMONSTRATION PLANT OPERATION
4. PLANT QUALITY MONITORING
5. HEALTH EFFECTS TESTING
6. FULL SCALE POTABLE REUSE PLANT DESIGN
7. FULL SCALE POTABLE REUSE PLANT OPERATION

Figure 8.

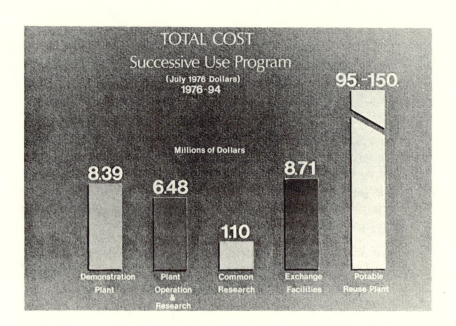

Figure 9.

V. SUMMARY

In summary, the Denver Water Department has been investigating the possibility of utilizing a once wasted resource. Extensive marketing, legal, economic, and technical investigations have led to a program which could add significant quantities of water to the Denver metropolitan area before the end of this century. The potential of successive use is limited, however, because only return flows derived from transmountain diversions are available for exchange or reuse. Successive use, therefore, must be considered as part of an overall program of water supply development including conservation and conventional supply alternatives.